LARRY WALSH

FORTY to FINISH

*Cycling to Victory on the
TransAmerica Bicycle Trail*

Editing and distribution by Bublish, Inc.
Published by Cabin Fever Press

ISBN: 978-1-64704-615-6 (Paperback)
ISBN: 978-1-64704-616-3 (Hardback)
ISBN: 978-1-64704-623-1 (eBook)

Forty to Finish is a true story. The author relied on Facebook entries, TransAmerica Trail maps, stored data on a GPS device, journal notes, photos, videos, and an imprecise memory to tell his story. Care was taken to preserve conversations' meaning and accurately depict events as they occurred. All organizations are real, and most names are actual racers. All photos are the property of the author. The Afterword is presented with permission from the Eastern Shoshone Cultural Center. Forty to Finish is based on the author's view entirely.

CONTENTS

PREFACE

"I hope you find my story interesting."

And with that, I recounted my journey to self-discovery with residents of the All-Seasons Independent Senior Living Center in Ann Arbor, Michigan.

While my bike rides across America span ten months between September 2018 and July 2019, memories will reach for a lifetime.

I'm no more a cyclist than any other middle-aged man searching for adventure and wanting to regain the self-confidence that had waned.

On the saddle, I learned the true meaning of a life well-lived is the journey—pedaling uphill to reach that mountaintop, taking in the vista for a job well done, then the downhill to reflect on what's next.

I'm often asked, "Will you do it again? Any other trips planned?'

My honest reply, "I don't know," adding, "Good things come in three's, so I never rule anything out."

When I returned home to New Jersey in July 2019, I felt the time was right to get a 'real' job. So, I did. Beginning January 2020, I wore business attire and attended meetings—presenting to and talking with customers seemed new again. I felt refreshed and ready to start a new journey in an industry where I had spent close to thirty years.

My flight to San Francisco on March 9th, 2020, was eerily quiet. About 10 percent of passengers wore masks. Covid was in the news, but as we know, those early signs portend the pandemic. My meeting in Palo Alto on March 10th went on without a hitch. I was the last vendor allowed in the building in a separate meeting on March 11th in South San Francisco. A business lunch in downtown San Francisco on March 12th preceded my forebodingly different flight back to Newark, NJ.

One other person walked through the central corridor inside the United terminal at the SFO airport.

This is crazy, I thought.

On Friday, March 13th, I woke up to a world that would change our lives.

The pandemic impacted my business and my job.

But this time, I welcomed the change.

Why would anyone care about my bike rides across America? I thought.

One day, it hit me like a ton of bricks.

A better question I asked myself:

Why wouldn't everyone want to hear my story of cycling 7,300 miles, crossing 18 states and through 528 towns?

I was fortunate to have the support, time, and resources to tackle such an incredible journey.

I felt empowered to share seeing "America Up Close" from a unique vantage point, on the saddle, one pedal stroke at a time.

I felt compelled to write.

Thank you for reading *Forty to Finish: Cycling to Victory on the TransAmerica Bike Trail,* a sequel to my #1 New Release, *Suit to Saddle: Cycling to Self-Discovery on the Southern Tier.*

INTRODUCTION

I wore my green Columbia Silver Ridge Convertible hiking pants on United Flight #2415 to Portland, Oregon. They were the same ones I had donned eight months earlier for a United flight to San Diego, when I began my three-month odyssey from self-doubt to self-confidence. A blue, long-sleeve Smartwool 100 shirt and silver Northside Brille lightweight water shoes rounded out the ensemble, giving me an appearance that revealed my enthusiasm for the occasion.

The clothing easily fit into the Salsa Half Frame Pack, with adequate storage capacity to carry only essential items for my journey. Beginning June 2, my Smartwool shirt would serve a much more critical purpose than casual travel attire—it would warm my torso as I cycled over five mountain ranges, including the Cascades and the Rocky Mountains, and into the heart of middle America in the Trans Am Bike Race.

The landing gear extended, the wing flaps opened, and the distinct roar of the airplane's hydraulic motor signaled the final approach. The loud thump and screech of the brakes triggered an immediate rush of high-speed air spewing out of the plane's engines. United #2415 touched down at 11:12 a.m.

I moved into the aisle and pulled a large, mesh, drawstring cinch sack carry-on from the upper bin. It carried all the clothing I needed for the next 40 days. Roger, my travel partner and cycling mate, pulled his backpack from the upper bin.

Roger and I exited the terminal and walked directly to the taxi stand.

"Hi! River City Bicycles on MLK Boulevard," I said to the driver. Roger and I gazed out the windows; Roger looked left, and I stared right, numb to my surroundings. During the 12-mile ride from the Portland airport to River City Bicycles on this sunny day, we were mostly quiet.

I wondered, *Am I nuts to embark on a 4,200-mile bike race across America?*

Tank, the same Surly Disc Trucker touring bike I rode months before, on the Southern Tier route, and Roger's recently bought All-City touring bike, appeared to be in great shape. Both had been rebuilt by mechanics at River City Bicycles after a long flight from New Jersey to Portland, with BikeFlights. We browsed inside the bike shop located in Portland's Central Eastside district. Many shoppers filled the store. *Portland must be a bike-friendly community*, I thought, as I scanned the walls, floor, and tables full of cycling equipment and accessories. The volume of merchandise on display was greater than I had ever seen before. Portland's reputation as an environmentally friendly city entered my mind.

Two mechanics were working on bikes hoisted on repair stands behind the cash register. Roger and I were in no rush to leave the store; our bus from Portland to Astoria would not depart for several hours. I thought the $100 bike assembly fee was excessive, but we paid at the register and left the establishment. A large mural covering the concrete wall next to the entrance grabbed my attention. I looked up and said to Roger, "How cool is that! Let's get a picture." The bright, multicolored abstract painting of an adult and a child facing the entrance created a focal point —and perhaps more foot traffic.

I opened a Portland city map, located the bus station, and walked toward the Greyhound station on NW 6th Avenue near Old Town and Chinatown. I lugged Tank and my 20-pound cinch sack across the Hawthorne Bridge over the Willamette River. Roger followed behind, single file. A slight haze blocked out the sun's intense golden rays. However, the balmy, early summer day created conditions under which I began to sweat before reaching the bridge.

My arms tired after a few minutes of pushing Tank from the left side. I switched to the right side, then back to the left, then the right, then left again, all the way to the bus station. We walked on Madison Street, turned north on Broadway, then right onto Burnside, zigzagging the last few hundred feet. Finally, after 45 minutes, we arrived. The tall buildings of downtown Portland dominating the city streets protected us from the direct sunlight on Madison and Broadway, making the walk much more pleasant.

It had been many years since I'd visited Portland. I saw three homeless people sitting on the ground on Madison Street, leaning against a window. Each vagrant sat next to a cardboard sign; one read, "Poor and Hungry." I quickly looked away and continued walking, without glancing at the second and third signs—not because I didn't want to help, but because I didn't know if the man had a genuine need. His filthy, unshaven face and worn clothing caked with dirt gave the impression he needed help. I did not know for sure, though, so I chose to continue walking.

My mind flashed back to a summer weekend in the late 1990s, when my wife, Kelley, and I visited Portland during the annual Oregon Brewers Festival at the McCall Waterfront Park on the Willamette River. To this day, the event attracts dozens of breweries, food vendors, and musicians, transforming the park into an outdoor carnival.[1] Hundreds roamed the area. When my wife and I went, many wore tie-dyed clothing. Well before their time, tattoos were commonplace, and one memory stands out of a pregnant lady walking barefoot, abdomen exposed, full of tattoos from head to toe. Shortly after the turn of the century, Portland embraced its unique culture by calling itself America's Capital of Weird, borrowing the expression first started in Austin,

---

[1] "Welcome to the Oregon Brewers Festival, Oregon's Original Craft Beer Celebration!," Oregon Brewers Festival, accessed July 12, 2022, https://oregonbrewfest.com

Texas.[2] Portland's unique culture and way of life were on display then, and again 20 years later; I'd been desensitized to seeing homeless people on the streets by my prior visits to the Capital of Weird.

The bus station occupied the corner of a city block. A fence cordoned off a construction zone across the street from the station. Except for the occasional three-to four-second bursts of sound made by a powerful jackhammer, the neighborhood surrounding the bus station was still.

I walked inside the terminal and immediately thought of Grand Central in New York, though without the throngs of people. I felt unnoticeable in the cavernous room. I walked up to the ticket counter and stood in line. When it was my turn, I asked, "Can you tell me if this is the right place to find the bus to Astoria? I have a ticket for the 6:00 p.m. departure, and I'm also transporting a bike."

"Yes," the attendant said. "You can pick up the bus behind me on the side of the terminal. It usually arrives about thirty minutes before departure."

"Thank you," I said. Before walking outside to join Roger, I bought a Good Humor Giant Vanilla ice-cream sandwich at a gift shop inside the terminal. I did not think consuming a 230-calorie ice-cream sandwich mattered because, beginning June 2, I would start burning between 7,000 and 10,000 calories per day until I arrived at the Yorktown Victory Monument in Yorktown, Virginia.[3]

A man and woman exited the terminal walking next to their bicycles and joined Roger and me in a compact, communal space next to the entrance.

"Hi, I'm Larry, and this is my buddy Roger," I said, extending my arm to shake hands.

---

[2]   Alexia Wulff, "How Portland Became America's Capital of 'Weird' and Embraced It," *Culture Trip*, January 29, 2017, https://theculturetrip.com/north-america/usa/oregon/articles/how-portland-became-americas-capital-of-weird-and-embraced-it/

[3]   "Calories Burned Biking / Cycling Calculator," Calories Burned HQ, accessed July 12, 2022, https://caloriesburnedhq.com/calories-burned-biking/

The two introduced themselves as Garth and Rylee, each taking turns to extend a warm greeting.

"Are you two together?" I asked. They shook their heads in unison to signal it was their first time meeting each other.

Garth asked, "Are you guys here for the race?"

"Larry is," Roger answered, "but I'm riding for about a week and then returning home to New Jersey."

"I guess the both of you are in the race?" I asked. Rylee and Garth each nodded in response. "Is this your first race? Do you have a goal?"

Garth replied, "Yeah, it's my first Trans Am. I want to finish in twenty-two days."

Rylee just shrugged when it was her turn to answer, apparently not interested in divulging that information.

I calculated the math and quietly marveled at the prospect of Garth cycling 190 miles per day for 22 straight days. Garth stood next to his bike, his left arm holding the bike frame, and his right hand mimicking a finger gun by his side. He wore a bright-yellow cycling shirt reminiscent of a Tour De France jersey covered with sponsorship and an orange reflective top with two prominent stripes over his shoulders and one around his waist. I focused my attention initially on his head and then on his arms and legs. A perfectly fitted, curved helmet, glasses to protect from wind and sandblast, a smile that extended from ear to ear, and muscular and well-defined arms and legs conveyed that he was ready to go.

A few feet away, Rylee stood, both hands balancing her bike. A confident stance and an equally magical smile evinced her excitement and anticipation for tackling this epic journey. Roger leaned his bike against the Amtrak Rail Passenger Station and flashed the shaka hand sign—a signal to relax and enjoy the moment. I snapped a photo, the first of many over the next 40 days. Rylee and Garth soon disappeared; they presumably had a different game plan for traveling to Astoria.

At 5:30 p.m., the Greyhound bus arrived at the terminal. Roger and I got up from the bench we'd sat on for most of the afternoon and walked around the corner to the parking area. Passengers gathered and waited for the driver to give the signal to step up onto the bus. Surrounded by passersby, we loaded our bicycles into the bus's underbelly. Our destination: Astoria, Oregon, point of departure for the Trans Am Bike Race (TABR). The sunny, 65-degree afternoon had given way to a calm, crisp, 50-degree dusk as the Greyhound began traveling north on Highway 1.

I stared out the window in something of a trance, gazing at the pine trees as the bus hummed along. I did not want to interact. I wanted to reflect, think, prepare.

Roger broke my introspection. "Larry, this is Michael. He's racing, traveling from Nashville."

I smiled and introduced myself but quickly shifted my gaze back to the outside world, contemplating and wondering. I was happy to be present, though I was unsure what had led me to this point.

Again, Roger broke my trance. "Larry, we'll be riding on this same road in a couple of days." I looked at the road and thought, *Yikes, that's a narrow shoulder to ride on.*

A few passengers disembarked at a bus stop in Seaside, the last before Astoria, 17 miles farther north. I dozed. The bus engine's rumbling white noise and the darkness supplied the perfect sleeping conditions. The Greyhound turned onto Marine Drive and stopped in front of the Astoria bus stop drop-off point. At 9:00 p.m., I stepped down onto a dark, quiet street and scanned my surroundings. I felt at ease. A sense of calm came over me.

I wanted to be in Astoria, but I did not comprehend the task ahead of me, honestly. We retrieved our bikes from the bus's underbelly and began the short, one-mile walk to the Commodore Hotel on 14th Street. Walking after dark, Roger and I had this sleepy town all to ourselves. On an otherwise dim street, blue, neon lights and bright, white bulbs lit up the hotel's front entrance. We saw a café attached to the hotel and were relieved to know we'd have a place to get coffee in the morning. The Commodore, built in 1925, is a chic hotel situated in the Downtown Historic District's heart. It's small and intimate; when I entered, I felt like a personal guest in someone's home rather than just a hotel occupant. The check-in desk was a mere opening in the lobby wall. Large, metal room keys hung on a wall inside the open space. I could have reached in through the aperture and selected any room key I wanted. Instead, I rang the bell to summon the front desk attendant. The young woman welcomed Roger and me to Astoria and assigned us two rooms on the second floor. The first floor housed the front desk, the small lobby, and a walkway to the café entrance.

"Is there any place open in town to get a bite to eat?" I asked, expecting a different response than the one I got.

"The Fort George Brewery has really good burgers. Just up the road on Duane Street. Walk up 14th, and you'll see it on the left," she shared, before handing the room keys to Roger and me.

The elevator and the room were small, barely large enough for both me and Tank to fit inside.

Nine months had passed since I'd last been employed. Finding a job had been my top priority when I returned home the day before Thanksgiving in 2018. Mentally, I was much better prepared to go about the task of discovering my next career opportunity. For one interview, early February 2019, I drove two hours to Princeton, New Jersey, in a snowstorm and sat through a three-member panel interview for a pharmaceutical sales manager job. I connected very well with the interviewers and thought I'd hit a home run. I did not get the job. I was disappointed but not discouraged. After reflecting on my responses to some questions, I realized I was more enthusiastic answering questions about my first cross-country bike ride than about the job itself. Whether the interviewers took that as a signal to pass on me, I didn't know.

I continued to network with friends and browse job sites, hoping to find something that would capture my imagination. But as days and weeks passed, I started to feign the dedication to my job search, because something else had grabbed my interest.

While searching for a job, I also began sifting through pictures and videos I'd taken on the Southern Tier cross-country ride. I knew my memory would fade over time, so I set out to complete a documentary before starting a new job. I wanted to memorialize the experience. I spent countless hours looking at pictures, videos, and extemporaneous notes from my 57 days on the saddle the year before. I disconnected in my office, taught myself iMovie, and produced a video with music and subtitles. I set forth to tell my story of cycling from California to Florida. OneRepublic's song "I Lived," Fleetwood Mac's "Go Your Own Way," and Lee Greenwood's "God Bless the USA," as well as other favorites, made for a perfect soundtrack to go with my journey from San Diego to St. Augustine, Florida.

I gave Kelley a sneak preview. "What do you think?" I asked.

She responded, "I love it. It's really good."

Kelley had been by my side for the past nine months and appreciated the positive impact the cross-country ride had on my mental well-being. She felt my story could help others coping with a similar situation—losing a job and dealing with feelings of depression. When she told me she loved the video, I knew I had a worthy goal to achieve—a dream that would challenge me to dig deep, discover my potential, and perhaps, in the process, help others.

Kelley and I invited friends to our home to watch the video on our 65-inch Samsung TV. Kelley created a theater experience by serving popcorn, soda, and a lot of candy. For Christmas 2018, my eldest daughter, Tara, had surprised me with a memory book that captured many of the pictures and descriptions I'd posted daily on Facebook the year before. Kelley placed the hardcover book on the coffee table in the TV room, hoping to inspire conversation. Our guests were engrossed, looking intently at the screen, periodically asking questions. I loved watching, reliving, and talking about my journey. When Lee Greenwood's "God Bless the USA" played and the credits rolled, my friends teared up.

And something else happened. Memories filled my mind each time I watched. I started to think about riding across the country a second time. I had an inner restlessness and a longing for something more. The sense that something was missing created an internal tug-of-war—my brain whispering to me to find a job, my heart urging me not to settle. I did not realize it at the time, but I still had the cycling itch.

I felt I could, and needed to, accomplish something bigger and more challenging than the Southern Tier. Cycling coast-to-coast, from the Pacific Ocean to the Atlantic Ocean, had brought me immense gratification. I'd answered a nagging question: Was I physically and mentally capable of completing a cross-country bike ride? Overcoming significant obstacles such as extreme weather, loneliness, numbness in my extremities, and a sore butt only added to my feeling of satisfaction.

In March 2019, I watched a YouTube video of the 2016 TABR. Lael Wilcox overtook Steffen Streich on the last day of the 4,200-mile race and won. She completed it in a little over 18 days, the second-fastest time on record. Streich was leading, with 110 miles to go. On the final morning, he started riding in the wrong direction—the effect of sleep deprivation. He realized his error when he met Wilcox in Bumpass, Virginia, cycling in the opposite direction. They rode together for a brief time, and Streich suggested they ride to the finish together. Reportedly, Wilcox responded, "This is a race," and sprinted the last 110 miles to become the first woman to win a major, ultradistance bikepacking race, beating Streich by two hours.[4]

I pondered what it would feel like to race across America, just like Wilcox did. Deep down, I yearned for the same feeling I'd had when I yelled, "I'm doing this!" in July 2018, when my heart won the tug-of-war and I committed myself to the Southern Tier Bike Tour.

I reflected for hours, sitting alone in my office. I yearned for the chance to once again pedal through small-town America—connecting with strangers, anticipating the next surprise. But I also craved something more. I wanted to experience complete solitude in the middle of America,

---

[4]   "Lael Wilcox finishes Trans Am Bike Race 2016 in 18 days 10 minutes," *Gypsy by Trade*, June 23, 2016, https://gypsybytrade.wordpress.com/2016/06/23/lael-wilcox-finishes-trans-am-bike-race-2016-in-18-days-10-minutes/

while pushing my physical limits. I put the Southern Tier ride in the rearview mirror and focused my full attention on competing in the 2019 TABR. The race began on June 2.

My inner restlessness and the gnawing sense that something was missing disappeared. That same crisp thinking that was my North Star in 2018 had returned. I did not have much time. I needed to decide. The distance: 4,200 miles, crossing 10 states and five mountain ranges. *Hell yeah! My name is written all over this race,* I thought.

> The TransAmerica Bicycle Trail began in 1973… as nothing more than an ambitious idea for a way to celebrate the nation's upcoming 200th birthday. By June of 1976, the Trail was ready; the maps and guidebooks were published… Given the name "Bikecentennial," organizers publicized the event, and thanks to strong word-of-mouth and… prodigious publicity, 4,000 cyclists showed up for the ride.[5]

In 2014, Nathan Jones, race founder and organizer, adopted the TransAmerica Bicycle Trail and created the Trans Am Bike Race (TABR). The original trail covers 4,200 miles, crossing 10 states and five mountain ranges. It is one of the most challenging ultradistance, self-contained races in the world. For many years, I imagined riding my bike in the California desert and through the Imperial Sand Dunes. Cycling over the Rockies was not something I had contemplated taking on so soon after returning home from my first cross-country ride. But now, I was fixated on cresting Hoosier Pass in the Rocky Mountains, cycling on endless Kansas roads, and looking up at that big Montana sky.

---

5   "TransAmerica Trail," Adventure Cycling Association, accessed July 12, 2022, https://www.adventurecycling.org/routes-and-maps/adventure-cycling-route-network/transamerica-trail/

Kelley supported my decision, but she hedged just a little. She asked, "How will you explain a second ride in a job interview?"

I did not have an exact answer. Instead, I replied, "I will figure it out." I had been out of work for almost a year at that point. I rationalized the gap in employment. *What difference would a few more months make?* I thought. Kelley had convinced me that tackling the first ride would make me a more interesting person. As a 56-year-old white male, it was a way to distinguish myself from others. I'd bought into her reasoning. But now, the roles were reversed. She was the one asking why. There was only one explanation that made sense then, and it still does today. It is this lesson I want my children to remember: follow your passion, enjoy your life, and do not let others define you.

My three kids' reactions were different—a muted response this time. I sensed they were curious, wondering why Dad was doing this again.

Registering for the race was an ordeal. The TABR website was not accepting new entrants when I first inquired in late February. Contact information for the race organizer did not exist. I sent an email to a nondescript address I uncovered on the race website. I heard nothing. Precious days passed. Finally, a couple of weeks later, Nathan responded, telling me he had been traveling the country, evaluating the impact spring rainstorms had had on the Midwestern states' infrastructure. Flooding had caused the closure of many roads in Missouri, Kansas, and Illinois—three states on the TransAmerica Bike Trail.

In that first correspondence I received from Nathan on April 6, 2019, he asked why I wanted to race across America.

> So, you want to race the Trans Am Bike Race? A good question is, why? Why do you want to do this? Is this your calling in life? There are many other great events out there with a drastically lower risk for injury and death. For years, we have told people that there are no guarantees out on the open roads, and we have lost friends and family in the process. Continuing to run

the race sometimes seems insurmountable, perhaps even foolish. We will continue, but we will evolve. People will continue to ask you why you do this. If you do not have an answer, we suggest you at least have an understanding and one that we wholeheartedly sympathize with.[6]

He signed off with "Cheers" and asked me to read the Racer Manual, complete the Stage 1 Application, and sign the waiver and the Racer Agreement. The unmistakable message was that the TABR was not for the fainthearted and I should consider other long-distance routes if I was not fully aware of the challenges, difficulties, and dangers associated with the race.

My email response was simple yet direct. "I want to test my physical and mental limits," I wrote, adding that I'd recently completed the Southern Tier route. I knew what it took, both physically and mentally, to pull off a long bike ride, but now, I explained, I yearned for something bigger. I also highlighted my military experience and successful completion of the grueling, two-month-long Ranger School. I thought it would not hurt to mention it and, if anything, might elevate my chances of receiving a positive response.

I was thrilled beyond belief when, on April 7, 2019, I received an email from Nathan. The subject line read: "2019 Trans Am Bike Race Application Approved." I paid the nominal $290 entrance fee. All race entrants are required to carry extreme sports insurance, obtain a medical clearance, and ride with a SPOT satellite tracking device. I bought a SPOT Gen3 satellite tracking device rather than rent one from the race organization, an option for entrants who believed they could complete the race in 30 days or less.

I scoured YouTube videos in search of bikepacking ideas. Many racers carried all equipment in a single frame and seat post bag, limiting

---

6   Nathan Jones, email message to author, April 6, 2019.

weight and air resistance. Lightweight titanium and carbon fiber bikes appeared to be favorites, designed with speed in mind. Anything that reduced drag was implemented, including helmets with curved and sloped surfaces to cut through the air. Many packed a bivvy, an air mattress, bike tools, food, a navigation device, and minimal clothing to weather any significant rain or snow event.

I did not need nor want to carry as much gear as I had on the Southern Tier ride. I split the difference but erred on the side of caution. On Tank, my CroMoly steel Surly Disc Trucker bike, I carried my Big Agnes tent, sleeping bag, air mattress, multiple pairs of wool socks, two long-sleeve Smartwool shirts, two cycling shirts, three pairs of cycling shorts, PEARL iZUMi long pants, riding shoes, and an extra tire. I placed personal identification, a pocketknife, a pocket light, a multi-tool, a waterproof notepad and pen, and pogey bait inside my handlebar bag. As much as I wanted to experience cycling through the Rockies, I did not want to be stranded at 11,000 feet, riding through a snowstorm without the proper gear.

If the Southern Tier was my first ultradistance ride without training wheels, the TABR was my Tour de France. I hunkered down. I needed to devise a plan. Where do I start? How do I begin to formulate a plan for a 4,200-mile bike race across the country? I would be on my own once the race started. There would be no stages, rest days, or help along the route. Every single decision would be the responsibility of the racer, period.

The first step in formulating my plan involved performing a simple math exercise. I had completed the 3,100-mile Southern Tier in 57 days, averaging 55 miles per day. Eighty miles was the highest one-day total. So, if I increased my average daily mileage total from 55 to 80 (which I believed was realistic), I would complete the 4,200-mile race in 53 or 54 days. Could I finish the 4,200-mile race in fewer days than it took me to complete a 3,100-mile ride? *That would be pretty cool*, I thought.

After returning home from my first cross-country ride, I had started to play pickup basketball again. Many of the guys I played with wondered where I had been the past few months. A few had heard about my ride from California to Florida, but most were unaware. Roger, a fellow hoopster and cycling enthusiast, was intrigued by my journey and said he wished to take on a long-distance bike ride, adding that he'd consider joining me if I ever rode again. I piqued his interest. On Tuesday night, April 9, 2019, two days after Nathan approved my registration, inside the Mendham Township Middle School gymnasium, I told Roger I had entered the 2019 TABR. Within a week, Roger decided to join me on my trip to Portland—not to race, but to ride across the state of Oregon. He planned to take a week off from work and cycle hundreds of miles before returning home via Boise, Idaho. By mid-April, Roger and I were both committed and began to prepare in earnest. We hunkered down in a mad dash of effort, our departure to Portland only about five weeks away.

In late April, Roger and I met at Simple Coffee in Mendham to review my bikepacking and riding plan. I wanted to bring Roger up to speed on the details of my plan as quickly as possible. Familiar people entered the shop to buy coffee and stopped briefly for casual conversations. Eyebrows were raised when friends learned of our plans to tackle such an epic journey. Looks of bewilderment and genuine fascination were conveyed through body language, often preceding "Good luck, guys." I wondered if anyone we did not speak to in that shop had a clue that two middle-aged guys were concocting a plan for a bike ride across the country.

From mid-April to mid-May, I increased my training intensity. I lifted weights three or four days a week and rode a stationary bike for 90 to 120 minutes every other day. I varied my training routine; on days not on the stationary bike, I climbed Calais Road, a twisty, winding, half-mile stretch of hill at a 15-percent grade, burning my legs to exhaustion on each climb.

Chet, the owner of Whippany Cycle in Hanover, New Jersey, offered to help me prepare for a grand ride once again. His recommendation to insert sealant inside the Schwalbe Marathon Plus tires' inner tubes the year before had contributed to my being the only member of my tour group who did not experience a single flat tire during the entire 3,100-mile journey. I hoped for a similar outcome with the TABR.

On Sunday, May 19, after attending my son's AAU basketball game, I took Tank to Whippany Cycle for shipment to River City Bicycles in downtown Portland, Oregon.

Kelley and I attended a live Styx concert on May 20 at the Mayo Performing Arts Center in Morristown, New Jersey. A throng of cheering fans packed the theater. With my chin high, chest out, and shoulders pulled back, I raised both arms above my head and clapped wildly when Styx started playing "Too Much Time on My Hands," anticipating the familiar lyrics that had entertained crowds for decades. Like the lead singer, Tommy Shaw, who in the song contemplates his own experience of spending time in a bar in Michigan, I wondered if I too was spending too much time searching for something I would never find. But then, "Come Sail Away" started playing. It was the one song that sent everyone immediately into a frenzy. Hundreds of cell phone lights appeared out of nowhere, everyone expressing their appreciation for the performance. The beginning lyrics touch on the nostalgia of the past, the ending verses a transition to follow your dreams by embarking on a journey into the unknown. An inner peace overwhelmed me, and I remember thinking I could not wait for the race to begin.

A family get-together in Isle of Palms, South Carolina, over Memorial Day weekend to celebrate my sister-in-law Gina's birthday was a fitting send-off, along with much raillery and kind wishes for a successful journey.

Early in the morning of May 30, Kelley drove Roger and me to the Newark airport. At the United terminal, I gave her a hug and a kiss. I remember thinking I would be 30 pounds lighter the next time I saw her. I stood in line at Gate 83, holding a cup of Starbucks coffee. I beamed, so happy to be on the road one more time. I was ready to go!

Chapter 1
ASTORIA, OREGON
May 31, 2019

Roger and I met at 7:00 a.m. in the café attached to the Commodore Hotel lobby. Refreshed after a decent night's sleep and three extra hours of West Coast time, I ordered a breakfast fit for a king: coffee, bacon, fresh fruit, and French toast smothered in maple syrup and sprinkled with powdered sugar. I delighted in every bite, not knowing the next time I would consume such a delicious meal.

After breakfast, we strolled through downtown. The first of many images of nineteenth-century Astoria appeared when I stumbled upon a weathered, cream-colored mural in the small Urban Core neighborhood off Marine Drive. I stepped closer, realizing it was a mural of the Lewis and Clark Expedition's trail, including routes, river passages, map contours, and brief descriptions of each. It was overwhelming and seemed out of place. Was I looking at a blowup of one of Clark's journal entries? I didn't know. I imagined myself using the painted, concrete surface to hit tennis balls.

I thought about Astoria in the winter of 1805 and Lt. William Clark's journal entry, "Ocian in view! O! the joy!" revealed by Stephen

Ambrose in *Undaunted Courage*, when Clark appeared at the mouth of the Columbia River and gazed at the Pacific Ocean.[7]

I stood next to Roger and read every word. I'd never cared to learn history in my primary and secondary education years. I thought, "What's the purpose?" However, since I joined the military in 1984, I had grown to appreciate the world from an entirely different perspective. What better way to experience history, to learn history, than to immerse oneself? The explorers on this expedition traveled in canoes and on horseback to make history; I was pedaling a Surly Disc Trucker to experience it.

The expedition established Fort Clatsop, located six miles south of Astoria, near the Columbia River, and settled in for the bitterly cold winter of 1805.[8] My journey to Yorktown would travel over the same mountains and plains the Corps of Discovery advanced through 220 years before. I read the names of expedition volunteers inscribed on the mural. My heart pounded when my eyes met the name: Pvt. William Werner.

OMG! I wonder if Wally's related? I thought to myself, at the prospect of a familial connection to someone from my Southern Tier tour group. I texted Wally. He replied, "Not that I'm aware of." Oh well.

Roger and I strolled to the Bikes and Beyond store on Marine Drive, just a short distance from the mural. I bought a bright, lime-colored Class 2 neon safety vest to complement the reflective decals I had attached to Tank's frame. In a previous communication to all race entrants, Nathan stressed he'd send anyone home who didn't comply with the safety guidelines. I took his challenge seriously, attaching four Planet Bike Superflash Turbo blinking, red, rear lights and three bright, white front lights and reflection decals to the front and rear tire rims. I hoped the Northwest pea soup fog would be no match for my carnival-colored, blinking bike.

---

[7]   Stephen E Ambrose, *Undaunted Courage: Meriwether Lewis, Thomas Jefferson, and the Opening of the American West.* (New York, NY: Simon & Schuster, 1997), 310.

[8]   Ambrose, *Undaunted Courage*, 318–336

Michael, from Nashville, had been dealing with a bit of a crisis. His mostly put-together custom bike clamped to the repair stand behind the cash register had arrived, but minus a tire. Michael paced back and forth, occasionally stopping to adjust something on his bike. His body language expressed a pinch of uneasiness, as if he was trying to shift his mind from the unthinkable—that after a year of preparation, the race might start without him.

To make matters worse, none of the shop's tire inventory fit his bike. We felt horrible for Michael; his dream to race across America was in jeopardy, and there wasn't anything any of us could do to help. I felt a little guilty knowing my journey to Astoria had begun less than eight weeks before and my preparation had been minimal. Michael had set his sights on conquering the TABR before I'd even considered purchasing a bike, let alone riding it across the country.

"Hey, Michael," Roger muttered, "we'll check back later—Larry and I need to run some errands. I hope the tire shows up."

I proposed, "Hey, Roger, let's divide and conquer; I need to get extra batteries for my SPOT device."

Roger met my suggestion with a consenting nod.

"Open Barbershop" was stenciled on a wooden placard on the pavement along Marine Drive. A clenched fist and extended index finger pointed to the entrance. I peeked inside and knew right away I wanted to return for a haircut—the one and only time I would fraternize and chew the fat with the locals inside a tonsorium on my race across America.

Eyes wide open, I smiled and hummed a tune as I strode at an energetic pace for 1.6 miles to a Safeway grocery store on the eastern edge of town. My usual dull, plodding gait transformed into a gliding stroll; I had a bounce in my step, as I was impatient to hear, "Let the race begin!"

I got extra Energizer Ultimate Lithium AAA batteries for my SPOT satellite tracking device as well as food, including protein bars and beef jerky to carry with me on race day. By early afternoon, menial chores finished, Roger and I turned into tourists once again, wandering around downtown on the main street, peeking inside stores, and pointing out interesting spots to each other.

We swung by the bike shop to see if Michael's tire had arrived before we returned to the Commodore Hotel.

Perusing the store merchandise, I coughed to get Roger's attention. He looked at me. I raised my eyebrows and cocked my head toward two cyclists who were standing and talking nearby. Gawking at them, I whispered, "Those guys look legit!" Their palpable intensity, leg muscle tone—characterized by a bulging teardrop over the kneecap—shaved lower legs, and large, defined, impressive calf muscles convinced me either one could win the event. It struck a nerve seeing their bodily appearance, steady demeanor, and expensive-looking bicycles. These two awe-inspiring individuals meant serious business. And here I was, mad enough to join them.

Each year, the bike shop owner eagerly awaited the Trans Am Bike Race coming to town. Their doors remained open for extended periods when a hundred cyclists descended on the modest town of 10,000 every summer. Except for the Christmas season, race weekend was their moneymaking highlight of the year. One by one, as racers entered the city, Astoria would become the epicenter for ultradistance cycling enthusiasts.

By 2:00 p.m., we had completed all chores, and by 2:20 p.m., I was sitting in a barber chair in Oly's Barber Shop for the only haircut on my trip across the country.

"Hi, I'm Larry. I'm in town for the race," I volunteered, assuming she would ask what I was doing in Astoria.

Oly responded with a familiar barber greeting. "What can I do for you today?"

"One on the sides and two on top," I replied, and for the next 20 minutes, we talked nonstop about Astoria. We covered a whole variety of topics. My usual barbershop behavior was to chat for a couple of minutes after sitting in the chair before closing my eyes for a 10-minute nap and opening them again to the smell of talc, a signal it was time to leave. But now, in Oly's, my eyes remained wide open, as I engaged in discussion from the first clip to the last.

At 6:00 p.m., Roger and I met in the hotel foyer to discuss dinner plans. We settled on eating at the Buoy Beer Company, a brewpub on the pier next to the Columbia River. The fish-and-chips tasted superb! I passed on dessert because we patronized the Frite & Scoop ice cream store on our brief walk to the hotel after dinner. A full, rewarding, and even relaxing day ended at about 8:30 p.m. Roger and I both settled into our rooms, one day closer to entering the world of ultradistance bicycle racing.

Chapter 2
ASTORIA, OREGON
June 1, 2019

W hen I arrived at the hotel café just before 7:15 a.m., Roger had the Adventure Cycling Association map section #1 laid out on the table next to his coffee and breakfast muffin. I sat across from him, ordered the same breakfast I'd eaten the day before, and prepared to complete the final prerace checks and services. We had studied the trail many times before arriving in Astoria, but now, with D-day approaching, prerace preparation took on greater importance. We studied the 65-mile route to Tillamook, our planned destination for race day one.

A man sat in the lobby next to a wide cardboard box that held his disassembled custom-made bike. Shipped from Italy, it had arrived the day before. I sat and watched while he built his racing machine part by part. He left us with the impression he too could win the race.

Since retrieving Tank from the Portland bike shop, where they assembled it after the cross-country flight from New Jersey, I still had not evaluated it to uncover any hidden issues before the race began. I rode Tank around town, only for a mile, checking brakes, shifting gears, and tightening screws to ensure the bike racks were adequately secured.

My abbreviated shakedown ride mimicked my minimal preparation to get to Astoria. I would soon test my body and bike to their limits.

The distance between my new Brooks leather saddle and pedal provided a comfortable, upright riding position. To my pleasant surprise, I hadn't had lower back pain or any other back soreness on the Southern Tier. I planned to repeat the same upright position rather than ride in the typical, hunched-over position most racers employ to reduce drag. (The majority of drag working against a cyclist comes from the rider rather than the bike. Most bikes use aerobars, which are designed to reduce drag, in the hopes of squeezing in an extra one to two miles per hour).

I performed PMCS (Preventive Maintenance Checks and Services) on the brakes, tires, and gear shifters. I added new brake pads and Schwalbe Marathon Plus tires and upgraded to microSHIFT MTB handlebar gear shifters. I packed, repacked, and packed again to ensure everything I'd brought fit into the same Topeak handlebar and saddlebag—a newly purchased Salsa triangle frame bag—and one 20L Sea to Summit weatherproof bag. The REI Big Agnes tent, co-op 35-degree sleeping bag, and wintry weather clothing I secured to the top of the rear rack.

The Columbia River Maritime Museum parking lot, the race starting point, was empty when I rode by that Saturday midafternoon. Attached to a 30-foot pole and flying half-staff, the American flag waved in the wind. Two large fishing boats were docked in the Columbia River next to the museum. Were they about to set sail? Perhaps the vessels had recently returned from a successful trip to sea, contributing their catch to my dinner later that evening.

I straddled Tank, tiptoes touching the ground, underneath a tranquil and clear blue sky and thought about a YouTube video I'd watched several weeks earlier. In that video, Nathan gave a pep talk before the start of the 2016 race, the same race Lael Wilcox won in an epic, come-from-behind win that triggered my desire to test my limits once again. All racers had lined up in a row before the cacophony of birds chirping to signal the dawn of a new day. On that dark and silent June morning, countless red lights blinked, dozens of cyclists ready to fasten their cleats to the pedal and begin the noble race. *Has Nathan planned a similar send-off for my group?* I asked myself. I would find out in less than 18 hours.

A smattering of the 73 race entrants from 15 countries had descended into the downtown locale. Astoria transformed from a sleepy, charming, turn-of-the-century Oregon town into an active, bustling one that overflowed with anticipation for the race to start. A few cyclists rode along Marine Drive and other streets that ran through the heart of downtown. In the parking lot of a convenience store on the south end of Astoria, Roger and I met Noel from Ireland, Crowell from Montana, and Ben from England, all clustered together for a friendly chat. Crowell, Noel, and Ben stood beside their racing machines, all three decked out in colorful cycling gear. Roger wore his bright cycling shirt, while I wore casual clothing. Noel stood next to his bike, which had two differently colored tire rims: the first was green with a white center, and the second a bright orange—a patriotic gesture to his Irish heritage.

As this was his second time competing in the TABR, Crowell was straightforward. He told the group a cycling coach had helped him train for this event. *A cycling coach?* I thought, but I didn't dwell on the notion for very long. Ben chimed in, informing us he had trained with his cycling partner, Mark Cavendish. (The name meant nothing to me. I learned later from Roger that Cavendish is a world-class cyclist of Tour de France fame.)

While I wished to greet as many racers as possible during our relaxing walk through downtown, I realized the primary communication channel would convert to social media after the race started. *How many cyclists will I keep in touch with, anyway?* I mused, realizing the purpose for folks being in town was not to make new friends. The group Facebook page and trackleaders.com, a live tracking site for events that pulls real-time data from the SPOT satellite tracking systems, would soon become the principal communication tools.

Downtown Astoria was not immune to the fate of small-town USA. Older establishments, including the Columbian Theatre—a cinema with one daily showing of *Captain Marvel* (children $2 and adults $4)—and

Schwietert's Cones & Candy, remained open for business. JCPenney on Commercial Street had closed its doors in 2017. Sears Appliance Repair on Marine Drive has since met the same fate.

I had grown accustomed to and cherished the small-town friendliness toward cycling through 229 hamlets nine months earlier. Fifty-six percent had a population under 1,000. I wondered if the TransAmerica Bike Trail kept to the same less-traveled roads as the Southern Tier. Little did I know that my two-day stay in Astoria foreshadowed things to come. Seventy-five percent of the 299 towns between Astoria and Yorktown, Virginia, had similarly small populations.

At 3:40 p.m., I reported to the Astoria Armory community and events center for the prerace inspection. A "Welcome Trans Am Bike Race 2019!" sign hung on the wall near the front entrance. I paused at the welcome sign, kitted out in my cycling gear—blue, short-sleeve shirt, lime-colored neon safety vest, black cycling shorts, and well-worn bike shoes—ready to meet fellow contenders. A powerful sensation overcame me. It was a feeling of belonging. Exuding self-confidence, I thought, *I have been here before.* I knew I could ride coast-to-coast. How fast could I make it across, I didn't know—but I knew I would complete this race.

I opened the door and entered the Armory. About a dozen people sat on chairs around one of the four round dining tables set up in the lobby. Some stood chatting, mostly in hushed tones. Others carried on lively conversations, but all were unintelligible. A handful of unfamiliar faces lined up single file, sitting on chairs next to the wall outside the gym entrance. Nervous energy permeated the room.

One guy sat alone at the first table, staring at something. Maybe in a trance? Some wore cycling gear. Others wore casual clothing. Another guy looked at me and pointed to the gymnasium entrance. I nodded, gave the thumbs-up sign, and walked Tank to the back of the line that had formed inside the gym. The familiar feel of an old, dank, dusty, and welcoming gymnasium was reminiscent of the Fort Polk, Louisiana, field house I had spent many mornings in during PT (physical training). *Oh, the memories.* The magical moment of winning the 5th Division

Basketball Championship in 1985 on that field house court. Charlie Battery. My team. I display a picture of that championship team in my office to this day.

I walked back to the lobby and sat in a chair next to a large man. "Hi, I'm Larry," I said, introducing myself.

"Hi, I'm Harry," he said. I later learned he was a bartender from New York City.

The overwhelming majority of the other cyclists were much shorter and leaner than my six-foot-four, 230-pound frame. But not Harry—at six foot four and 250 pounds, his muscular arms, tree-trunk sized legs, and thick, reddish beard symbolized an adventurous spirit. After that, I had a brief conversation with Wade from Rhode Island, a man who gave the appearance of a successful corporate executive pausing his career to follow a dream. Wade would scratch several days later, returning to complete the 2021 TABR and finishing 10th, arriving at the Yorktown Victory Monument in less than 30 days.

Carl—a North Carolina native and the most colorfully clothed person by far—seemed eager to start the race. He wore bright-yellow compression socks and a bright, multicolored jersey and projected unmatched positive energy. He commanded the room like a good politician, walking around, interacting, and conversing with fellow racers.

I could barely hear myself over the din of the growing crowd. I served myself a plate of cheese, crackers, and assorted fruit, waiting for Nathan to arrive. Platters of food sat on the ledge of a walk-up, pass-through window. I thought about my high school cafeteria and daily approaching a similar window many years before with a dime to buy an extra ice-cream sandwich.

Nathan walked into the lobby at 4:30 p.m. and welcomed all of us to Astoria. He put us all at ease when he said, "I just want to be clear—everyone will pass the inspection."

Seventy-three racers entered the gymnasium and stood next to bikes lined against the wall. When it was my turn, Nathan signaled for me to walk toward him to the front of a plastic, rectangular, six-foot-long table—the first station. I handed my medical clearance and proof of extreme sports insurance to him. He glanced at Tank, eyed the two documents, and pointed to his right. Had I just passed the prerace inspection? The most critical inspection I could remember preparing for was over in less than 30 seconds. Nathan had given me the green light to move on.

I approached the next station—the weigh station—and introduced myself to Thomas, who stood next to a hanging scale. I did not realize it, but Thomas was a legend in the ultradistance cycling community. He would become a household name for all racers and "dot watchers" (cycling enthusiasts who follow the event online). At 78, this was Thomas's fourth TABR. He gave no sign he could take on such an enormous challenge by his appearance and gait. I shook Thomas's hand, raised my bike, and placed it on the industrial scale. Thomas looked at me and said, "That's a heavy one—seventy-two pounds." My CroMoly steel Surly Disc Trucker touring bike weighed at least 25 pounds more than the average carbon fiber framed bicycle that swarmed the gymnasium. An entrant standing behind me in line gave me a puzzled look. I bet he perceived me as one less person he'd have to compete with. (Carbon fiber and titanium framed racing bicycles cost several thousand dollars. My Surly Disc Trucker touring bike cost $1,500.)

After the prerace inspection ended, all racers assembled in the middle of the gym, clustered close together, sitting on rickety, white folding chairs. A few sitting close to me spoke in low voices, holding mumbled conversations. Others stared straight ahead, appearing lost in the moment. Directly behind me, two racers sat next to each other. One guy looked down at the ground. The second cyclist yawned, perhaps anxious, thinking about what lay ahead.

I extended my hand and introduced myself to Jared, who sat next to me. Originally from Australia, he now lived in Gig Harbor, Washington. He appeared to be in great physical shape. I wondered if his mild manner obfuscated his cycling prowess. "What kind of training did you do to prepare for the race?" I asked. He looked straight ahead, not making eye contact, and told me he rode short stints to and from work each day. On weekends, he extended the mileage and camped out, trying to replicate the bona fide experience that would greet all of us in a matter of hours. After hearing Jared share his focused and intense training plan, I appreciated the monumental challenge ahead of me. Had I trained well enough to complete the race? I would find out soon enough.

I did not know it at the time, but Abdullah Zeinab, from Australia, sat next to Jared. By the end of June 4, race day three, Abdullah would be so far ahead of all other racers that it was a foregone conclusion he would win. Eventually, he would win in record time: 16 days, 9 hours, and 56 minutes, averaging 254 miles per day.

Nathan stood on the gym's raised, stage platform, glanced at the multitudes, and, for the second time, welcomed all of us to Astoria and the TABR. The crowd quieted down in a matter of seconds, and all eyes directed to the stage, anxiously waiting to hear Nathan speak. I captured the moment on video—the opening scene to what I knew would be one hell of a journey.

Nathan started the orientation by telling us how the TABR began. He had lived in a Missouri town on the original TransAmerica Bike Trail and often wondered why a Trans Am race didn't exist. An avid cyclist, he acted on his curiosity and founded the TABR in 2014, which has since become one of the most challenging, self-contained, ultradistance races in the world.

Nathan went on to describe sections of the route in Midwestern states that remained impassable because of flooding caused by widespread spring storms that dropped historic amounts of rain. Residual snow in the Cascade Mountains meant Santiam Pass (4,817 ft) replaced McKenzie Pass (5,325 ft) as our ticket over the Cascades. For a fleeting moment, I considered taking an alternate sanctioned route through Nebraska rather than the primary route through Wyoming to Pueblo, Colorado, before turning east. The alternate route bypassed flooded roads in large swaths of Kansas. However, my desire to experience the endless Kansas highways overshadowed any concern about lingering floodwaters. Plus, I had a greater chance of seeing a tornado if I rode through Kansas!

Nathan then shifted his attention to Thomas and praised him in front of the entire assembly. The tragic death of John Egbers during the 2018 TABR—he'd been struck by an automobile while riding eastbound on Kansas Highway 96—made Nathan reflect long and hard on whether to continue the event. He gave Thomas credit for guiding him, concluding that the race must continue. I had been aware of Egbers's death before arriving in Astoria, but I had not fully appreciated his impact on the cycling community. Many in the gym had been dear friends and had ridden with him for many years. The year before Egbers's death, during the 2017 TABR, a car struck Eric Fishbein's bike and killed him on the same Kansas Highway 96. To compound events further, three months before Fishbein's death, an automobile struck and killed Mike Hall, winner of the 2014 inaugural TABR, while he was riding in the 2017 Australia Indian Pacific Wheel Race. One prerace communication warned of a high probability that at least two collisions would occur. It was a chance I took and a detail I didn't share with my parents—I told Kelley, though.

Nathan shared two parting thoughts before wishing us well and sending us on our way. First, he reminded everybody, "It's just a bike ride—nothing more, nothing less." He then added, "If you're thinking about scratching, sleep on it for a night before deciding." He appreciated what we were all about to embark on, having finished the inaugural 2014 TABR.

With the last of the prerace instructions over, we all rose, reclaimed our bikes, and moved toward the exit. I met Rolf on my way to the door. He handed me some baseball-sized cards with a request to distribute them at random markers along the route. Each laminated card revealed a message I would repeatedly see on my ride across America: a picture of Egbers riding his bike, followed by the statement, "Four Deadly Words… 'I Didn't See Him'—Eyes Up!" A kind gesture and a hint to cycle carefully.

After eating at the Fort George Brewery, Roger and I returned to the Commodore Hotel. We agreed to meet outside at 4:30 a.m. The elevator opened on the second floor.

"Sleep well," I said.

"You the same," Roger replied.

I entered my room and made sure I packed everything and that Tank was ready to go. I uploaded the alternate routes Nathan had shared with us. I lay down on the bed and shared on my Facebook page, "Not in a million years did I ever imagine riding coast-to-coast a second time. The mind works in mysterious ways, and in about 7 hours, I begin again. This time on the TransAmerica Bike Trail, Astoria to Yorktown. Only this time, I'm racing." I added that I was excited to get started and test my limits and that I would do my best to give daily updates.

The morning would arrive quickly. I thought about my wife and kids before falling fast asleep.

Raring To Go
Astoria, Oregon
June 1, 2019

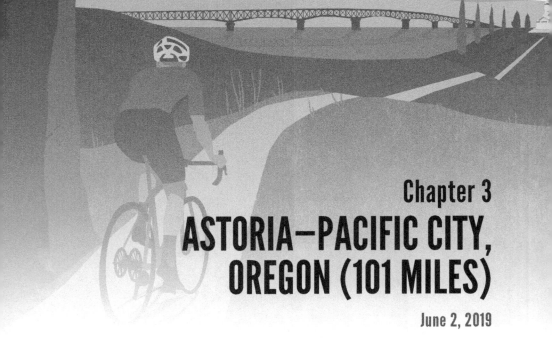

Chapter 3
ASTORIA–PACIFIC CITY, OREGON (101 MILES)

June 2, 2019

T he alarm sounded at 4:00 a.m. sharp. I sat up and looked around the room, which was so small that it would not suit someone affected by claustrophobia. I collected my thoughts, processing the early morning hour. I popped out of bed, brushed my teeth at the sink inside my room, and swallowed 100 mg of Zoloft and 100 mg of Wellbutrin, continuing a morning routine that began in 2018. I donned the cycling gear I had placed on a chair next to the bed the night before: a blue, long-sleeved Smartwool base layer top underneath a blue, short-sleeved, 100-percent polyester cycling shirt. As a Class 2, the lime-colored, neon, outer layer vest I bought the day before guaranteed I would remain visible during the predawn hours. (The American National Standards Institute certifies safety vests Class 1, 2, or 3. Class 1 for low-risk work environments; Class 3 for the highest risk.) I inspected Tank and thought, *Anything missing? Nope.* I was ready to leave my room at 4:30 a.m.

I quickly walked Tank through the hallway, careful not to wake hotel guests. Moments later, I exited the elevator and entered a quiet, empty hotel lobby. I walked outside into a peaceful, dark, chilly morning. Waiting for Roger to arrive, I looked around, caught in the surreal sense that everything that had happened the past several months had a purpose. It was hard to process the moment. I was about to begin one of the world's most challenging ultradistance, self-contained bicycle races. In less than 30 minutes, I would begin a journey like no other.

"How'd you sleep?" I asked Roger when he appeared in the morning darkness.

"Good. How about you? You ready?"

"I'm ready to go."

We hopped onto our bicycles and began the short trek to the Maritime Museum. Pedaling away from the Commodore Hotel brought me a sense of calm.

Like many times before, I thought, *Don't try to keep up with the leaders.* The lesson of the tortoise and the hare, one of Aesop's Fables, had entered my mind countless times when deciding on my strategy. *Don't be careless, be resolute. Slow and steady wins the race.* Roger stopped at 14th Street and Marine Drive, about half a mile from the starting point. He would enter the queue along Marine Drive after all racers passed his location. I arrived at the Maritime Museum parking lot at 4:37 a.m. and was one of the first to get there.

White lights beyond the Columbia River shoreline poked through the haze and darkness in the distance. The museum parking lot would soon become the point of convergence for the ultradistance racing community. I saw a couple of cars parked in a lot next to the museum as well a few people milling around, presumably there to wish us well. I rode across the parking lot to the assembly area and leaned Tank against the museum's glass facade. I looked inside; a radiant security light spotlighted an empty gift shop. A single, bright, white light projecting from a fishing vessel docked next to the museum along the banks of the Columbia River caused me to lose my vision. I quickly looked away. The lot swiftly and quietly filled. Anticipation filled the air. Thirty seconds. One minute. Two minutes. The number of blinking, red, rear bike lights grew to create a symphony of light. The predawn gathering was coming to life. Reflective tape attached to several lime-colored vests illuminated in the darkness. Each person displayed a quiet intensity, whispering to others within earshot. Some made last-minute bike adjustments, ensuring everything was secure and ready to go. That is what I did.

At 4:47 a.m., Nathan broke the silence when he addressed the assembled masses. "Sixty-four of y'all, sixty-six of y'all, are ready to go. We got eight people left. Come talk to me if you haven't yet pinged." He implored everyone to ensure their satellite tracking device was operational. At 4:50 a.m., Thomas, standing next to the flagpole in the center of the meeting place, welcomed everyone to the starting line and said, "It's tradition to start the race with a toast." He walked around and handed several individuals standing next to their bikes a plastic party flute filled halfway with champagne. Others, including me, walked toward Thomas and waited to be handed a champagne flute. We all raised our champagne, giving Thomas our undivided attention.

"Everyone, ride safely, and good luck getting to Yorktown," he toasted.

I heard a muffled "Cheers!" and other unintelligible gibberish before the muster drifted back into silence.

I raised my flute, looked at Thomas, and nodded my head, agreeing with the words he shared. However, I only touched my lips to the rim. Anything that dulled my senses, including alcohol, was off-limits until I finished the race.

Nathan gave a one-minute warning. And before I knew it, the race started. The sound of cowbells filled the air, bringing to life the quiet, still morning. I waited until most racers departed before I began riding away from the Maritime Museum. I crossed over railroad tracks, a section of the now-closed Astoria & South Coast Railway, and turned south onto Marine Drive, riding into the darkness. Two thoughts entered my mind. The first was that I would never see most of these people ever again, and the second was a reminder to pace myself, to ride my race and only my race. "It's all about the finish," I said to myself, hoping I would remain disciplined in executing my strategy.

Seventy-three racers formed a pseudo-peloton, like an amoeba. The single mass of humanity slowly extended for the first two miles before reaching the Old Youngs Bay Bridge on the edge of town. From that point on, everyone was on their own. When I reached the bridge, most blinking red lights had disappeared—no caravan of motorized vehicles tagging along like many professional race events. No medical van, police escort, or other vehicles with flashing lights took part in the send-off. Nathan and his copilot, Anthony, the official race photographer, led the pack out of Astoria in a small, blue sedan.

Except for the measured send-off at the starting point, the ride out of Astoria was similar to the typical, quiet, early morning training ride in my hometown of Mendham, New Jersey. All alone, not concerned, I had fallen to the rear of the pack. It was too soon to know if I would take home the title of Lanterne Rouge when all was said and done. I thought about Nathan's parting words the night before. "At the end of the day, it's just a bike ride—nothing more, nothing less." I set my pace. My body felt good; my leg muscles came to life with every pedal rotation. The cool, 60-degree temperature and mild humidity made for perfect riding conditions. My upper body felt snug underneath my long-sleeved Smartwool base layer.

I saw a few blinking red lights in the distance at 5:20 a.m. when I reached the intersection of Lewis and Clark Road and Logan Road. *Which way do I go?* I wondered. My GPS directed me left. Racers before me veered right, onto a road with no name. "What the heck is going on?" So early in the race, and I was already second-guessing the route? That could not be a good sign and was perhaps an ominous warning for things to come. I veered right, onto the path the others had taken. Surrounded by tall pine trees on both sides of the narrow road, I became concerned that Roger might not have seen me veer right. Suddenly annoyed, I mouthed, "WTF!" I stopped, turned around, backtracked, and turned right onto Logan Road when I reached the intersection. I learned later that Roger had been delayed leaving Astoria due to helping a fellow cyclist with a flat tire. After they both continued pedaling toward the outskirts of Astoria, the cyclist clipped a car and fell off his bike. Thankfully, no one was injured and the bike wasn't damaged. When Roger shared this story with me later that morning, I thought back to the prerace communication materials I had read: "There is a good probability two collisions would occur somewhere along the 4,200-mile route." I wondered who the second victim would be.

Why had the others gone in a different direction? I put that thought in the back of my mind. Nathan mentioned nothing about an alternate route 10 miles outside Astoria. The leaders of the pack had thrown me a curveball. It was déjà vu. For on September 17, 2018, the first day of the Southern Tier, my group gear nearly fell off my front rack just 10 miles outside of San Diego, the starting point for that journey. That trip ended well, and I hoped that would hold true for this one!

I wondered if I had made the correct decision when I found myself in this dilemma. Oddly enough, I welcomed testing my mind and body. I wanted to confront the unexpected. My sense of gratification heightened each time I conquered the unknown.

The route would throw me many curveballs on my way to Yorktown, Virginia. Would I make wise decisions? Moved by a strong desire to test my boundaries, there had been many circumstances in my adult working career when I'd met the proverbial fork in the road. Challenged to carry out my chosen path, I frequently chose adventure over comfort. My thirst for stepping into the unknown drove me.

But I lacked the courage to make one decision: leaving a well-paying pharmaceutical sales and marketing job. Between 2007 and 2018, I considered resigning many times because of a toxic work environment. But the money and benefits were good. I lacked the strength to leave my comfortable, corporate lifestyle.

I fretted for the next five miles, not knowing if I had taken the correct route. "What the hell!" My gut churned at the possibility that, less than an hour into the race, I was already riding extra miles. It seemed like an eternity. Twenty minutes later, I saw a bike leaning against a tree on the side of Logan Road. When I reached it, I scanned the wood line; a racer stood facing away from the road, relieving himself. *I wasn't the only one who went this way,* I thought. Then I thought about how this racer was in for a long ride if he had to pee an hour into a 4,200-mile bike ride!

A couple of miles later, I passed the side road others had taken when they veered right, reconnecting with Logan Road. *Aren't we all adhering to the same route?* I wondered, not sure why my GPS directed me onto Logan Road. I didn't realize that the side road and Lewis and Clark Road were the same. To this day, I'm still puzzled why my GPS directed me onto Logan Road. The race organizers had levied penalties against cyclists in previous races who didn't abide by the race rules. Satellite tracking devices going dark for an extended time was a common infraction. The extra lithium batteries I carried would reduce the chances of my SPOT device dying in the middle of a desert.

No use dwelling, I thought. At 5:45 a.m., on June 2, 20 miles outside of Astoria on Lewis and Clark Road, I decided to trust my instincts from then on. Several days later, trusting my instincts would serve me well in Jeffrey City, Wyoming.

At 6:44 a.m., I reached Seaside (population 6,457) and the intersection of Wahanna Road and North Promenade, a one-and-a-half-mile stretch that runs parallel to the Pacific Ocean. A man, woman, and dog greeted me. They'd missed the sendoff at 5:00 a.m. Realizing their mistake, they drove 17 miles to greet racers at the coast to cheer us on. When the woman asked if I had seen the documentary *Inspired to Ride*, about the 2014 inaugural TABR, I had to admit I hadn't even heard of it. The 90-minute documentary features Mike Hall, Juliana Buhring, and others who competed in the race. The film takes the viewer on an "invigorating road trip amidst the jaw-dropping beauty of the TransAmerica Bike Trail as the racers battle lack of sleep, injury, and sheer competition." This couple, who I've since lost touch with, followed my progress across the country, reaching out to congratulate me when

I reached the finish 37 days later. Kelley and I watched *Inspired to Ride* the day after I returned home.

At 7:44 a.m., nine miles south of Seaside, I stopped at the Cannon Beach Bakery in Cannon Beach (population 1,690). I sat alone on a stool next to the window, drinking coffee and gazing outside on this quiet Sunday morning. I chose not to talk to anyone while waiting in line to buy coffee and a muffin. Here, a conflict entered my mind for the first time, and it wouldn't be the last. *If I am trying to race across the country, can I also enjoy myself?* I had to wonder if my desire to enjoy this experience was incompatible with my desire to finish this race. The brief stops in Seaside and Cannon Beach would be the first of many on my journey across the country. My desire to engage with folks faded as the race developed. My attitude gradually shifted to a single desire— finishing the race.

Thirty minutes after entering the bakery, I was on the saddle. A marine layer blanketed the sky. Much of the route hugged the coastline. I was riding south on US Highway 1, the same road Roger had pointed out on the Greyhound bus two days earlier. Roger and I reconnected along the highway south of Cannon Beach. We paused to look at the famed Haystack Rock, a 235-foot sea stack claimed by the locals to be "the third-tallest intertidal structure in the world."[9] It dominated the beach landscape. The image of Lady Liberty buried in the sand in the 1968 film *Planet of the Apes* entered my mind as I peered at the rock formation. The silhouette of the massive landmark on the sandy Pacific Ocean beach was unmistakable against the soupy sky. The calming sound of the crashing waves was only a whisper.

Still hugging the coastline, I approached the iconic Arch Cape Tunnel entrance, the gateway to Oswald West State Park. First opened

---

[9] "10 Fund Facts About Haystack Rock in Cannon Beach," *The Local Arrow*, The Hasson Company, April 30, https://www.hasson.com/blog/2021/04/fun-facts-haystack-rock-cannon-beach/

in 1940, the 1,227-foot-long, one-lane, narrow tunnel[10] road on coastal Highway 101 caught my attention when I looked through the dark, semicircle opening built into the side of the mountain. Tank's white front light and three blinking red rear lights were on. I activated a beacon that signaled to motorists that a bicycle was entering the tunnel and then nervously entered the dark, cave-like stretch, knowing I had little room to maneuver.

When I emerged, blue sky appeared above the low cloud cover, shining over the ocean at the top of a short but steep ascent over Neahkahnie Mountain. Several curious bystanders watched paragliders flying high out over the sea. Using a small gravel section of road that had been carved out as a makeshift launch pad, paragliders soared over the water, close to the enormous Tillamook Headlands that dropped from the road's edge hundreds of feet into the crashing waves below. According to one paraglider, wind conditions were ideal for paragliding in this area.

Harry had stopped to change a tire halfway up the hill we had just ascended.

"Hi, Harry. Do you need help?" I asked. My pace had slowed to a mere crawl due to the steep grade.

"No, just changing a flat. Thanks, though," he responded.

I remember thinking Harry was in for a rough haul if he already had a flat tire less than 50 miles into the race.

In Manzanita, I stopped at a vista overlooking Tillamook Bay. Several older folks approached the opening to view the breathtaking scenery. "Where are you going?" somebody asked—a familiar question, which prompted me to share my story.

"On December 17, 2017, I injured my foot playing basketball, so I started riding my bike for exercise. Now, I'm riding my bike across the country a second time." It was an account I had proudly broadcasted

---

[10]   "The Arch Cape Tunnel," The Cannon Beach History Center & Museum, posted November 13, 2014, https://cbhistory.org/blog/general/the-arch-cape-tunnel/

many times before. When I pedaled away from the vista, I thought about how my life had come full circle. The injury to my foot prevented me from playing hoops. Riding my bicycle for exercise triggered my desire to ride coast-to-coast. And now, for reasons that seemed improbable, I found myself on a vista overlooking the Pacific Ocean, talking to strangers who coincidentally were hoopaholics, just like me.

Downtown Tillamook was sunny and warm when Roger and I entered at 1:00 p.m., eight hours after leaving Astoria and 65 miles south. It was too early to stop for the day. I had plenty of gas remaining in my proverbial tank. I wondered how Roger felt and asked if he wanted to continue. We were not in a rush. Roger, Harry (who caught up in Tillamook), and I walked into the Dutch Mill Diner on Main Avenue in the heart of downtown. The three of us sat on vinyl, backless, 1950s-vintage stools and placed our arms on the laminate tabletop. I washed my greasy bacon cheeseburger and fries down with a large vanilla milkshake. A local patron overheard our conversation. He suggested riding to Pacific City (population 1,035), about 25 miles south of Tillamook.

So, that's what we did.

Ekloff Road took us through a clear-cut logging sector. Surrounded by an empty, harvested forest, I thought, *Thank God for my Schwalbe tires*, when the asphalt road turned to gravel. Self-doubt crept in once again. Had I made a wrong turn? I pulled out the Adventure Cycling Association map and waited for Roger to join me at the summit. I felt much better when I realized a paved Whisky Creek Road—the primary route—was only 0.2 miles ahead.

I reached Pacific City about an hour before Roger and two hours before sunset. We were all alone at the primitive Cape Kiwanda RV resort campsite, located across the street from the Pacific Ocean. It would be our first night camping under the stars. We walked to the Doryland restaurant, which was near the resort entrance and across the street from the ocean. It felt good to stretch my legs. An intense white, yellow, and orange sun overwhelmed the sky out over the sea. Within minutes, the color morphed into a pink sky as the sun sank into the sea.

With the first day on the saddle now behind us, Roger and I chatted over a rich carbohydrate and protein meal of pizza, pasta, and chicken wings. We were invigorated to have ridden over 100 miles, but we were disappointed to be no farther east than when we left Astoria 12 hours earlier. We agreed not to press too hard the next day. However, when I said good night and entered my tent, deep down, I wondered if I could go 100 miles again on day two.

I sat on the ground inside my Big Agnes tent and curled up inside my sleeping bag. I watched a Facebook video taken earlier that day. The footage showed three racers sprinting in the tuck position in the middle of South Hemlock Street in Cannon Beach. If I didn't know any better, they could have been on Water Street in Yorktown, pushing the last two hundred yards to the Yorktown Victory Monument finish line. I couldn't fathom how these pack leaders were pedaling so hard with over 4,100 miles to go!

Tired and contented, Roger and I were ready for a solid night's sleep and a more reasonable start the following day. Vivid images of the day flashed through my mind. Conversing with individuals I met brought me an abundance of joy. But I recognized this ride had higher stakes and the satisfaction I experienced would wane as the days passed.

Racing across America demanded a singular focus that didn't include stopping to chat with folks as much as I had done on the Southern Tier. Still, sometimes I hungered for the same sense of satisfaction I had each time I greeted a stranger and swapped tales with families who lived in rural America. The farther I fell behind the leaders, the more the conflict played out in my mind. Ignoring the freedom to meet decent individuals in small-town America took away from the authentic experience that comes with a cross-country bike ride. I kept this internal conflict to myself. The cognitive dissonance: race or enjoy the ride. Could I do both? This nagging, internal quarrel stayed with me from June 2 until June 8, in Baker City, Oregon. From then on, it was all about the race.

Abdullah was 140 miles ahead of me when I checked the leaders' site as I snuggled inside my sleeping bag. *Unbelievable*, I thought. I was determined to remain disciplined, to never waver from my strategy to ride in daylight and rest when the sun went down. I also believed in the *start slow, assess how I'm feeling, and then finish strong* approach. I did, however, fall victim to "Abdullah's watch." By June 4, he had grown into a folk hero, leading the next closest racer by two hundred miles.

Ouch! My Leg Muscles Ache
Pacific City, Oregon
June 3, 2019

Chapter 4
PACIFIC CITY–CORVALLIS, OREGON (93 MILES)

June 3, 2019

Deciding how long to ride, sleep, eat, and rest each day was all part of the intrigue. "We planned to stop [in Tillamook], but I feel we should continue," I had urged Roger at the Dutch Mill Diner the day before. Roger agreed. By then, the 54-day game plan had morphed into a general guide, no longer a comprehensive, controlling formula for success. At this early stage, I didn't have a refined master scheme. I'd reflected on a famous phrase among many respected historical military figures—"No plan survives contact with the enemy"—as I'd saddled up for the last leg to Pacific City.

At 6:10 a.m., I grasped the Big Agnes zipper and drew open the inside tent and rain cover. The liners, weighed down by the morning dew, slowly crept back to the closed position. I flung the liners open again, this time rolling them and tying them so they remained open for the morning light to shine through. The intense adrenaline rush from the morning before, when racers gathered predawn, anxious to leave but bound to wait until 5:00 a.m., was gone. We were no longer confined, now free to begin each day at our discretion.

I felt refreshed after a fantastic night of sleep. The morning mind fog that often greeted me—to only be subdued by caffeine—was absent. My thigh muscles felt sore after completing a century ride the day before. When I stepped outside into the morning light, I saw Roger stirring about inside his tent. A few parked RVs dotted the campsite. The sound of silence was deafening. Morning clouds blanketed the coastline. Farther south, blue sky appeared beyond the marine layer. Surprisingly, the neon vest and yellow windbreaker I'd hung on a pine tree the night before had dried.

I packed and secured my equipment, item by item. Every morning was the same routine—a process I had perfected to help transform my 57-year-old body into a 57-year-young competitor. However, what had become my routine was not the same for Roger. The night spent camping in Pacific City was Roger's first time sleeping on the ground in many years. "I didn't sleep so well," Roger shared when he poked his head out of his tent. The original 54-day plan called for staying at campsites and motels; ideally, camping when the weather was good and staying in a motel when it wasn't.

At 8:54 a.m., we reached the intersection of Highway 101. Blue sky entered into the picturesque landscape, appearing above the low marine layer hovering over the ocean. A middle-aged man greeted us outside Stimulus Coffee and Bakery, triggering a chance encounter with a basketball junkie.

His greeting drew me in. "Good morning. A fantastic day for cycling."

"Sure is. We're riding across the country. And, hopefully, we start heading east soon," I replied, tongue in cheek. Emphasizing my point, I added, "Virginia is east. That's the direction I want to go!"

Our discussion turned to women's basketball. He'd coached at the high school level for 42 years.

"My two girls—Tara and Jaclyn—played high school varsity basketball," I boasted, adding, "I did not appreciate women's basketball growing up with four brothers."

After Tara and Jaclyn started playing in grade school, I became a fan, to the extent I loved coaching and now prefer watching women's basketball; they play the game the right way!

Between 2005 and 2007, we lived in Chagrin Falls, Ohio. I played ball in a 25-and-older competitive league at the Mandel Jewish Community Center in Beachwood, Ohio. A traditional draft selected for each team, and coaches picked players they wanted for their roster. The basketball league was stocked full of accomplished players, many of whom had competed at a high level in college, including at the University of Dayton and the College of Charleston. Before the 2006 season, my team gathered inside the gym before tip-off to introduce ourselves. Our coach had selected Christine Rigby, the only female in the league. At six foot six, Christine led our team in block shots and three-point shooting percentage and helped guide us to an overall second place league finish. Christine played at UCONN and was a 1999–2000 National Championship Team member. In 1997, she led the Canadian Women's National Team. How I misjudged a woman's ability to play high-level, competitive basketball when I was a young guy! I wouldn't make that same mistake in the world of ultradistance cycling, that was for sure.

After hugging the shoreline for a full day and 110 miles, finally, the route swung east and inland at Nestucca Bay on Highway 12, near Neskowin (population 134). The crisp morning air chilled my torso when I began in Pacific City. The combination of cool climate, elevated humidity, and low cloud cover made it challenging to dress appropriately. Layering properly had challenged me ever since riding the Southern Tier. I sweated profusely, which often resulted in my torso becoming cold, wet, and extremely uncomfortable. I never figured out the ideal layer combination.

Highway 12 turned into Old Scenic Highway 101, which flanked the Salmon River. In August 1805, after crossing the Continental Divide on their westward expedition, Lewis and Clark first ventured down the Salmon. The area bordering the river was considered sacred ground by Indigenous people due to the abundance of food.[11] The clear, fast-running water burbled through the wood line, the pitch increasing when water and rocks collided, creating white, foamy rapids. The marine layer had dissipated, and towering evergreen trees provided a canopy covering the narrow road. Some of the trees had branches extending the entire length, starting just off the ground. Other species' branches grew from the trunk about 30 feet from the ground. Towering ponderosa and cottonwood trees intercepted the sunlight, filtering it like a net. It fell in dapples over the road, disguising serpentine cracks and ankle-deep potholes. I avoided riding over any irregularity in the surface of the road. The extra precaution served me well on the Southern Tier and would do the same on the TABR.

When I noticed a sign for the Salmon River Fish Hatchery, I was reminded of the fall of 1996. Our friends Arlene and Milt, from Oakland, California, visited Kelley, me, and our two daughters at our home in Issaquah, Washington, where we lived from 1996 to 2001. During their stay, we ventured to downtown Issaquah for Salmon Days to watch salmon return to Issaquah Creek from their arduous journey at sea, battling against the current hundreds—if not thousands—of miles to spawn at their chosen place. Remembering the salmon splashing and struggling to swim upstream, working overtime to get to their destination, I imagined the same arduous journey awaited me as I continued on Old Scenic Highway 101, approaching Santiam Pass, Oregon—our gateway over the Cascade Mountains.

My body felt strong. Every pedal stroke propelled me a fraction of a mile closer to the Yorktown Victory Monument. Close to Dallas, Oregon, on Highway 22, I looked to my left and squinted to see a large landmass protruding skyward in the distance. Once my eyes adapted, a snow-covered Mount Hood came into clear view, its location 136 miles away. I looked at the ground and followed the journey to Mount Hood one frame at a time. The late afternoon breeze rippled through acres of wheat fields,

---

[11] Ambrose, *Undaunted Courage*, 289–291

transforming into rolling, grassy slopes that led to the picturesque Cascade Mountain Range. Mount Hood, centered and framed by the Southern Oregon landscape, resembled a table centerpiece. The marine layer, cool climate, and cloud blanket that had monopolized the coastline from Astoria to Neskowin had transformed into a brilliant, clear blue sky and mid-seventies-degree weather on my way to Corvallis, Oregon.

Many of the towns I went through in Southern Oregon—Grande Ronde (population 1,661), Monmouth (population 9,534), and Adair Village (population 526)—kept the quality and feel of what had vanished in vast swaths of American society. The folks I met lived under an accepted code of "small-town friendly." Each interaction, while often brief, seemed sincere. The small talk ran deep; everyone made eye contact. Each human encounter seemed like more than a handshake between two strangers. Store employees genuinely appreciated each time I bought food or other items from their establishment.

At a Dairy Queen in Monmouth, Roger and I did not think twice about leaving our bikes outside unattended. The irresistible pull of a vanilla ice-cream cone was too potent to avoid. Roger and I had agreed to ride at our own pace, but we maintained contact through text messaging, often arranging to meet at a rallying point, as we did at DQ in Monmouth.

Red blotches had formed on the tip of my nose. Upon closer inspection, I saw blood had dried on my blistered lower lip. The skin had peeled away from my nose because of the harsh sun beating down on me all afternoon. I'd forgotten to apply sunscreen and ChapStick before leaving Pacific City hours earlier.

My head was on a swivel while pedaling to Corvallis, turning left and right to snatch a glimpse of anything of significance. Like riding in one of those miniature choo choo trains on a visit to the zoo, my eyes and ears were laser focused on getting a glimpse of a caged monkey or hearing the roar of a mountain lion. I was enjoying myself too much. *I'm supposed to be racing*, I thought—an internal conflict that played out repeatedly. I kept these musings to myself. Roger didn't need to hear my internal argument. About 15 miles before entering Corvallis (population 54,462), the home of Oregon State University, we caught up to Carl (from North Carolina). Carl had worn a brilliant, colorful cycling kit at the prerace orientation and had been full of spirit, mingling with race entrants. He had worked the room like a seasoned politician—the life of the party.

"I'm going to ride ahead and reserve rooms," I offered, confident Roger and Carl would welcome each other's company for the few remaining miles to Corvallis. I took full advantage of the excellent riding conditions, increasing my speed to 25 mph on the smooth, paved NW Highland Drive leading to Corvallis.

Roger called me about an hour after I reached Corvallis. The rate he got at a Days Inn was $10 lower than what I could bargain for at the Super 8. To save money, we decided to stay at the Days Inn, even though its location was a mile off route. I saddled up and met Roger and Carl there. The Super 8, our original lodging destination, was on the route next to the Willamette River, which we would cross on our way out of town.

Roger, Carl, and I strolled about 300 feet through the Days Inn parking lot to Elmer's.

"Carl, what's the deal with no shoes?" I asked, wondering why he only wore socks.

"Trying to keep bike weight down," he replied.

I raised my eyebrows and nodded, but I thought, *Not sure that's the best idea*, foreseeing the endless ways in which shoes would come in handy over the next 4,000 miles. We sat in a wall booth—Roger and me on one side, facing Carl. I craved pancakes. At 7:30 p.m., in the empty dining room, I ordered a large stack with a side of bacon and washed it all down with a large vanilla shake.

"Hey, Larry, we rode close to one hundred miles again, the second day in a row," Roger shared, his voice signaling surprise, pride, and concern. "Not sure my knees can repeat one hundred miles every day."

I felt conflicted, unsure how to reveal my honest thoughts. "I know, it's crazy. I want to press, but without going too hard. I don't know if my body will hold up," I said. Could I ride 100 miles per day all the way to Yorktown? *That's insane*, I thought.

I went on, "Let's just take the same approach tomorrow and evaluate things midday, before deciding how much longer to go."

I could tell Roger did not want to hold me back when he said, "I'm here for the ride. You're here for the race, Larry."

We ate our meal, making light conversation to pass the time.

"I bought a Brooks saddle about a month ago. It feels good so far, but I fear it's not sufficiently broken in. My biggest worry is developing saddle sores. I got them on the Southern Tier, and I can tell you they aren't much fun," I shared, as our conversation evolved to equipment.

Carl replied, "I bought a $400 custom saddle from a guy in California. It's got an open funnel in the center designed to prevent saddle sores and ensure continuous blood circulates to the groin."

Another moment of self-doubt hit me. "God, I hope my butt survives this ride!"

Abdullah had extended his lead to over 300 miles by the end of day two. The next closest contenders were about 50 miles behind. Europeans (Omar, Jani, Paolo, Maximiliano) and Americans (Peter, Garth, Keith, and Tom) pressed hard to keep pace with Abdullah. One of 10 female racers, Lea had proven herself a contender, pacing in the top 10. I held to my game plan—sleep at night, ride during daylight. I was racing against time, against *myself*—not 72 contenders. My daily goals varied based on weather conditions, available services, and body strength. I genuinely believed a clear vision and executing a defined strategy would give me the best chance to finish the race—perhaps in fewer days than initially planned.

I'd willingly joined the rat race to climb the corporate ladder when working for Pfizer Pharmaceuticals, starting in 1991. Ten years later, I moved my family from Issaquah, Washington, to Ridgefield, Connecticut, after a promotion from district sales manager to director of leadership development in Pfizer's prestigious training department. I joined a small team responsible for training Pfizer's first-line sales managers in the art of selling, coaching, and performance management. I had entered my new role after five successful years as a district sales manager, earning the prestigious Vice President's Management Cabinet Sales Leadership Award twice. I knew I could contribute to helping newly promoted district sales managers develop into effective sales leaders. During that time, promotion into the training department was often the entry position to an alternative career pathway. For others, like me, it was a stepping-stone to a more senior field sales leadership position. Those positions were limited—only about 10 percent of district manager assignments—and they were hard to come by. Performance was key. So too was "who you know." I had to learn the art of networking at the Pfizer New York City corporate headquarters. The competition was fierce. Although I always felt supported and valued, even by those vying for the same roles, I had to figure out how to leave my mark to create a personal brand—a way to separate myself from others with the same dreams.

Making sound business decisions was a hot subject at Pfizer when I joined the department. After three months in my new role, I devised a decision-making training program for newly promoted district managers—the content valued by senior management—that I felt was my ticket to promotion. Trainers who had arrived before me developed numerous programs to strengthen their brand and regularly received that sought-after promotion. This cycle perpetuated, accounting for Pfizer's voluminous library of training materials when I showed up. Many selling models, leadership approaches, and social-style selling platforms were all collecting dust.

Guest speakers and outside consultants closed many training sessions by sharing a poignant message and a call to action. New district sales managers would leave training energized to return home and lead their sales team. While I found many guest speakers' stories entertaining, I often wondered if they were authentic, personal accounts or another person's tale. I struggled to share original, personal anecdotes when I facilitated a training class, constantly rehashing stories I had heard. Why? I don't know. I had served my country in a hostile conflict, deploying to Panama in Operation

Just Cause. Indeed, there were lessons learned there that I could pull from and parlay into a training session. More than once, I walked away from the stage feeling displeasure because I had not been genuine. I knew it. I felt it. I just never connected my own life experience with the notion of owning a unique leadership style. One seminar, however, echoed in my mind more than others. Noel Tichy, author of *The Cycle of Leadership: How Great Leaders Teach Their Companies to Win*, describes a teachable point of view as a leader's view on what it takes to win, an approach to leadership from actual life experiences.

Tichy describes leadership as "authenticity." Tell your version rather than representing someone else's. And why not? None of us have the same collection of experiences, and we all have a different approach to life.

It took me years, but I finally discovered the courage to walk away from the corporate rat race. I had battled depression, cycled from California to Florida, and now dared to compete in this epic race. And this would be my race. I needed to experience living on my terms, and I could, with my family's support. Here I was, smack-dab in the heart of one of the world's most challenging cycling events. I did not, however, appreciate how demanding the days ahead would be.

Chapter 5
CORVALLIS–MCKENZIE BRIDGE, OREGON (97 MILES)

June 4, 2019

F orce myself to stop.

    On many nights, I jotted down reflections from the day in a yellow, all-weather journal. The entries reflected a purposeful attempt to capture details likely to be forgotten with time.

> Journal entry on May 30: *Rylee-Yosemite, Garth-LA, Michael-Nashville.*
> Journal entry on May 31: *Haircut, relax.*
> Journal entry on June 2: *Documentary, gravel, hug coast, hills.*
> Journal entry on June 4: *Force myself to stop.*

    This practice faded as the days passed and my frame of mind shifted from adventure to indifference. When all was said and done, on the good days and the bad, I recounted highlights from about 50 percent of the days I spent riding Tank through the heartland of America. There were days, primarily in Kansas and Missouri, when I didn't jot anything down—including a 15-day gap between Yellowstone National Park to Elizabethtown, Illinois.

Like a terrifying dream in which you're trying to run but your legs won't move, I felt the competition getting away from me. I reflected on countless 10K running races I had entered. I often finished strong after a slow start. I never won, but I always sprinted at the end. (If there were a Clydesdale category, I would have won every race!)

I wondered if I could come from behind and earn a respectable finish in this contest as well. My competitive spirit whispered to me not to lose too much ground. But I didn't want to shove away the chance to meet people along the way, so I forced myself to stop. Roger would have encouraged me to pick up my pace and leave him behind. That day would arrive a few hundred miles farther east.

The Southern Tier and TransAmerica bike trails were similar in that I rode through hundreds of small towns, pedaled on paved roadways (some ripe with potholes), and devoured food. However, there was one striking difference: I owned every decision during the race, from the moment I left Astoria until 3:10 p.m. on July 10, 2019, when I arrived at the Yorktown Victory Monument. *Do I turn left or right or continue straight? Should I stop or ride through the storm? Where do I eat? What happens if my derailleur is damaged?* It was all up to me.

At 9:00 a.m., Roger and I pedaled to the Corvallis post office on 2nd Street— the first of several side trips to a local post office. I shipped nonessential equipment home to New Jersey. I carried a two-pound, bulky spare tire. Before leaving New Jersey, I hemmed and hawed whether to take the two-pound security blanket. I had remembered Wally (a member of my Southern Tier group) reaching our campground in Mimbres, New Mexico, late in the afternoon on October 2, 2018, carrying a souvenir. His rear Marathon Schwalbe Plus tire had exploded earlier that day—the same type of tire propelling Tank. He had held on to the destroyed tire to show the group.

If this could happen to an experienced cyclist, then it was not farfetched that something like that could happen to me. The chance of a mechanical problem or a flat tire on a 4,200-mile race was high. However, I had begun trusting my instincts by the time I reached Corvallis, now more confident in the event of a mishap; I shipped the tire and a couple of other small items home. The lighter bike was a bonus. Roger collected my things and entered the post office while I waited outside, minding our bikes. A middle-aged, disheveled woman stepped down from inside a dull, rusted, old-style van. She walked with a noticeable limp and passed next to me. I made eye contact and said, "Good morning," while contemplating an offer to help her maneuver up the stairs to the post office entrance.

She paused and replied, "Hi, where are you heading?"

Despite her failing health, she had a cheery, warm temperament. She opened up about her challenges dealing with an autoimmune disorder that affected her walking ability and added, "The van is my transportation and shelter."

A visit to the Bike N Hike Shop on SW 3rd Street turned out to be the correct decision. Extensive and all-inclusive, the store was stocked full of bikes, clothing, and accessories organized on the floor, racks, and walls. We escorted our bikes to the mechanic's workshop in the back. Visiting bike shops was a ritual I'd started on the Southern Tier. "Both of your tires' pressure is low, around forty PSI. How high do you want to go?"

I told the guy, "Eighty PSI." Hand-squeezing the tires each morning to gauge pressure was not an effective practice apparently. Properly inflated tires meant a much smoother ride ahead.

After I'd passed over the railroad tracks and turned south onto Marine Drive on June 2, somebody about to pass on my left side muttered sarcastically, "That's a lot of equipment you're packing." He was perhaps looking at the spare tire attached to Tank's rear rack. The remark annoyed the hell out of me. I thought, *Why not say hello or tell me to have a safe ride?* Something—anything—other than what he said. I do not know if his remark was a dig, but deep down, at that moment, his comment was petrol for the soul. He had lit the fuse that fueled an inner drive. I didn't respond to his snarky comment. I recall thinking I would let my actions speak louder than my words. I never found out if he ended up completing the race—but I know I did.

Our destination was unknown when we left Corvallis at 10:00 a.m. Carl had left the inn about 30 minutes before us. When I looked at the "Welcome to Harrisburg—Established 1866" sign (population 3,567), I thought about my upbringing near Harrisburg, Pennsylvania, which was first settled around 1715 to 1718.[12] Seeing this sign triggered a trip down memory lane. But unlike many sections of the Southern Tier, I was now riding through virgin territory that brought about new experiences and rekindled my interest in the Lewis and Clark Expedition of 1805.

Highway 126 flanked the McKenzie River. A canopy of lush, green trees shaded us from direct sunlight. Running, turquoise-blue water flowed over rocks, creating white caps. Light shot out of the sky in rays, the heat of its reach dampened by a delicate breeze. The world was as hypnotic as a kaleidoscope—so full of color and synchronized movement. I paused on a dirt patch along the narrow, two-lane road west of Walterville, Oregon, and listened to the gentle, steady roar of the McKenzie River. The music of water falling from the cliffs and onto the pavement—the result of thawing snow flowing from the Cascades—was mesmerizing. But then, a car whizzed by and disturbed my tranquility.

Twelve miles west of McKenzie Bridge, Oregon, near Blue River on Highway 126, a mighty, snowcapped mountain came into view. Roger and I stopped pedaling and gazed upward to absorb the natural beauty that surrounded us. Mountainous peaks loomed, unobstructed. Pine trees reached for the sky along the narrow highway, creating a V-shaped channel that directed my eyes to the top of Lookout Mountain (5,276 feet) and O'Leary Mountain (5,530 feet). I grabbed a picture of the fantastic view and unknowingly captured Roger's tanned, smiling face. He looked content, away from the hustle, bustle, and grind of work. The sunshine pouring through the

---

[12] "History of Harrisburg, Pennsylvania," U-S-History.com, accessed July 12, 2022, https://www.u-s-history.com/pages/h2088.html

mountain passes disappeared the farther east we rode on the scenic byway. Our ticket over the Cascades lay ahead: Sawtooth Ridge to the south, Lookout Ridge to the north, and Santiam Pass in between.

Harry had caught Roger and me at 7:00 p.m., when we reached the town of McKenzie Bridge. Since leaving Astoria, Carl, Harry, Roger, and I had ridden at about the same pace. We hadn't planned to; it just happened that way. At Elmer's restaurant, Carl mentioned he might detour to Eugene, Oregon (30 miles off the main route) due to a snowstorm forecasted to strike Santiam Pass the next day. At breakfast, Roger and I talked about the weather forecast and concluded the threat for snow was low. In the McKenzie General Store parking lot, on the west end of McKenzie Bridge, we three men—physically spent and out of food—had no place to sleep. The sun was quickly dropping behind the mountains; time was running out to find shelter before dark. The Adventure Cycling Association map indicated Cedarwood Lodge was located a couple of miles east on the main artery. The three of us split up. Harry and I rode ahead, searching for the lodge. Roger bought food at the store and would meet us at whatever shelter we found. We had a plan. The race to find cover before dark was underway. I looked forward to a hot shower and a warm bed. An intensity like we had not experienced since the race began set in, part exhilaration and part panic. I became distressed when I saw the red sign at the Cedarwood Lodge that read: "NO VACANCY."

I continued pedaling, holding hope. Ten minutes later, Harry texted me he had reached the Willamette National Forest Paradise Campground two miles east of my location and was waiting for me at the campsite entrance. A mad dash to reach Harry ensued. The isolated campsite was 500 feet down a narrow, twisting trail, nestled close to the McKenzie River. Scattered sunlight sparkled through the lush forest. I texted Roger, letting him know where to find us. I pitched my tent on soft pine needles, next to a firepit and a picnic bench and 20 feet from the McKenzie River. The echo of crystal-clear, running water rushing over boulders was like music to my ears.

I immediately became disheartened when I saw a sign outside the restroom: "No running water." I thought, *No shower, no washing clothes, and no drinking water*. My 2.5-liter Osprey backpack water bladder was empty. I shook each of the five water bottles I carried, hoping to feel the presence of water moving around inside. One bottle, a CamelBak insulated container, carried about 15 ounces. The river water moving swiftly would have been a suitable source of drinking water, except for one problem: water-purification tablets didn't make the packing list. Thirty minutes before nightfall, Roger arrived and walked to the table, extending his arm to give me a sandwich and can of Coke. My dinner. "Thanks," I said. I quickly ate the sandwich and had a few sips of the soda. I retrieved my lightweight water shoes, wrapped my REI personal body towel around my waist, grabbed a bar of soap and a face cloth, and proceeded to walk through the thicket and over jagged rocks to the water's edge.

Water broke over partly submerged rocks, the journey both beautiful and violent. I stood, taking in the sight of the rapids, so white they looked like gleaming teeth. The sound was a continuous bubbling with a meditative quality—a natural noise machine to drown out all else. I thought about my buddy Jeff from Mendham, who loved the wilderness and often shared experiences he had camping with his sons on Boy Scout trips. Another thought came to mind—that of a flaming Cuyahoga River. In 1969, the Cuyahoga River near Cleveland, Ohio caught fire. The inferno was caused by waste and other pollutants seeping into the river.[13] We lived in Cuyahoga County for a couple of years. When I drove over the cleaner water in 2006, a nasty image of a river in flames revealed itself in my mind.

I gingerly entered the rushing water, mindful of slippery rocks underneath the surface, and scrubbed, focusing primarily on my crotch. When I came back to the campsite, I approached Roger. "With no running water, we need to make do with what we have. There's a coffee

---

[13]   Michael Rotman, "Cuyahoga River Fire: The Blaze That Started a National Discussion," *Cleveland Historical*, May 2, 2022, https://clevelandhistorical.org/items/show/63

shop a couple of miles east of the campsite before the big climb to Santiam Pass." I took a few more sips of soda and preserved the precious remaining water. Roger had not bought water, thinking we could fill our bottles at the campground. Harry settled into his tent on the opposite side of a thin line of pine trees. I hung my washcloth and drying towel from a tree branch, expecting them to dry quickly in the gentle breeze.

"I'm okay," I texted Kelley, using the SPOT device's texting feature before settling in for the night. The SPOT texting feature came in handy on half a dozen occasions when cell service was poor or nonexistent. (The satellite coverage includes a substantial part of the planet. The trackleaders.com site links multiple trackers onto a group event map and supports many well-known events like the TABR.)[14]

While discussing plans outside the general store, Roger had mentioned that Carl sent a text message hours before pressing Harry, Roger, and me to join him in Eugene. No one had given Carl's concern about a snowstorm serious attention. But it crossed my mind all day as we began our 4,000-foot ascent to Santiam Pass.

The next day, we heard Carl had scratched. He developed saddle sores that prevented him from continuing and wisely put his health above all else. I reflected on our conversation at Elmer's the night before. The extra precaution Carl had taken, investing in a custom-designed saddle, hadn't been enough to prevent an early exit. The notion that an experienced cyclist had scratched so early due to saddle sores raised my level of concern. (Thirteen days later, in Jeffrey City, Wyoming, saddle sores almost ruined my ride as well.)

Three days in and 300 miles closer to Yorktown, I contemplated on the saddle the possibility of averaging 100 miles a day. In my yellow notepad, I wrote, *Strategy—54, ahead of it.* I also recorded, *Physically—knees, feet*, which served as a cautionary reminder that riding 100 miles each day had taken a toll on my body.

---

[14] "Leaders of the Track," TrackLeaders.com, accessed July 12, 2022, http:// trackleaders.com

Chapter 6

MCKENZIE BRIDGE–PRINEVILLE, OREGON (97 MILES)

June 5, 2019

Reaching the Santiam Pass summit and putting the Cascade Mountains in the rearview mirror was the only inspiration I needed when I awoke. The soreness in my leg muscles had disappeared, and my mind felt clear when I unzipped my sleeping bag and raised my body. I wiped the crust away from my eyes. My morning routine started once again. My cycling kit on, I took my daily medication. Neither Roger nor I uttered a word when we stepped out of our tents to begin a new day.

God, I hope the coffee shop is open. The calm white noise of the McKenzie River tempered my enthusiasm to begin moving. Harry remained inside his tent when Roger and I rode past him at 7:30 a.m.

Dehydrated, I felt vulnerable—and so did Roger—but we had no choice but to make do with the remaining 10 ounces of water we had. We couldn't count on a vehicle passing on the less-traveled Highway 126. We focused all of our energy on reaching the café, which was two miles east of the campground. *Pancakes, orange juice, coffee, and five full water bottles.* The image of the perfect start to another exciting day on the saddle was about to unravel. Refueling our bodies was our immediate consideration when we exited the campground to begin the 32-mile ride to Santiam Pass. Three miles later, riding side by side, we looked at each other and, in unison, asked, "Where's the café!?" We knew right away. *There was no café.* All alone, with only 10 ounces of water to survive on, surrounded by God, forest, and silence, we stopped on the shoulder of the road, owning a feeling of concern. I pulled the water bottle from the cage. We took sips that didn't do much more than temporarily wet our lips. That parched, dry-throat feeling that's hard to ignore gave rise to a heightened level of anxiety. Each pedal rotation and lungful of air robbed more water from my body. White paste formed on my lips and the corners of my mouth. I closed my mouth and sucked hard, trying to help stimulate my salivary glands. Every few hundred feet, we stopped and took small sips, wetting our lips. Fifteen minutes later, we ran out of water.

The need to replace fluid lost during exercise is basic. In my case, I craved water and Gatorade. Anxiety, stress, and worry were sapping my energy. *Do we stop and wait for a vehicle to pass, or do we continue moving and hope for the best?* Our singular focus became finding water, the holy grail, and that focus was all-consuming.

We continued pedaling. I saw a campground sign on the opposite side of the highway about 100 yards ahead. I glanced in the rearview mirror, cut across the road, and made a beeline to the campground manager's mobile trailer home.

The morning calm was interrupted when I reached the trailer. A dog began barking from inside the structure. A woman opened the lone door and stepped out to greet us.

"Hi, good morning. Sorry to disturb you so early. Any place to get water?" I pleaded.

"Sure, let me get a water jug. You can fill as many bottles as you want," she answered.

Relieved beyond belief and nearly in tears, we waited patiently for the jug to arrive and immediately filled and downed one bottle of cold, thirst-quenching water. We filled our remaining water bottles to the brim. Acquainted with the race, the woman—who we learned was named Stella—mentioned that Noel from Ireland had stopped for water two days before. Stella said Noel didn't stay long to chat; he'd pedaled away after filling his water bottles. (Noel finished the race in 23 days, 14 hours, and 59 minutes, averaging about 180 miles per day to secure 17th place.)

Before starting the decisive advance to Santiam Pass (4,817 feet), Roger, Harry—who caught up shortly after we said goodbye to Stella—and I stopped at the Clear Lake Resort. According to the map, we could find camping, lodging, and food services at the location. But when we left Highway 126 (Lake Belknap Springs Hwy) and began riding down a steep, two-mile descent, I recall thinking we had made a poor decision. Returning to the main route required us to climb back up the same road. *Why on earth are we doing this!?* The question haunted me as I pumped the disc brakes to control my speed. I glanced to my right at the mountain base and saw a series of log cabin–style buildings. I rounded the last turn before entering a parking area full of cars and RVs. I looked to my right, and Clear Lake appeared in all its beauty. *What a stunning view!* I thought, while looking out at the hidden gem. There was a gorgeous blue sky, snow-crowned peaks in the distance, and clear, turquoise-colored water all around. Once again, I thought, *Aren't I supposed to be pushing myself and not enjoying myself so much?*

Harry, Roger, and I walked inside the small café. I bought a sandwich and a drink. I walked outside and stood next to the lake. Roger snapped a picture of me, snow-crowned mountains in the background, holding an Arnold Palmer. I sent my dad the picture. He always orders an "Anee Pama"—it's his favorite drink. Our family chuckles when a server tries to figure out what my dad's saying with his distinctive New England accent.

The slow, two-mile climb to Highway 126 rekindled my race mentality. The ride to Santiam Pass would begin shortly after returning to the main route. My memory of the last 3,000 feet to the summit is fuzzy. I recall seeing lava fields, stick-figure trees dotting the wilderness, and massive rock formations. A single cliff reminded me of Mount Rushmore in the Black Hills region of South Dakota, minus the faces depicting four US presidents. I was entranced by the Western Cascade Range smack-dab in the middle of Mt. Washington Wilderness in this scene. I knew I was close to conquering the first of five mountain ranges when I looked at a yellow road sign warning: "Downhill grade next 5 miles."

In the distance behind us were the unmovable mountain peaks we had ridden over. The road disappeared about 200 yards behind Roger due to the sharp descent on the downside of the mountain we'd just climbed. Wally, from my Southern Tier group, sent me a text at the summit congratulating me on reaching Santiam Pass. Two months before the race began, I'd contacted Wally to seek his advice. In September 2018, when I met Wally in San Diego, he mentioned he had recently completed the TransAmerica Bike Trail with a tour group led by the Adventure Cycling Association. He had planted a seed. I knew he knew what it took to complete this much longer ride, and he knew my capability. He was an experienced cyclist, and I valued his opinion. He told me flat out that I should not enter the race, even though he considered me a strong cyclist. He shared a story about meeting two racers at a convenience store in Kansas during the 2018 race. He emphasized that both racers looked sleep-deprived, describing their sunken eyes, unshaven faces, and skeletal upper bodies. "I don't think it's safe," he stressed. I acknowledged his concerns and thanked him for his opinion. We agreed to meet for dinner when I reached his home in Colorado. As I reflected on Wally's insights, I wondered why I asked for his opinion in the first place. I had already made my decision to enter the race. But hearing Wally focus his concerns on sleep deprivation reinforced my decision to strategically ride during day and sleep at night.

Receiving Wally's congratulatory text was the first time I realized strangers likely followed the TABR on the Track Leaders' site. How many, I didn't know—perhaps dozens, maybe hundreds. The satellite tracking system listed first and last initials only, with dots on a map to indicate each racer's location. Wally had seen "LW" on top of Santiam Pass when he texted me. How often each racer pinged their SPOT device to the satellite would reveal a real-time location. For the first two days, 73 racers' initials all blended. It was hard to distinguish between the leader and Lanterne Rouge on a three-inch United States map. By day four, initials had begun to separate as the distance between front and back widened. "LW" now stood out as a solitary speck amid the spacious western wilderness.

The Cascade Range was a bed of lava fields—one vast volcanic landscape. A border of red clay separated the road from mounds of lava rock that at one time generated excessive heat, impeding the growth of trees seen from the road's edge. A dull, brown road sign pointed to the Pacific Crest Trail. I noticed a white van stopped in front of the sign. I was curious, so I also stopped. And for a moment, I visualized the hikers that had crossed by this spot and Cheryl Strayed's recounting of her solo hike along the PCT in 1995, brought to life in a memoir titled *Wild: From Lost to Found on the Pacific Crest Trail* and a movie of the same name starring Reese Witherspoon.

I likened the setting to a cyclist approaching a small town—the chance for a little human contact before reentering the great outdoors. I had read about trail angels (people who volunteer to provide direct kindness, generosity, and food to hikers) setting up food tables welcoming hikers who crossed through villages or over roadways. I took a picture of the sign and sent it to my buddy Jeff, who walked the entire Appalachian Trail from Georgia to Maine in 2017. I religiously followed his daily posts. The Pacific Crest Trail,[15] one of three that make up the triple crown of hiking (the other two being the Appalachian and the Continental Divide), traverses the Cascade Range near Santiam Pass. The 2,650-

---

[15] "Discover the Trail," Pacific Crest Trail Association, accessed July 12, 2022, https:// www.pcta.org/discover-the-trail/

mile trail runs along the high points of the Cascade and Sierra Nevada mountain ranges.

In the Deschutes National Forest, I saw snow-covered Mount Washington, 25 miles south of my location. It stood out like a sore thumb. With an elevation of 7,794 feet, it was a thing of beauty, majestic. Its base was broad and snow-covered, like the sweeping hem of a wedding gown, with a peak that pushed against the sky itself.

A strong tailwind propelled us from the vista overlooking Mount Washington to Sisters Valley on the west side of town, a 10-mile distance and 1,000-foot elevation drop. I rode ahead of Roger and reached Sisters, Oregon, at 4:30 p.m. I called the Blazin Saddles bike shop to investigate store hours while waiting at a Chevron gas station. When Roger showed up, I told him Tank had been making odd noises. If we hurried, we could make it to the bike shop before 5:00 p.m. We hustled, making it before closing. While the mechanic attempted to diagnose the problem, Roger called every motel in town, searching for a vacancy, but he couldn't find a single room. That Wednesday afternoon, there was not a single vacancy at any of the 10-plus motels in Sisters (population 2,038). I had to assume this was because it was just two days before the annual Sisters Rodeo was in town; known as the "biggest little show in the world," the Sisters Rodeo is held the second weekend in June.

The mechanic couldn't find anything wrong with Tank. He also shared that there was not much between Sisters and the next closest town, Prineville, which was about 50 miles farther east. We had a decision to make. *Do we take a chance and continue to Prineville, raising the odds we'd ride several miles after dark? Or do we find a place in Sisters to pitch tents?* The mechanic heard Roger and me discussing our predicament. He proposed that we continue pedaling east on Highway 126, a more direct way to Prineville, shaving 20 miles off the official route. The sanctioned route detoured from Highway 126 east of downtown, meandering through the surrounding countryside on a less-traveled road. The mechanic noted that other racers who had stopped at his store days before had taken Highway 126 when they left town.

What ultimately drove our decision to continue was the desire for a hot shower and a comfortable bed. Two hours of sunshine remained. Roger stayed on Highway 126, and I continued on the primary trail. The intention was for Roger to reach Prineville and secure a motel room before I arrived. Six miles east of Sisters city limits, at McKenzie Canyon Reservoir, I swung north onto Holmes Road and attacked the entire 46 miles with every ounce of energy I could muster. I did not stop, except for one time to gaze at a herd of alpacas in Terrebonne (population 1,257).

For the first time, I felt like I was racing. My leg muscles burned, pumping strenuously in the highest gear, taking advantage of the favorable tailwind. The cloud cover limited direct sunlight, but my pace put me on track to make it before darkness set in. Roger reached town one hour before I did. On the west end of town, near Ochoco Wayside State Park, Roger informed me the Econo Lodge was the only place with a vacancy on the east end of town. The overabundance of visitors attending the rodeo had overwhelmed the motels in Prineville, too. We were extremely relieved. Harry was already in Prineville when we arrived. He stayed in our room because he could not find another vacancy. A single room with two queen beds? Earplugs!

A dot watcher made a plea on the public Facebook page, asking the community for support. Someone was thinking about scratching. His friend reached out, asking for advice. It was not my nature to engage on social media, but I expressed my view on how I had persevered. I thought I might be able to help. I wrote, *Take it one day at a time. Break up each day into workable segments, sleep well every night, ride your race—not someone else's. Experience the countryside, and by all measures, chat with the residents.* My exchanges with ordinary folks instilled that extra spark needed to continue pushing forward. I added, *Heed Nathan's advice—if you're considering scratching, sleep on it. Avoid making a hasty decision.* Three days later, the racer scratched. I wished my words had helped more. Perhaps they enabled him to go on an extra day or two. In a heartfelt post, another racer informed us that she would end her race, too, her note revealing just how tough finishing this race would be: *It turns out that my being a 'racer' just isn't who I am...* I remembered meeting this energetic person in Astoria. She had prepared for a long time and was excited and ready to go. It served as a powerful message and reminder for me to ride my race, not concern myself about others. I wondered if she tried to keep pace with the leaders, riding through the night. Did sleep deprivation lead to her scratching?

When I cleared the crust from my eyes, lifted my torso, and scanned the room, I had a flashback to my army days. After a night out with the boys, my bachelor officer quarters would appear to have been hit by a twister the following day—battle dress uniforms (BDU) strewn on the floor, field gear on top of the dresser and hanging on light fixtures. A putrid smell—a mixture of stale beer and human gas. Here, sweat-saturated cycling gear replaced BDUs, beer cans, and spittoons.

The motel manager had told Roger the room he had reserved accommodated two guests. The three of us had devised a plan to sneak upstairs unnoticed. The operation unfolded; I entered from a side parking lot door, tiptoed up the back stairway and 30 feet along the hallway to our room. Harry provided overwatch, eyeing the motel lobby to warn us of any signal the manager had gotten wind of our scheme. Roger followed, and then Harry completed the mission. I rationalized the childish behavior by saying, "We gotta do what we gotta do." We repeated the operation the following morning.

I had confessed to Harry when I met him in Astoria that finishing the Southern Tier did not wholly satisfy me. An eagerness to complete a more considerable challenge pulled me onto the saddle once again. I hungered for purpose and something that would satiate my adventurous appetite. Then, perhaps I would return to an everyday life—and a regular job.

"I took thirty days off from my bartending job in NYC," he said, revealing his desire to reach Yorktown in the allotted timeframe. His studly appearance and titanium bike were perfect for such a lofty goal. But now, nestled inside the close quarters of our one-room hideaway, it struck me that Harry was not on pace to finish in 30 days. He needed to pick up the tempo, leave Roger and me in the dust. It was a thought I kept to myself.

A handful of the 73 racers had scratched by day five. In the motel room, I wrote *50 percent attrition* in my journal as a reminder to remain disciplined and not try to emulate others. During prerace communications, Nathan had briefed the mobilized masses that about 50 percent of riders scratch every year. That and the statistic that two cyclists would get struck by a vehicle continued to weigh heavily on my psyche.

Nathan required each racer to send a selfie every day. He came up with the idea as a way to monitor safety. The request didn't seem very practical, but I honored it. I didn't lose sight that Nathan, with the support of Thomas and others, ultimately decided to carry on the race after mulling over the future of the TABR. The selfie I sent Nathan at 10:30 a.m. revealed a thinning face, matted salt-and-pepper facial hair, and an exuberant smile.

At the Econo Laundromat, 0.3 miles from the Econo Lodge, I felt a prickly feeling in my buttocks while waiting for a load of laundry to dry. Ever since Carl had scratched from the race, I'd been acutely aware of the risk of saddle sores.

The next stop was the Prineville post office. Each subsequent trip to the post office reduced carrying weight by only a few ounces. My body had also begun reshaping itself. My calorie intake wasn't keeping up with the thousands of calories I was burning while cycling 12 to 14 hours a day. My metamorphosis from touring to racing had begun.

June 6 was the most demanding day on the saddle. I wore cold-weather gear for the first time. The temperature had plummeted to the mid-forties overnight. My hands and torso withstood the worst, riding in icy, wet, and blustery conditions. Cycling with the wind penetrating my clothing, combined with sweat trapped next to my skin, was miserable.

Cresting Santiam Pass was not as demanding as I'd expected it to be. My legs felt powerful. The weather had cooperated. Pedaling through the Cascades had been enjoyable, hemmed in by such beauty. I felt a sense of achievement when I arrived at the top. When Wally congratulated me, I no longer felt entirely isolated.

Now, well east of Prineville, I looked at a yellow, diamond-shaped warning sign. "Next 7 miles," it read, with an image of a truck descending a steep decline. I braced my arms for an exhilarating ride down the east side of Ochoco Pass (4,722 feet), the highest peak along Highway 26 in the Ochoco Mountains. The effort to reach the summit of Ochoco Pass—a 33-mile, 1,700-foot elevation climb from Prineville—took all the strength I could muster. Finally, at the top, I could bask in nature's beauty. For many, ascending a mountain is the furthest thing from easy. Not for me. Each wheel revolution reeled me in further so that my mind focused entirely on closing in on the peak, one foot at a time. At the top, I halted, looked at the vast wilderness that surrounded me, and felt so small. In this endless backcountry, I was alone and loving every minute of the feeling of achievement after conquering another milestone. It's an addictive feeling to have made it to the top of another significant climb. I thought about the remaining climbs that would test me before the ultimate one in the Rocky Mountains, which was still several days away. The surrounding scenery was full of rich colors; different shades of dark green carpeted the remote sierras. Closer to Highway 26, a wild, light-green meadow and clusters of pine forests loomed.

The grass swayed as a slight cross breeze blew south to north across Highway 26. One car passed me, but otherwise, I had this pristine beauty all to myself. I cruised in the vehicle lane for the next 16 miles, descending 1,700 feet to Mitchell (population 130), one of several towns I rode through that has hung on from the early mining days. A little over an hour had passed when, from a distance, I heard cowbells ringing and people cheering. I squinted, staring ahead. Along the highway, a handful of individuals stood outside a small, one-room building, waving their hands over their heads. I quickly realized this was a welcome party, and they had stepped outside to meet me.

The building—a community church and bike hostel known as the Spoke'n Hostel, which is well recognized among the cycling community—brought a smile to my face. A sign affixed to a wood beam advertised: "Racer Support—hot food, hot shower, warm beds, Wi-Fi, coffee—Spoke'n Hostel." I stopped pedaling when I reached them, greeted the well-wishers, and stayed there for a much-desired rest. The pastor, Patrick (and mayor of Mitchell), his spouse, Janet, and the others had tracked the race on a giant TV monitor mounted on a wall in the church basement. They knew when each racer passed through their sleepy town. Every racer who rode by received the same hospitable reception. I walked inside and leaned Tank against one of the empty wooden bunkbeds lining the aisle leading to the sanctuary. I walked gingerly down a narrow set of stairs, mindful of each time my cleats clacked against the wooden stairs. When I arrived, Harry was sitting at the kitchen table, almost done eating. I sat next to him, across from a few others, and beamed. "Yes! Thank you so much. Your hospitality is amazing," I replied when asked if I would like a plate of lasagna. It had been six days since I'd last had a decent, nutritious meal at the Commodore Hotel Café. When Janet placed a full plate of meat lasagna, salad, and warm bread in front of me, my body said, "Thank you." But after I finished, I realized that wasn't all—the meal included a bowl of vanilla ice cream, a fitting end to a delicious lunch.

The Spoke'n Hostel relies on donations to survive[16] and hosts hundreds of cyclists a year from all over the world. Their website states, "An oasis for cyclists and adventurers"—a description fitting the experience. The first floor reminded me of a military barracks, as it had bunk beds on both sides of a single aisle. But rather than cold, metal bedframes, the beds were crafted from light-washed pinewood. The narthex inside the entrance was reminiscent of an ordinary church lobby—a door off to the side leading to a private room for meetings with the pastor. A basket filled with religious pamphlets sat on a table at the entrance to the main church. The pastor explained he and his wife originally bought the building to provide religious services for citizens of Mitchell. After they learned the TransAmerica Bike Trail passed directly in front of their church, they created a cyclists' way station with an experience second to none. They extended an offer for me to stay overnight, but I needed to cover more miles if I was to achieve a 100-mile per day average distance. I knew I had to take advantage of the opportunity to continue when I felt strong and several hours of daylight remained. After making a generous donation, I thanked Patrick, Janet, and the rest. I snapped a few pictures and then, after about an hour, I walked outside to meet Roger, who had texted me earlier that he had begun descending from Ochoco Pass. Harry had continued riding about 30 minutes before I finished eating.

When I saw Roger approaching, I hollered, "You're going to love this place!"

As Roger got nearer, he slowed down. I saw his eyes reading the sign. He mustered the energy to respond, "Wow, wow… Now this is what you'd think… Right! Right! Hot shower! Warm bed!" One of Roger's knees had caused discomfort the preceding couple of days. I hoped pushing to ride 20 miles more on average each day wasn't the reason. We were both in superb physical shape, especially given we were both in our late fifties.

---

[16] Dan D'Ambrosio, "Spoke'n from the Heart," *Adventure Cyclist* 48, no.6, (July 2021): 40–41, https://www.adventurecycling.org/adventure-cyclist/adventure-cyclist-online/2021-issues/

My knees had held up on the Southern Tier. And so far, they felt fine—indeed, better than what I recalled from the early days on the Southern Tier. I believed Roger would treasure Patrick and Janet's reception, and it didn't surprise me when Roger accepted the pastor's invitation to stick around for the night. Maybe the extra rest would lessen his knee pain.

Roger and I had traveled 438 miles when we stood together outside the Spoke'n Hostel. We had enjoyed each other's company for five cycling days, preceded by two pleasant preparation days in Astoria. When we embraced and bid adieu, I felt I had begun a different stage of the race. Roger prearranged to meet a friend who would take him to Boise, Idaho, for a return flight to New Jersey and the transition back to the working world. I would miss Roger shouting "Car back!" to warn me of approaching vehicles. Now, I was on my own until Yorktown.

At 4:05 p.m., I stopped when I saw a syringe on the gravel shoulder—the only unnatural thing I saw until 7:11 p.m., when I reached Dayville (population 149). The skies remained gloomy and overcast all day. The continuous ups and downs of climbing Peggy Butte (4,787 feet), Keyes Creek Summit (4,382), and Juniper Butte (5,400 feet) had been exhausting but incredibly rewarding. Every gulp of water tasted better than the one before. Life would quiet down for a brief moment at each summit.

Time was on my side, as I didn't have any other distractions for the 40-mile distance from Mitchell to Dayville. Not a single vehicle passed me in either direction. The last five-mile ride into Dayville was an absolute thrill. I rode parallel to Mountain Creek and the John Day River, "one of the longest free-flowing rivers in the continental United States and the longest undammed tributary of the Columbia."[17] In their written account, Lewis and Clark had mentioned the John Day River but did not explore the region when traveling along the Columbia River

---

[17] "John Day Wild and Scenic River," U.S. Department of the Interior Bureau of Land Management, accessed July 12, 2022, https://www.blm.gov/programs/recreation/permits-and-passes/lotteries-and-permit-systems/oregon-washington/john-day-river

in 1805. A rocky hill hugged the road, reaching skyward in a sharp, vertical ascent. The river foamed to my left, while sunshine glowed like a halo above the bluffs. As day succumbed to dusk, the rugged terrain, deep-set ravines, and rocky cliffs grew more prominent around me, like monsters coming to life in the dark. I pedaled down a mountain spur, past the John Day Fossil Beds National Monument, to the valley below. Highway 26, my beacon to Dayville, was guided by a fading, blue sky above, the Cascades to the west, the Ochoco Mountains to the south, and the Blue Mountains to the east.

I reached Dayville (population 150) at 7:50 p.m. The three restaurants in town had closed by the time I arrived. I had previously made reservations to camp at the Fish House Inn and RV Park. The manager set me up in a permanent, tent-like structure located on the back side of green, park-like grounds. While unpacking Tank, I noticed my bike pump was missing. It must have fallen off between Mitchell and Dayville. I also carried CO_2 cartridges, a backup solution to inflate a flat tire. I had taken meticulous care of Tank since leaving Astoria, and in turn, Tank rode well. I hadn't faced any mechanical problems up to this point.

I ate two breakfast bars, a bag of peanuts, and a few strings of licorice I had stashed away in my handlebar bag. Then I strode about 100 feet to the Fish House Inn laundry room to wash my dirty and sweaty clothing. While standing in the dark outside the laundry room, I struck up a conversation with three people who I learned were the manager, his wife, and the manager's friend. "Last night, another racer stayed in the same tent," the manager stated, adding, "He called ahead, ordered three PB&J sandwiches, and asked me to put them inside the tent." The manager emphasized the next point, "He gave me his credit card number and told me to charge whatever." The following morning, when the manager opened for business, the cyclist was already gone. He had arrived after dark and disappeared before daybreak.

When I returned to my tent, I wondered if I should modify my strategy and push harder in order to squeeze in more miles each day. I was falling farther behind the leaders with each passing day. Riding 100 miles helped me get a good night's sleep. Extending time on the saddle a little each day could only help with sleep, I thought. (I never did change my strategy. If I ever race the TABR again, I would start riding before dawn. It's calm. It's peaceful. No wind, cooler temperatures. Adding a couple of extra hours on the saddle each day would contribute to finishing in fewer than 38 days. Riding after dark would remain off-limits.)

Refreshed and stocked full of energy each morning, I had ridden farther than I thought possible. I was pleased but not satisfied and obsessed over whether I should push myself harder. As the days passed and more racers scratched, my strategy felt like a winning formula for success. Finishing would be a notable feat. "Finish strong!" became my mantra, a phrase I repeated to cultivate a particular state of mind meant to transform any negativity that dared seep into my subconscious.

Barring unforeseen circumstances, it was almost guaranteed that Abdullah would finish first. The TABR Facebook page was abuzz. He had been averaging close to 250 miles per day, sleeping as little as three hours a night. His performance that first week had been hard for me to comprehend. I couldn't imagine riding 250 miles in one day, let alone *consecutive* days. During the same conversation outside the laundry room, I described Abdullah's extraordinary performance as "insanely crazy."

The manager's friend chimed in, "You realize you are one of those crazies, too, don't you?"

"I guess so," I said, nodding in agreement and chuckling.

It occurred to me then that I still did not consider myself a racer. Sure, I was an ultradistance cyclist. But I was not a contender to win. For that reason, I never put myself in the same category as the elite racers. Racing with this group of crazies felt the same as when I played pickup basketball with legitimate, big-time players. I had always felt energized competing against Duke-level cagers on the same court, but we were not in the same talent league. This race was a carbon copy of big-time hoops.

Chapter 8
DAYVILLE–BAKER CITY, OREGON (112 MILES)

June 7, 2019

Journal entry on June 6, 2019: *Thinking a lot.*

The Fish Inn manager recommended I visit the Growler Station before leaving town. "They make excellent breakfast sandwiches," he pointed out. At 5:30 a.m., I entered the quiet and empty store and introduced myself to a man clad in sweatpants, a T-shirt, a ball cap, and slippers. "The Fish Inn manager told me you guys make great breakfast sandwiches," I said, waving hello.

"I'm making a few right now. It will take a couple of minutes," he replied.

A woman at the front counter appeared to be getting things in order before the morning crowd arrived. Crafts, artwork, and other knickknacks were either displayed on tables, hanging from the ceiling, or affixed to the walls.

The guy handed me a cup of fresh-brewed coffee. The heat transferred from the mug to my hands. With the mug barely touching my lips, I sipped, making a slurping sound to pull the liquid through my mouth. When the caffeine hit my taste buds, I sighed with relief. The man told me he prepared sandwiches every morning before working at a local, family-owned tree farm. His wife, the store owner, walked from behind the counter dressed in jeans and a T-shirt underneath an open, long-sleeved Patagonia button-down. At 6:00 a.m., a young man in his twenties entered the store and said, "Good morning, Dad." Ten minutes later, their second son walked in. By 6:15 a.m., the family of four had gathered, ready to begin an honest day's work.

We sat in high-back chairs at one of the two oval, wooden dining tables in the center of the store. I sipped coffee, scarfed down two breakfast sandwiches, and shared stories of the people I'd met and the places I'd seen since leaving Astoria. The family was acquainted with the race. A Presbyterian church in town had hosted cyclists since the 1970s. The conversation shifted. I listened to the boys tell their parents about daily plans. One son talked about a meeting he scheduled with a customer interested in buying lumber. The second son updated Mom and Dad on the status of a new home under construction on the family farm. The man turned toward me and said, "This is our typical morning routine." A family get-together to kick off each day. Selling lumber from their juniper tree farm was their livelihood. While technology had altered things at lightning speed, rural America seemed to move at its own pace. This family wouldn't want it any other way. *Folks in this part of the country truly work for a living,* I thought each time I grasped another large, leathery, calloused hand to say goodbye.

I gazed at the silver, cloud-covered sky, surrounded by green grasslands and mountains on the scenic byway, about to take a journey through time. A massive log—about 20 feet long and 4 feet in diameter—caught my eye. Two messages had been plastered on the log: "Remember Benghazi—Hillary for Prison," next to "This is a UN-Free

Zone—United Nations, Keep Out!" Each served as a reminder of the great divide separating rural communities from city life.

Farther along on Highway 26, I entered Mount Vernon (population 527). Outside of an auto repair shop, I saw three adults standing underneath the American flag next to a sign with "Land of the Free *Because* of the Brave" on the front, and "We Will Always Remember" on the back side. The notion that many rural Americans vote Republican, Libertarian, or Independent didn't strike me as farfetched from what I'd gathered while riding through Southeastern Oregon. The American flag fluttered in the breeze in most towns I went through, reminding me fondly of my time serving in the military.

Reflection

"The only thing new in the world is the history
you don't know."—Harry Truman

Around every turn, I anticipated the next surprise. If only I'd been wiser, more willing to pay attention in history class. When I was younger, to a large extent, I'd taken things for granted, caught up in experiencing new environments and situations. But the "newness" quickly faded and became routine—a new job or visiting a foreign country for the first time. The focused intensity dwindles, turning new and exciting to familiar and boring. For years, I had fallen victim to lack of appreciation for the limited time we all have on this earth. I went through the motions— showing up to work, no doubt giving it my all, but rarely enjoying myself. Then, on March 5, 2018, when I lost my job—a blessing in disguise—I regained time. Time to appreciate the blessings of family, friends, and country. Every mile traveled exposed me to new land, new people, and the past. I witnessed one-stoplight, small-town America in all of its glory, where famous and not-so-famous heroes were raised. I often thought about the United States marines who raised the flag on

Iwo Jima, that iconic image symbolizing victory over defeat. Ira Hayes, a United States marine and member of the Gila River Indian Community in Arizona, and Frank Sousley, a marine from Hill Top, Kentucky—the flesh and blood who pulled off that amazing triumph—were from small towns. As I write this on April 18, 2022, I'm grateful for living in the United States of America. We are all so incredibly lucky, especially when one thinks about Ukraine—so much suffering. Now, my mind is quiet; I feel relaxed, and the simple things all seem so fresh. I was so proud to have answered the call when President Bush issued the order for my unit to deploy to Panama in support of Operation Just Cause on December 19, 1989. My sense of pride in America had begun to blossom in my early twenties. I tear up listening to "The Star-Spangled Banner," and it gives me goosebumps when I look at our flag and hear those words, "Oh, beautiful…" I wonder how many Ira Hayes and Frank Sousleys drove on the same roads, ate at the same cafés, or frequented the same gas stations that had become my daily grind.

"Don't just dream, do."—Anonymous

"Infuse your life with action."—Anonymous

Storm clouds had developed by the time I reached John Day (population 1,744) at 9:30 a.m. A 6,000-foot climb in elevation awaited me after a second breakfast at Grubsteak Mining Company Bar & Grill on Main Street. Customers didn't bat an eye when I strolled through with Tank by my side, before leaning it against a wall in the lobby. A smattering of people ate breakfast on this quiet Friday morning. The weekend was ahead for most, but not for me. Every day was a workday until the finish. My second breakfast of pancakes and bacon washed down with orange juice, hot chocolate, and several cups of coffee really hit the spot.

The temperature had dropped by 10 degrees in two and a half hours. As I was leaving town, the conditions became more brumous. Like a dog's highly developed sense of smell foreshadowing the arrival of a familiar face, I followed my gut and found shelter underneath an awning in front of a group of stores minutes before the sleet and hail started to fall. A snowstorm had moved through John Day a couple of days before. Lucky for me, the storm's remnants didn't present as much of a threat compared to what those who arrived before me experienced.

But the idea of riding through snow on Friday gave me a nervous feeling in the pit on my stomach. I thought the 3,200-foot elevation east of John Day would be child's play compared to 11,500-foot Hoosier Pass in the heart of the Colorado Rocky Mountains, 1,000 miles southeast of my location. *I wonder what the chance is for snow when I get to Breckenridge?* I thought while donning my REI cold-weather gear, consisting of Junction Cycling Rain Pants, a red PEARL iZUMi winter rain jacket, full-fingered cold-weather gloves, and cheaply made shoe covers.

Ten miles farther, west of Prairie City (population 909), a mix of hail and sleet pelted the pavement. Low-hanging storm clouds swept above the valley toward the Strawberry Mountain Wilderness. I wasn't sure if the storm would result in much accumulation but I stopped underneath a bush to shelter from the hail that would no doubt create slippery and unsafe riding conditions. The wind whistled through leaves and branches, which shook with each gust. The image of an Italian racer, 500 miles ahead, riding in the dead of night through a snowstorm in Yellowstone, entered my mind. A dot watcher had taken a video and posted it on Facebook. A mix of wonder and trepidation filled my mind. Fearful that I too might meet the same predicament, I put those thoughts in the basement and closed the door behind them. I snapped back to the present moment and, with much relief, looked east at the blue sky. The storm had disappeared, and I hopped back on the saddle by 11:30 a.m.

My destination, Baker City (population 9,828), was 60 miles and three big climbs away and was my ticket to another 100-mile ride. I dreaded descending Dixie Pass (5,279 feet), Tipton Pass (5,124 feet), and Sumpter Pass (5,082 feet) because body sweat combined with colder temperatures and increasing winds would leave me feeling frozen and shaky. I attempted to shift my body to reduce the sweat-filled base layer from clinging to my skin—each slight movement causing that unpleasant, biting sensation.

As I began the big climb to Dixie Pass, I stopped at Conestoga Wagon Landmark—a rest stop for travelers that is also a vista overlooking the majestic view of the grand John Day Valley and Strawberry Mountains. Low cloud cover eliminated any chance to witness the surrounding mountain ranges, but the land that generations had traveled on their westward migration was crystal clear. My mental task was to reify the emptiness with an image of families in wagons kicking up dust while in search of their new homeland. Named after the Conestoga River in Lancaster County, Pennsylvania, the Conestoga wagon had been a favored mode of transportation for the eastern migration, but less so for the western migration.[18] The landmark was out of place and much larger than the commonly traveled in covered wagon or converted farm wagon, called a prairie schooner. Nevertheless, seeing the Conestoga wagon made real the dangers encountered by settlers over 200 years ago.

The Strawberry Mountains and the Blue Mountains came into view when I reached the Dixie Pass summit. I thought it was odd I didn't see residual snow from the storm that passed through days before. Towering ponderosas sprung up along the tree line, while smaller fir trees hugged the road shoulder. The TransAmerica Bike Trail is the country's longest, established cycling route and built-in obstacle course—the cyclist's equivalent of the Ranger School Darby Queen Obstacle Course. That two-mile slog through varied terrain and 25 obstacles tested this ranger candidate's mettle in that first week after arriving at Fort Benning, Georgia, to begin the grueling, months-long training course. Twenty-eight years later, I accepted a new challenge—my singular focus on burning up 4,200-miles over five mountain ranges, passing through 10 states.

---

[18] "Conestoga Wagon," History, updated August 21, 2018, https://www.history.com/topics/westward-expansion/conestoga-wagon

I preferred climbing rather than descending the back side of a big hill. When I shifted to the granny gear, leaning forward, gripping the handlebars, I locked in on the road directly in front of me. Every pedal stroke drew me closer to the top. Eyes directed at the asphalt, looking for irregularities, I pedaled to exhaustion until I reached each summit. Huffing and puffing each time my right foot completed a rotation, my breathing was labored because of the strenuous effort. My mouth was wide open, and each huff of air caused my lips to dry, creating an unquenchable thirst for water.

The mere thought of racing across America had been refreshing when I first imagined doing so in the comfort of my home in Mendham, New Jersey. During those eight miles from Prairie City to the summit, riding parallel to Slaughterhouse Gulch, I began to question why I entered the race. Was I seeking to prove something? Was I running away from my responsibility to care for my family? A few of the same questions I had on the Southern Tier popped into my mind in the middle of Oregon. I anticipated the seven-mile, 1,000-foot drop into Austin Junction would be a miserable ride—and it was.

Unknown to me at the time, Harry stayed at the Presbyterian church in Dayville the night I slept on the grounds of the Fish House Inn. We crossed paths in Prairie City and rode to the top of Dixie Pass at a similar pace.

During the seven-mile descent, I maintained a speed under 30 mph. I squeezed the brakes until the grip handle was flush against the handlebar. The cables were loose, coupled with a slippery road, which reduced the efficacy of the disc pads. I was worried about slipping on the wet surface. The air ripped right through my torso, chilling me to the bone. One mile before reaching the valley below, I lost my capacity to grip and control the handlebars. My forearms burned, and my hands were numb from the driving wind and cold temperature. When I reached the bottom, my core body temperature had fallen. I shivered uncontrollably and felt miserable. I needed to warm my body immediately. Harry had already gotten off the saddle and was waiting for me in the Austin House restaurant parking lot. I was relieved and thankful when I looked at this oasis in the wilderness.

I recall thinking as I reached Harry and hopped off the saddle, *A place to rest, eat, warm my chilled-to-the-bone body, and dry my soaked clothes.* I placed my gloves and yellow windbreaker on the ledge next to a wooden booth. Sunlight peaked out from behind the cloud cover, bright enough to cause me to squint when I looked outside through the large window. I thought the window might magnify the sun's intensity and dry my clothing. In place of a regular dryer, we improvised by using the bathroom hand dryer. Neither approach was effective in pulling moisture from the soaked material.

"I'll have the chili," I said, thinking a hearty meal would hit the spot and prepare me for the expectedly grueling ride ahead. Harry and I sat across from each other, peering out at the sun peeking through the gray sky. The chili tasted good and provided a much-needed supply of protein, with a boost of energy sure to follow. After an hour of waiting and hoping for the clouds to disappear, we decided to continue riding and deal with the miserable riding conditions we had just escaped from, even if only for a short time. We rolled away from the restaurant and immediately turned north onto Highway 7.

Thirty minutes later, my stomach felt queasy. I wondered if I had eaten bad chili. There was hardly any traffic on Highway 7 as I focused on making it to Tipton Pass. My stomach churned, and the threat of potentially crapping my pants was overwhelming. I scanned to my left and right, looking for a place to stop. *I'm glad I'm carrying extra toilet paper.* I carried three packages instead of one of Coghlan's toilet paper rolls of 150 sheets. I tried to ride upright to relieve pressure on my stomach. Gas buildup led to stomach bloating, followed by cramps and the urgent need to have a bowel movement. I moved to the side of the road, hastily dismounting and hurrying to a bush, invisible to any passing cars. On one occasion, just shy of Tipton Pass, when stomach cramps suddenly overwhelmed me and the urgent need to go forced me to stop, I dropped my cycling shorts in plain sight and squatted on the road shoulder. Fortunately, no vehicle passed while my shorts were at my ankles, my legs spread, and my ass exposed to God and country. Nothing was more miserable and pathetic than the handful of times I stopped to relieve myself between Austin Junction and Baker City. Squeezing my butt cheeks didn't work. On a dozen occasions, at least, before making it to the side of the road, I thought, *Did I just shit my pants?* I didn't, but it was a nasty feeling, nonetheless.

Not calling to secure a motel room before reaching Baker City created unwelcome anxiety. According to the ACA map, a couple of campgrounds, each one to two miles off route, were a possibility if I couldn't reach Baker City before dark. Because of my stomach problem, I did not want to camp outside. I desired a hot shower, a comfortable bed, and a washer and dryer to clean my filthy cycling kit. Thirty minutes before dusk, at 8:00 p.m., I entered the south edge of Baker City. The first two motels did not have a vacancy. The next stop: the Oregon Trail Motel & Restaurant on the south side of town. When I saw a lit vacancy sign, a feeling of relief overwhelmed me. I hopped off Tank, leaned my bike against the office building, and walked inside the lobby. I buzzed for an attendant. I was the only person inside for 15 minutes. Another man then entered. We both waited and waited and waited. I called the motel phone number and left a message. I waited patiently for 30 minutes.

I had lost hope that I would locate a vacancy anywhere in town so late in the day. I made one last call before resorting to finding a park to set up my tent—and I'm glad I did. The Knights Inn on Broadway Street, 0.6 miles away on the west side of town, had a room for me. The motel manager answered and shared the best news I had heard all day. "I have one vacancy," he revealed in a heavy Indian accent.

"That's great news. Thank you!" I said, overcome with joy.

When I reached the motel, the owner wanted to comp the room when he learned I was a race contestant. "Thank you, but please take $40," I requested. I respected this man's gesture of appreciation for cross-country cyclists fueling the economic engine of small-town America.

I called Harry and suggested he contact the Knights Inn as well. Harry called to tell me there weren't any vacant rooms at the Knights Inn or any other motel he called. I offered for him to sleep in one of the two queen beds in my room.

Two racers scratched earlier that day. Saddle sores were the reason for one person, and knee pain for the second. I was no longer surprised when I read about someone else scratching. It seemed days three, four, five, and six were the peak days that dealt several racers a final blow to their long-sought dream to complete the TABR. I wondered if this trend would continue. My determination to finish the race increased with each passing day. I understood the odds, knowing only about 50 percent of the racers would make it to Yorktown.

At about 1:00 a.m., I was awoken by Harry's loud snoring. I tossed and turned and, at one point, relocated to the ground in front of the bathroom. I turned on the fan, hoping to generate white noise to drown out the sonorous, grating, log-sawing sound. No luck. The worst night of sleep ended when I stepped outside the following morning. I told myself, *No more bunking with Harry or anybody else.*

By now, I had grown accustomed to riding alone. *Think a lot, alone,* I reflected in my journal entry. My hope to experience isolation had become the world I currently occupied. Little did I realize the isolation I felt riding through rural Oregon paled in comparison to the isolation brought on by the untamed Montana and Wyoming wilderness.

Restless Sleep in Baker City, Oregon
June 8, 2019

Chapter 9
BAKER CITY, OREGON– CAMBRIDGE, IDAHO (110 MILES)

June 8, 2019

I dressed quietly and tiptoed through the dark room at 6:30 a.m., careful not to disrupt Harry's sleep. I walked 0.3 miles south on Broadway Ave to Main Street in downtown Baker City, scanning left and right, searching for an open café. I could hear a pin drop. There were only a few cars parked on both sides of the street. Not a human being around, and nothing had opened. Baker City was still dormant. I faced south, the direction I had come from 10 hours before, and marveled at the breadth of the Blue Mountains—this creative, powerful, and pristine force of the universe.

For a moment, I wondered if I was looking at Sacajawea Peak, 42 miles north of Baker City, named after the Shoshone girl who traveled with the Corp of Discovery in 1805 to 1806. At 9,843 feet, it's the second highest peak in the Blue Mountains.

The broad main street reminded me of the wide streets in downtown Salt Lake City, Utah. When horses and wagons roamed this region, transporting people and hauling freight from railheads to their destination, wagons needed to turn around, which created a need for the wide streets.[19] This vintage, old western town stood still.

One pedestrian walked on the sidewalk, heading south on Main Street. When I caught up to him, I inquired, "Excuse me, do you know of any place open in town for coffee?"

He pointed for me to continue the same way and added, "A coffee shop is a little farther up on main Street."

At 6:55 a.m., a woman opened the doors to The Little Bagel Shop. I went in and approached the lone employee, who had been setting up the display case and placing pastries on the shelves underneath the counter. She instantly halted, glanced at me, and said, "Coffee will be ready in a couple of minutes." Either she could read my mind, or my haggard and tired look gave it away. I sat down with two blueberry muffins and an orange juice, while waiting patiently for a freshly brewed cup of coffee. I kept to myself, watching the employee ready the store for the first patrons. "Here you go, sir," she said, placing the cup of joe on the table. The plume of steam rising above the black liquid triggered me to prepare my mind and body to shift to another demanding day on the saddle. There is something about starting a new day with a freshly brewed cup of coffee. Aside from caffeine's stimulating effect, sipping that liquid warmed my torso and reignited my mind. Well before taking the first sip, anticipating the caffeine hitting my taste buds helped me start that transformation from grogginess to alertness. The aroma immediately put me at ease. "Wake up and smell the coffee" is more than a metaphor for the morning after a brutal century ride.

Harry was asleep when I returned to the Knights Inn at 7:45 a.m. I collected my belongings and softly stepped to the exit with Tank by

19   Rob Owen, "Back to the past in Oregon's Baker City," *Seattle Times*, April 7, 2012, Travel, https://www.seattletimes.com/life/travel/back-to-the-past-in-oregons-baker-city/

my side. I slowly opened the door to avoid any sudden commotion and took off, hoping to keep the morning light from peeking through the narrow door opening. At the motel lobby, I had counted on seeing the manager again to thank him for his generosity the night before. The man's wife stood behind the counter. She had the morning shift. I asked if she would pass my message of gratitude to her husband. At 8:22 a.m., I hopped on the saddle and started cycling east on SR 86.

Unknown to me at the time, Adam, whom I did not meet at the prerace orientation, was returning to Baker City in a pickup truck. While at the café, I'd looked at the race's Facebook page and read Adam's call for help. He had been stuck on the side of the road about five miles outside of Baker City with a damaged bike derailleur. Several days later, when we finally met up in Jeffrey City, Wyoming, he recalled seeing me riding out of Baker City that morning. Adam returned to racing the next day after repairing his bike. (Race rules allow for transporting a bike in a vehicle to a shop for repairs if the racer returns to the exact location before continuing.)

Abdullah's lead expanded with each passing day. Twelve hundred miles separated us. If I kept my pace and averaged 100 miles a day, I would finish in 44 days—10 days ahead of my original plan. I recall thinking this was the one opportunity to ride as fast as possible across the land. Now that I recognized I could go much farther each day, consecutively, my mind shifted to a racing, laser-like focus. I assumed the days ahead would be equally challenging, if not more so, and I needed to take advantage of my strong body and mind. (Kelley and Roger knew about my ambition to go a century each day, but I didn't broadcast my goal because too many things could still go wrong.)

I had completed a metamorphosis from bike touring to bike racing. The larva of a contender showed up in Astoria. The pupa was spreading, a racer forming after two century rides. The chrysalis was revealed in Mitchell, and the racer fully developed on Campbell Street leaving Baker City. The life of an itinerant man riding during the day, sleeping at night, never in the exact location more than once. I wanted to enjoy the ride, but, more than anything else, I also set my heart on proving something to myself.

Coping with unforeseen hardships and pedaling over 12 hours every day were the most demanding facets of the race. Setting my Garmin device to ping in 10-mile increments had served me well on the Southern Tier and acted as a way to maintain sanity and occupy my mind away from the eastbound journey. Adapting the same mental manipulation technique, the GPS would ping and display average speed and elapsed time. I would process the metrics and think about the adjustments needed to achieve my daily goals. "If I stay at this pace, I'll ride ninety miles; I need to pick it up so I can hit one hundred again," I'd say out loud to myself, a recurrent psychological technique that worked remarkably well.

And here, east of Baker City, was the first occasion I thought averaging 100 miles per day was *actually* achievable. *If I extend my pace a little, I could average one hundred ten miles per day, and that would put me in Yorktown in fewer than forty days! Am I frickin' insane to think this is possible?* But the more I thought about it, the more attainable it seemed. At least, it did in my mind. I played it out. *Everything over one hundred miles would move into a mileage bank. Kansas would be the wild card. With favorable winds and fair weather, I could exceed two hundred miles at least one day. That would add significant miles to the bank.* I also calculated that I needed to extend the daily average to 175 miles to arrive at the Yorktown Victory Monument on July 4. *How cool would it be to reach Yorktown on Independence Day?* The image had a romantic appeal to it.

High above downtown Baker City, five miles east on State Route 86, I halted when I reached Flagstaff Hill (3,684 feet) and the Oregon Trail Memorial. I turned my body and bike to scan behind me. For centuries, countless souls searching for a better life had stood in my exact location, staring at the rolling, sagebrush-laden hills, rugged terrain, and unrestricted views of the Elkhorn Ridge. Downtown Baker City, a tiny stamp, was overwhelmed by the vast wilderness. The memorial, a 20-foot-high stone obelisk, and the National Historic Oregon Trail Interpretive Center tell the story of frontier pioneers. After fighting their way from

Missouri through rough and rocky terrain, settlers knew their journey to the Willamette Valley would soon end when they reached Flagstaff Hill overlooking miles and miles of the Oregon Trail that extended across Virtue Flat.[20] This was one of the few occasions I stopped to read about history and immerse my mind in what it must have been like to go back in time 150 years. The region today attracts many off-road vehicle enthusiasts. Movies, such as the 2010 film *Meek's Cutoff* set in 1845, have told the stories of the earliest times of the Oregon Trail and the hunger, thirst, and fear families faced on their pursuit to reach the Cascades.

The boundless landscape surrounding me was awe-inspiring. A solitary, brown horse, with a white mark streaking from head to nostril, stared at me. Wonderstruck, I turned back to Baker City and gazed at the towering Blue Mountains I had ridden over a couple of days earlier. This area and the Oregon Trail were first blazed by John Jacob Astor in 1813.[21] And in 1842, long lines of covered wagons traveled along the 2,000-mile Oregon Trail, creating deep ruts that are still present today.

A roadside sign and the sight of mountains, a narrow gorge, and a riverbed snaking through the canyon got me thinking about when this area sat beneath a hundred feet of water. Hells Canyon, 10 miles wide, borders the eastern Oregon, eastern Washington, and western Idaho boundaries. Hells Canyon is "North America's deepest river gorge,"[22] more profound than the Grand Canyon. The Nez Perce Indians and the Shoshone, both tribes that played a role in the Lewis and Clark Expedition, were the first

[20] "Flagstaff Hill—Baker City, Oregon," National Historic Oregon Trail Interpretive Center, National Park Service, updated April 14, 2022, https://www.nps.gov/oreg/planyourvisit/national-oregon-trail-center.htm

[21] Oregon Encyclopedia, s.v. "Astor Expedition (1810-1813)" by Larry Morris, updated March 24, 2022, https://www.oregonencyclopedia.org/articles/astor_expedition_1810_1812/

[22] "Hells Canyon," Visit Lewis Clark Valley, accessed July 12, 2022, https://visitlcvalley.com/hells-canyon/

to occupy this landscape.[23] The long mountain stretches gradually meet the valley, forming the vast canyon. I was surrounded by blue sky and wispy clouds above and snowcapped mountain ridges in the distance.

Had Katharine Lee Bates, creator of the anthem, "America the Beautiful," visited eastern Oregon, the same views could have inspired the words, "O beautiful for spacious skies, for amber waves of grain. For purple mountain majesties above the fruited plain…" The skies were vast. Majestic mountains and the tender breezes brought the fields to life as tumbleweeds moved across the highway, dispersed, and disappeared into the canyon.

At 1:00 p.m., I reached the town of Richland (population 156), nestled on the northern tip of Brownlee Reservoir, about halfway through Hells Canyon and close to the city named Halfway (population 288). I took off my helmet, removed my cycling gloves, retrieved my wallet, leaned Tank against the outside wall, and entered the Richland Café on the west end of town. Alone, I sat at a table in plain view of Tank and the surrounding area.

"Hi, I'm Larry from New Jersey, riding across the country. Hells Canyon is a cool ride," I shared, extending my hand to a woman who approached the table.

"Hi. I'm Jaclyn, the café manager," she replied.

"Those cinnamon rolls look great. I'd like two and a cup of coffee, please," I said, scanning the glass case underneath the front counter.

"We have many cyclists stop here because there isn't much between Baker City and Cambridge," Jaclyn said, adding, "The owner of the café lives in New Jersey. My husband and I raise cattle on a farm just outside of town."

"I imagine living here is very different compared to New Jersey," I replied, as Jaclyn refilled my coffee mug to the brim.

The conversation evolved. Jaclyn added, "Everybody who lives in Richland owns a horse for primary transport."

---

23 William Ashworth, "Hells Canyon: Man, Land, and History in the Deepest Gorge on Earth," *American Heritage* 28, no. 3 (April 1977): 1–2, https://www.americanheritage.com/hells-canyon

Learning from a history book is one way to do it, but cycling brings you back to how people lived over a century ago. Time stood still.

Harry stopped at the Richland Café about 30 minutes after me. I told him about the cinnamon rolls. We decided to ride to Cambridge (population 328), Idaho—about 65 miles. Making it before dark would be a challenge, given the distance and hilly riding conditions.

Just east of Richland, a steep, 1,000-foot rise and seven-mile stretch shocked my body back to the moment. The valley, known as Immigrant Gulch, revealed an expansive and stunning vista to the west. Foster Gulch to my right revealed an equally vast wilderness. The Snake River cut through the land. I felt like I had traveled back in time, immersing myself in the experience so many had during the great westward migration 200 years before.

I stopped at the summit (3,653 feet) to absorb the American wilds, an area "untrammeled by man, where man himself is a visitor who does not remain."[24] The perfect location for a posse of cowboys or a band of Indians to assemble in advance of the next hunt. The ideal setting for the scene in *Dances with Wolves* where Union Army Lieutenant John Dunbar (Kevin Costner) welcomes Lakota Sioux at Fort Sedgwick, a deserted military post on the western prairie during the American Civil War.

A Silver Dodge 4x4 with a cab whizzed by, gunning it to reach the top, but otherwise, I had the land all to myself. Nestled in a faraway ravine south of my location, I saw the Snake River for the first time. The river is the largest North American river that empties into the Pacific Ocean. Native Americans have lived along the Snake for thousands of years, eating salmon that spawned after their harrowing journey from the Pacific. As I surrendered myself to contemplation, pondering their passage, I knew the miles would add up quickly.

I initially heard and then saw an automobile approaching from the opposite lane. The blue sedan decelerated immediately after seeing me at the summit. The car pulled off the road into the gravel along the shoulder

---

[24] Kevin Proescholdt, "Untrammeled Wilderness," *Minnesota History Wilderness Concepts*, vol. 61 (Fall 2008): 37, https://wildernesswatch.org/pdf/Untrammeled.pdf

and stopped. I squinted to identify the occupants. Nathan stepped out of the driver's side, and Anthony stepped out the front passenger's side. I drifted across the highway, stopped, and reached out to shake their hands, saying, "It's great to see you. Why are you heading west?"

They had been cruising between towns, following the race just like everybody else. Nathan mentioned that in years past, he would continue east for a couple of weeks, riding until the top two or three leaders separated from the others. He said this year would be much different. He flat out told me, "Abdullah will win the race."

I asked, "What's his secret?"

Nathan's reply was immediate. "He's twenty-five years old and focused."

Abdullah was in a league by himself, a pack of one. I'd expected a more nuanced explanation: riding technique, physique, equipment, genetics—something other than age and attitude. *Oh well,* I thought.

Anthony snapped a couple of photos with the three of us smiling at the camera. "Check out the website tonight. I've been posting pictures of the racers we run into," Anthony offered. Then we went our separate ways.

For 13 hours and 110 miles, I rode surrounded by God and country. I spent the time thinking about American history. My desire to meet interesting people, which fueled my mind on the Southern Tier, had given way to a desire to pedal through the uninhabited region alone. I enjoyed complete solitude, when there was not a single concern on my mind—every decision, big or small, was mine to make. Good or bad, I would be accountable for the result.

Traversing the Cuddy Mountain pass on the way to Cambridge, the splendor so unique and unfamiliar, piqued my desire to keep pushing. I was out in the bundus, unknown to most. This was the sort of fantastic adventure people only dreamed about.

During the 13 miles between Seid Creek Road at the top of Cuddy Mountain and the descent along Pine Creek traveling southeast on highway 71, I embraced the realization that I had entered an extreme racing competition. Not one to shy away from a test, my desire to finish in fewer than 40 days overwhelmed all else. I wanted to pull off a feat that I would've considered unthinkable just days before.

Later, when asked by friends which state I liked traveling through the most, I'd reply, "Oregon."

The 700-mile trek through Oregon, the first stage of my journey, was the most enjoyable to ride through. It may have been a mix of fresh legs, a clear mind, and natural Northwest beauty, but my seven days in Oregon were my pregame for the challenging weeks ahead.

In Oxbow, Oregon, near the Oxbow Dam, I turned south onto State Route 71 and started cycling parallel to the Snake River. Originating in Wyoming, the river runs through Jackson Hole and a gorge between the Teton Range and the Gros Ventre Range, crossing into southern Idaho, Oregon, and finally emptying into the Columbia River at Tri-Cities, Washington. The 1,100-mile Snake River, the largest tributary of the Columbia River, had taken many names since Meriwether Lewis first sighted it in the early 1800s, including Shoshone River, Mad River, Saptin River, and Lewis Fork. Explorers had misinterpreted the Shoshone tribe, who had made S-shaped hand gestures to signify they lived near a river with many fish. The motion appeared to the explorers to stand for a snake.[25] The 200-yard-wide river's striking beauty, a green mountain backdrop, the blue sky, and sunshine joined to form shades of blue, pastel, and deep-green pastures, sparking my will to endure.

At 5:36 p.m., I crossed over the Snake River, joining the Brownlee Dam, one of the three dams that form the Hells Canyon Project.[26] The

[25] "How the Snake River Got its Name," Dave Hansen Whitewater & Scenic River Trips, accessed July 12, 2022, https://www.davehansenwhitewater.com/how-the-snake-river-got-its-name

[26] "Hells Canyon Complex Hydroelectric Project," Idaho Department of Environmental Quality, accessed July 12, 2022, https://www.deq.idaho.gov/permits/water-quality-permits-certifications/water-quality-certifications/hells-canyon-complex-hydroelectric-project/

map elevation profile revealed a steep, serpentine, 13-mile climb from the Brownlee Dam to a mountain pass at a 4,131-foot elevation. Harry and I had stopped at the Gateway Store & Café at the mountain base to buy Gatorade and snacks for the 2,000-foot climb ahead. Harry, a powerful rider, left the store about 10 minutes before me. I foresaw it taking two hours to travel 13 miles up the 8-percent-grade ascent. If my assumptions were correct, I would reach the summit between 7:30 and 8:00 p.m., still 15 miles west of my destination, Cambridge, Idaho. The sunlight shone bright but had begun to retreat behind the rising cliffs that commanded both sides of the narrow roadway. Riding on pavement without shoulders, occasionally blinded by the seeping sunlight, sweating profusely, and working hard to arrive at the mountaintop, I contemplated stopping at a campground below the summit. I knew I was cutting it close to make it to Cambridge before nightfall. I decided to press on because I had made reservations at The Cambridge House Bed & Breakfast. The attraction of a home-cooked, hot breakfast following a night of sleep in a cozy bed outweighed sleeping on the ground and nibbling on protein bars. I finally reached the summit and rode along the plateau for two miles on Seid Creek Road, followed by a 13-mile descent into Cambridge. I had favorable riding conditions, a slight tailwind, and a paved road absent any vehicles. I controlled the lane, not concerned about anything except arriving in Cambridge before the sun went down altogether.

A couple of restaurants in town—a taco and a burger joint—had closed when I reached Cambridge a few minutes before 9:00 p.m. I bought my favorite snacks at Jay's Sinclair gas station and convenience store, which was still open for business. Peanut butter packets had become my go-to energy food. I grabbed a few single-packet peanut butter cups and then made a beeline for the candy aisle to replenish orange jelly and sugar-covered candy slices that quelled my craving for sweets almost daily. Three Slim Jim beef sticks were the final food group to make the shopping cart.

I reminisced about my Nana's home in New Bedford, Massachusetts, when I walked through the Cambridge House B&B's front door on 1st Street, located down a quiet, country road outside the small downtown business district. Every summer as a kid, I vacationed with my family in the home across the street from Clark's Cove, where my dad grew up. A Cape Cod–style home built in the 1940s, the Cambridge Inn was charming, irregular, and made from dark wood just like Nana's. The interior was full of character. If only walls could talk! Old furniture topped with patterned cloth material, creaky wooden floors, family pictures on walls and set on tabletops all blended to create an ambiance that made the stay that much more rewarding. Going to sleep that night knowing a hot breakfast awaited me in the morning helped calm my nerves as I thought about the challenging days ahead.

When I finally settled into my second-floor room, seven days had come and gone since I left Astoria on June 2. I had ridden a century three of the seven days and averaged 99.4 miles per day. I had taken a sledgehammer to my original 54-day goal. Assumed constraints, a term often used in business to address performance challenges, can manifest in negative internal dialogue or excuses as to why something isn't possible. In my case, I had limited myself by shallow thinking—not because I didn't think I could do it, but because the goal was "good enough." The enemy of my soul had led me to settle for good when excellence had been a possibility.

I sought to end each day fulfilled but restless to begin the next. When I set my head on the pillow, I thought of the leaders who had continued riding well into the night. This mental conflict would never end. I got a call from Roger, who had reached Baker City earlier that day. "You're not going to believe my story," Roger began. "Sitting at a bar, minding my own business, a young guy asked where I was going," he continued.

"I'd love to try a long-distance ride someday myself," the guy shared, likely not expecting what happened next.

"I've got a deal for you. My tent is yours if you commit to taking a ride within one year," Roger stated. Then he presented the hook. If you don't make the trip, I ask that you ship the tent back to me in New Jersey."

The offer now on the table, the guy responded, "It's a deal," with much appreciation in his voice. Roger handed over his high-quality, recently purchased tent.

"You gave away your tent?!" I asked, summing up the initial part of our conversation.

It was a friendly gesture for sure, and a not-so-subtle hint that the nights we camped under the stars were not as pleasant for Roger as they were for me! The following day, Roger's friend met him in Baker City and drove him to Boise International Airport to return home to New Jersey. After returning home, he reclaimed his bike from the Whippany Cycle shop, shipped by BikeFlights.

Roger had ridden 600 miles when he reached Baker City. His time on the saddle had come to an end, and it was time for him to go home and return to work. We had ridden through much of Oregon's incredible scenery, encompassing lush hillsides, flowing rivers, and snowcapped mountains, often pausing to capture the magical vistas unique to Oregon. We fully supported one another during the tough early days as we adapted. I'm grateful to Roger for joining me. He began the transition to the real world while I continued my journey to victory.

Week 1: 696 total miles (99.4 miles/day)

Recharged!
Cambridge, Idaho
June 9, 2019

Chapter 10

CAMBRIDGE–WHITE BIRD, IDAHO (92 MILES)

June 9, 2019

I n the video I watched for the second time while getting myself ready for the day, the Italian gripped the handlebars. A gator that covered his face and neck, nose-to-forehead goggles, and a helmet prevented heat from escaping his exposed body. He looked straight ahead. Big snowflakes fell from the sky. On my walk downstairs to eat a much-anticipated breakfast, I wondered, *What happens if he can't continue? Did he carry enough cold-weather gear to deal with this?*

At the same time the Italian was making his way through Yellowstone National Park, several racers got stranded in West Yellowstone, Montana. They were holed up in motels because the entrance to Yellowstone on Highway 20 was closed. Nathan posted a vivid account of the treacherous ride. "They were all in the middle, battling some form of snow, hail, rain, wind in various forms. It was quite the day, with many hunkering down early. Spirits still high with the lot of them, and we're rooting for them all!"

Nine hours earlier, I'd sunk into the soft bed, covered myself in a thick down blanket, and fell asleep instantly.

At 7:00 a.m., I tiptoed down the hallway, trying to keep the old, creaky wooden floors quiet. A couple stayed in the room next to mine. As I tread softly down the narrow stairway and came to the first floor, the smell of freshly brewed coffee and bacon gave me a surge of motivation. I couldn't wait to eat Sheila's homemade breakfast! "Good morning," I said to no one in particular when I heard noise coming from the kitchen. Sheila, the Cambridge House B&B proprietor, was in the kitchen when I entered the dining room. "Your place is so cozy." I kicked off our conversation when Sheila appeared, holding a carafe full of freshly brewed coffee.

She poured me a cup of coffee and said, "The casserole's almost finished."

"Thanks. Orange juice, if you have it," I responded.

It was an odd juxtaposition, staying at the charming B&B, indulging myself with an experience reserved for a vacation getaway, while simultaneously pedaling to exhaustion every day. The Cambridge House was initially built in 1916 and had been the home of the local family physician for many years.[27] Very similar to many old towns that try to maintain the look and feel of twentieth-century America in a twenty-first-century real world, it had changed hands in the 1980s but then was left uninhabited for many years. In 2008, Sheila and her husband bought the home, refurbished it, and opened the B&B business. Sheila manages the bed-and-breakfast, and her husband works the family-owned farm.

Egg casserole, assorted fruit, sausage, pancakes smothered in maple syrup, pastries, and fresh-squeezed orange juice made for a surplus of calories that would burn off in hours.

The only time I broached politics, I asked Sheila what her thoughts were about the tariffs President Trump had placed on specific imports

---

[27] "History," The Cambridge House Bed & Breakfast, accessed July 12, 2022, http://www.thecambridgehouse.net/history.html

from China—a piece of news that dominated the national conversation and had the potential to affect US farmers. "What do you think about the tariffs and President Trump's overall approach to trade? Have they had any impact on your farm business?" I inquired, curious to hear Sheila's point of view.

She told me her farm had not been affected but she assumed other local farms had been. She continued, "It's too soon to know. Eventually, it could affect us, too," adding that she thought President Trump had America's best interest at heart.

(The $120 rate, higher than many nights, was worth it, as it included a feast fit for a king. Motels ranged from $40 to $150 per night. Often, the rate included a hot or continental breakfast. Campgrounds cost between $8 and $25. A couple of nights, I slept free of charge, hunkered down in a makeshift shelter. Churches that hosted cyclists relied on donations. The honor system was alive and well in every church—a donation box was typically located in the kitchen.)

At 8:45 a.m., I opened the Cambridge Inn's front door and walked outside with Tank by my side. Sheila and I stood on the front porch for a couple of minutes. I was checking the brakes, chain, and tire pressure, preparing for the day's ride, and Sheila was soaking in the morning air. She had to repeat the breakfast experience for the couple who were waiting in the dining room. It was time for me to get back to the business of racing.

I rode until around 2:00 p.m., when I stopped to assess my situation. Waiting until the middle of the afternoon to secure lodging almost backfired in Prineville and Baker City, Oregon. Waiting that late in the day to confirm lodging had been risky, but I'd decided this approach allowed me the highest chance to achieve a century ride each day. Today, I took a different approach. At 8:45 a.m., before leaving the inn, I called the White Bird Motel in White Bird, Idaho, to book a room. "I have plenty of availability. Racers stay here often," the woman—who I learned was named Barbara—responded.

I said, "Terrific! How about two rooms? My buddy also needs one." Harry had slept at a campground on the east side of Cambridge.

"Yes, when you get to town, come to the main office," Barbara instructed. When I left the Cambridge Inn, a calm came over me, knowing shelter was secured.

At 9:00 a.m., I stopped at a Sinclair gas station on W. Hopper Ave, the same store where I'd bought food the night before. I packed my CamelBak hydration pack with ice and bought Gatorade and snacks. The towns I would ride through to get to White Bird—Mesa, Council, New Meadows, and Riggins—each had a population of fewer than 1,000 people. Services would be limited, so I stocked up in Cambridge. Typically, I began each day carrying 5.5 liters (185 ounces) of water plus a 20-ounce bottle of Gatorade.

I met two cyclists who had stopped to rest in Sinclair's parking lot. Our journeys were both on the TransAmerica Bike Trail, but theirs started in Yorktown, traveling west. It was a crushing blow to my psyche after I processed that these chaps had 1,000 miles to go while I still had 3,200 miles to complete my quest! One guy wore a golden, yellow-covered helmet, just like me. The other guy's helmet was two-toned, with a white top section and red lower area. Both riders displayed a positive enthusiasm, each smiling from ear to ear. I recall thinking how thrilled they must have been to be so close to the coast. Both also displayed a lot of facial hair. One guy's beard looked akin to that of my Southern Tier tour group member Doug, who sported a full Santa Claus beard after 67 days without shaving when we ended in St. Augustine, Florida. The second guy's patchy, scruffy beard resembled my own.

A historical marker 14 miles east of Cambridge described the history of the 1,400-acre Mesa Orchards. It read that, for over 50 years during the first half of the twentieth century, the country's largest apple orchard covered the surrounding land.

For 90 miles to White Bird, I rode north on US 95—alone in a part of America I had never experienced. Virtually every inch of ground I rode over was new to me; there was nothing to trigger a memory.

Recounting stories about the history of the wild, wild West that I had only learned about in the classroom occupied my mind. Near New Meadows (population 490), my trance was disrupted by a road sign: "45th Parallel–Halfway between the equator and the North Pole."

It was an emotional blow when, at 3:37 p.m., I passed a sign near a bridge over the Salmon River that read: "Entering Pacific Time Zone." *What?* Was I in a bad dream? I'd been pedaling for days, and yet I was no closer to the East Coast—even after hundreds of miles on the saddle. *Was I going the wrong way!?*

My attempts to remain optimistic were already shaky—but once I saw that sign, I felt completely defeated. I could hardly imagine the mental fortitude required to get me through the remaining 3,000 miles. *This is bullshit*, I thought, and for the first time, I felt like a zombie on a bicycle.

Instead of my normal cycling gait—arms stretched, head raised, back vertical, bum on the saddle—I hunched myself over and stared at the pavement in front of me, focusing on one pedal stroke at a time while restlessly waiting to hear the GPS ping.

The mental power needed to not dwell on reentering the Pacific Time Zone was significant. My tunnel-vision obsession with experiencing America one mile at a time had been replaced with a singular goal to reach my destination.

At 4:47 p.m., I entered the Nez Perce National Forest about 10 miles south of White Bird. I glanced up at nature's grace on full display. The White Bird Ridge and Hells Canyon Wilderness to the west, the Grass Mountains and the Salmon River Mountains to the east, and the John Day Creek, Slate Creek, and Slippy Creek tributaries all leading to the picturesque Salmon River reenergized me. Mountains towered above to the north, with the Salmon River acting as my beacon to White Bird.

Harry and I arrived in White Bird (population 91) at 7:00 p.m. I didn't want to wait for a so-called "guided tour," so I searched online and read about the Battle of White Bird Canyon in 1877. It was the first conflict of the Nez Perce War and a notable defeat of the US Army.

White Bird had been the chief of the tribe, and in 1891, the town was established and named for the Nez Perce chief.[28]

We hopped off our bikes at the White Bird Motel, found in a valley on the most southern edge of town and south of the Nez Perce National Historical Park. I opened the front office door and saw Barbara sitting on a couch, with the television turned on, volume low.

After exchanging a pleasant greeting, Barbara stated the obvious. "You guys are way behind the leaders."

I embraced her sense of humor. "What can I say?" is all I could muster in response.

While standing in the parking lot of the White Bird Motel, Barbara shared a brief history of White Bird and pointed to a memorial erected on the opposite side of US Highway 95. A prominent focal point in the center of town, the White Bird Idaho Veterans Memorial displayed the names of 107 of the Nez Perce who had served and fought for the United States. Barbara recounted that the Nez Perce had been peaceful and amenable to living alongside White Americans when the hordes began migrating west in the 1800s. Many years after that, in 1855, a US Treaty guaranteed the Nez Perce these lands they had occupied for thousands of years. After discovering gold here in 1863, the US Government pressed the Nez Perce to abandon millions of acres of their land. Many chiefs, including Chief Joseph and Chief White Bird, refused to move, but a handful of chiefs agreed, and in 1863 signed away 90 percent of their ancestorial land.[29] Then, under threat of a cavalry attack in June 1877, Chief White Bird, who had opposed any treaty that took away land, led resistance in the region known today as White Bird. The Battle of

[28]   Emerson, "The Idaho Town in the Middle of Nowhere That's So Worth the Journey," *Only In Your State*, posted November 24, 2017, https://www.onlyinyourstate.com/idaho/white-bird-id/

[29]   "History," Nez Perce Tribe, accessed July 12, 2022, https://nezperce.org/about/history/

White Bird Canyon was the Nez Perce War's opening battle with the United States.[30]

According to Stephen Ambrose in *Undaunted Courage*, Lewis and Clark first met the Nez Perce when the Corps of Discovery made its way to the mouth of the Columbia River. The Nez Perce helped Lewis and Clark prepare for the treacherous journey over the Bitterroot Mountains in the winter of 1805. A trust had developed; the expedition left supplies with the Nez Perce that they planned to retrieve on their return trip east during the spring of 1806.

As I listened to Barbara talk, the account of White Bird and the Nez Perce tribe fascinated me. I stood at the Veteran's Memorial and imagined the days of cowboys walking across the dirt road to the saloon for the afternoon gathering, their spurs kicking up dust with every step. I imagined a horse-drawn buggy coming down the same dirt road I had to bring much-needed supplies that would last for several weeks. The TV shows *Lone Ranger* and *F Troop* romanticized the communities where Whites and Native Americans lived alongside each other, a place I had found myself in on this day. I loved watching those shows growing up. At the time, I didn't fully understand the complicated nature of the relationship between settlers and Native Americans.

The White Bird Motel, Silver Dollar Saloon, Red's River Café, and a couple of modest churches on the city's northern edge made up this postage-stamp community. A weathered-looking man, most likely younger than his appearance suggested, sat outside the Silver Dollar Saloon. He wore a "Trump 2020" cap. Inside Red's River Café, Harry and I greeted Erica, our server, who supplied five-star customer service. We each ordered a large pepperoni pizza. Erica, so full of positive energy, connected with me on Facebook and followed my trek to Yorktown. It was gratifying to know strangers, friends, and family were invested in my daily updates.

---

[30] "White Bird Battlefield History," National Park Service, updated May 30, 2021, https://www.nps.gov/nepe/learn/historyculture/white-bird-battlefield-history.htm

Harry had a dilemma when he entered White Bird. His right bike pedal threads had stripped, causing the pedal to loosen for no reason. Each time he drove the pedal down with his right foot, he wondered if it would snap off. He didn't carry a spare pedal. A local, who had joined the earlier conversation with Barbara in the parking lot, offered to help Harry in the morning. I wondered if she would transport him on the back of the Harley-Davidson she stood next to.

Harry didn't know what he would do in the morning; he was noncommittal as to whether he would attack the climb with or without replacing the pedal. We walked out of Red's River Café after devouring the pizzas. I decided to call it a night and returned to the motel. Harry decided on a nightcap at the Silver Dollar Saloon, the inside of which was reminiscent of the Long Branch Saloon in Dodge City, Kansas, featured in *Gunsmoke*.

"What time do you want to leave in the morning?" I asked, as I extended my arm for a goodnight handshake.

"I need to fix my pedal. I don't think I can make it up the mountain. I'm afraid the pedal might fall off," he replied, a tint of resignation in his voice.

That handshake would be the last time I saw Harry. When I was ready to leave in the morning, I texted him, "I'm leaving. What's your plan?" I waited for a few minutes for a reply. Harry didn't answer. I assumed he decided to sleep in and fix the pedal before returning to the race. I took off at 7:30 a.m. and began my ascent to the top of White Bird Battlefield through the Nez Perce National Historical Park.

For the next couple of weeks, Harry and I maintained contact through text messaging until Walden, Colorado, where his race suddenly concluded. By that point, my journal entries had become less frequent but more poignant. No longer content to state a simple fact, I added details to convey how I truly felt.

Journal entry on June 9: *Difficult riding alone.*

All Alone
White Bird, Idaho to Yorktown, Virginia
June 10, 2019

Chapter 11
WHITE BIRD–GATEWAY PARK CAMPGROUND, IDAHO (119 MILES)

June 10, 2019

A t a 2,000-foot elevation, White Bird sits on the southern tip of White Bird Hill Summit. The history Barbara shared came to life for two hours while grinding my way up through the White Bird Battlefield and the Nez Perce National Historical Park. Climbing to the skies, going slow motion, and my body revolting had become a strange addiction I welcomed. The brutal switchbacks ran for 12 miles to the 4,200-foot perch overlooking Baker Gulch and the surrounding Nez Perce National Historical Park. I turned and looked in the distance toward White Bird Bridge. The vast wilderness swallowed the town from which I'd just ridden. It was like trying to find the irregularity in an X-ray without the support of a trained radiologist; downtown White Bird was there, somewhere, but I couldn't find it. It's the aura of the mountains, that feeling of achievement, that sense of being so small and insignificant against a monumental backdrop. Scenes unfolded in my mind's eye: the Nez Perce perched high on the peaks, camouflaged, about to confront the US Army. Julie Andrew's arms outstretched, beaming over the German Alps near the Austrian border in the opening scene of *The Sound of Music*. "The hills are alive with the sound of music…" sings Maria, spinning and soaking up the fantastic beauty. Instead of that splendid alpine meadow, I peered at a green, treeless field sloping to where the Battle of White Bird Canyon of the Nez Perce War took place in 1877.

I took in the pure mountain air and then began my descent on a gravel section of Old White Bird Hill Road, the kind of road that can wake up a community at the crack of dawn when the tires roll over material brought to the site from a local quarry. I reentered Old Highway 95 and began a nine-mile trek to Grangeville (population 3,141).

Every so often, I craved a specific food. I strode into Cloninger's Marketplace on the main street, making a beeline for the produce aisle and stopping in front of large, succulent navel oranges. I imaged eating the flavorful, thirst-quenching fruit wedges one by one. I bought five oranges, protein bars, a couple of packets of peanuts, and two 20-ounce Gatorades. Outside, I relaxed on a picnic bench underneath an awning away from the sun. I savored every morsel, taking my time to peel away the rough, shiny orange rind, wondering if the next would taste better than the one before.

I bought packets of Sathers or Braches orange jelly, sugar-covered candies every chance I could. My breakfast of choice was a box of Hostess white-powdered donuts. I ate orange slice candies during the day to keep my sugar levels elevated, and on many nights, I devoured an entire bag before snuggling inside my sleeping bag. Periodically, I ate Baby Ruth or Milky Way candy bars and substituted red licorice for orange candy slices.

At 12:34 p.m., I stopped pedaling at a sign that read: "Kooskia 3 miles, Lowell 27 miles, and Missoula 149 miles." The sign reminded me of the summer of 2018, when I talked to Emma in the Adventure Cycling Association tour department located in Missoula, Montana.

I swung east in Kooskia (population 607) and started on US Highway 12, also known as the Lewis and Clark Trail. It took me writing my book *Suit to Saddle* to realize the true impact of cycling across America. Pedaling my bike from state to state, leapfrogging from time zone to time zone, allowed me to unknowingly reclaim the person I wanted to be, the one I used to be.

It took riding the Trans Am Bike Race on the same roads where generations of Native Americans lived, wagon trains rolled during the westward migration, and much of America's complex history was born to reinforce in me the wonders of our great nation and to bring home a greater appreciation for tying the past to the present.

The Adventure Cycling map revealed there were no services for the next 89 miles until Elk City, west of Lolo Pass and near the Montana border. At 1:39 p.m., I began pedaling on Highway 12, which bordered the Middle Fork Clearwater River, absorbing the pristine landscape and listening to the soothing sound of flowing water. Not knowing if I would find a campsite or motel before day changed to night was unsettling.

At 2:56 p.m., I stopped at the Wilderness Inn Motel & Café on Highway 12 in Lowell, Idaho. A man, woman, and child sat inside the café. I sat down next to them and asked if they knew of any nearby lodging options. They were driving home from a camping trip, heading west on Highway 12. They recommended the Gateway Campground, which was 30 miles farther east but, importantly, on the west side of Lolo Pass. Not wanting to climb Lolo Pass after dark, Gateway Campground sounded like the perfect place to spend the night. I thanked the family and then walked to the front counter to pay for my burger and fries. A line of camouflage, baseball-style caps for sale displayed on the wall behind the cash register sported "Trump 2020" on the front visor. Rugged individualism described many folks I met along my trek to Virginia. I felt of a kindred spirit with the locals as I rode through rural communities in the northwestern sections of the country.

I continued north on Highway 12, paralleling the Lochsa River, en route to the Gateway Campground. The word *lochsa* is a Nez Perce word meaning *rough water*. The Lochsa River's flow is unregulated, and in late spring, when snow melts and water drains from the cliffs, the Lochsa River is rated as one of North America's finest for whitewater rafting.[31] In mid-September 1805, when Lewis and Clark traveled westward along the Lolo Trail, they descended from the Lochsa Gorge, close to the present-day Lochsa Historical Ranger State, about one mile from the Gateway Campground. In their journals, Lewis and Clark describe this area, where they spent unplanned time because of early winter snowfall.

Bounded by a clear, running river on one side and cliffs on the other, the natural surroundings drastically reduced visibility. When I came to the 30-mile mark without passing the Gateway Campground, I became worried. The couple had said it would be easy to miss the campground entrance. I didn't panic. I continued riding. At the 32-mile mark, I saw a sign for the campground that said it was a quarter mile ahead. When I turned off Highway 12 and entered, I felt fortunate, knowing the ride through Lolo Pass would come after a night sleeping under the stars, fully rested. I cruised around the circular campground road. Only one RV site was available. I hastily pulled into the gravel parking space and leaned Tank against a wooden picnic table. Green trees and bushes encircled the site. I knew the campground was full, but I felt isolated in this space nestled off the main road. I walked to the entrance and deposited the $12 fee inside the collection box. On my return walk to my campsite, it was so quiet, I could hear a pin drop. The peaceful sound of silence filled the air.

It had been challenging to ride a bike on paved roads, and I couldn't imagine forging a path on virgin soil to the Pacific Ocean over the Rockies, Bitterroots, and the Cascades as the Corp of Discovery did over 200 years before. They hadn't known what to expect west of the Rocky Mountains. What our forefathers experienced and withstood to create a land unmatched is worth noting in history books and worth

---

[31] "The Most Dangerous Rapids in the World," *The Active Times*, posted August 2, 2016, https://www.theactivetimes.com/water/most-dangerous-rapids-world

remembering to share with younger generations. When I sat on the picnic bench, waiting for darkness to set in, I felt like a time machine had brought me back to the winter of 1805, but with the understanding that I knew what was on the other side of Lolo Pass.

My encounter with the family at the Lowell café was not dissimilar to Lewis and Clark's reaching the Nez Perce, who had advised and guided the Corps of Discovery over the snow-covered Lolo Pass in 1805, which was reported as the single greatest challenge faced by Lewis and Clark on their trek.[32] Lolo Pass (5,233 feet) is the highest point on the Lolo Trail, also known as the Nez Perce Trail. It is still the primary route over the Bitterroot Mountains into Western Montana and the northern Great Plains and was traversed by the Nez Perce and other tribes long before Lewis and Clark ever stepped foot in the area.

It's one thing to read about something; it's another to hear about it. And it's entirely possible to form a wholly new perspective with an open mind if you experience it. That's what riding a bike across America can do for the mind and soul—and along the way, the body gets a good workout!

[32] "Lewis and Clark Expedition," History, updated March 16, 2021, https://www.history.com/topics/westward-expansion/lewis-and-clark

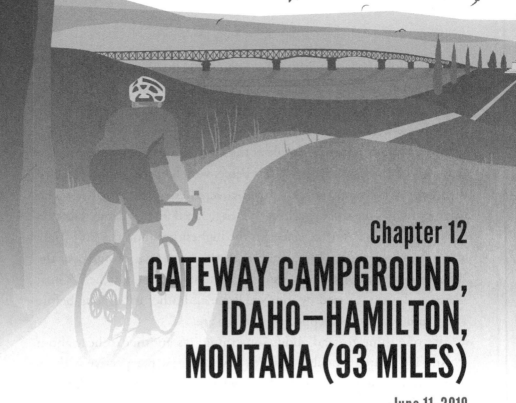

Chapter 12
GATEWAY CAMPGROUND, IDAHO–HAMILTON, MONTANA (93 MILES)

June 11, 2019

At 2:00 a.m., I unzipped my sleeping bag, wiggling my body to free my legs. I turned on my headlamp and slid outside to confront the stillness that greeted my gaze. The light cut through the brush, and my head was on a swivel, looking left and right for any critter that may have wandered to my campsite. Nothing. *Good news*, I thought. The rest of the world seemed so distant. I imagined other racers had continued to pedal through the night while I was fast asleep. Others were probably waking up after a three- to four-hour catnap before continuing their journey. Once again, I questioned whether my strategy was sound. I found a slightly downhill plot of ground free from leaves and twigs so my pee stream wouldn't splash onto my feet. I returned to my Big Agnes and quickly fell back asleep.

At 6:45 a.m., I exited my sleeping bag relaxed, content, and ready to tackle the day with vigor and vitality. The exterior rain cover had done its job. The tent liner was dry as a bone. The outer cover captured the moisture that had formed overnight. I gathered everything, ate two breakfast bars, and gnawed at pieces of Jack Links slow-cooked and hardwood-smoked original beef jerky. I was ready for the big climb up Lolo Pass, now 50 miles northeast on the western edge of the Bitterroot Mountains.

At 7:30 a.m., I pedaled away and meandered through hairpin turns, passing near Bald Mountain (6,526 feet), Indian Grave Peak (6,441 feet), Grave Butte (6,190), and Ashpile Peak (6,400 feet). The clear, fast-flowing Lochsa River bordered my southern flank. The beauty, peace, and tranquility created a fantastic cycling atmosphere. I had expected to see people fishing, kayaking, or canoeing during this fair-weathered summer morning. I did not. Farther east, near Elk City, 12 miles south of Lolo Pass, history came alive again when I rode by a historical marker that described how Lewis and Clark had crossed this section of road on September 15, 1805. The contingent had spent the previous night four miles upstream, in Powell, close to Whitehouse Pond. Over the years, history buffs and curious travelers have found solace in visiting this area to study Lewis and Clark's journey. The DeVoto Memorial Cedar Grove, located off Highway 12 near Lolo Pass, describes this location where Bernard DeVoto, conservationist and author, camped while studying the journals of Lewis and Clark. After his passing in 1955, DeVoto's ashes were scattered over the area for another vignette documenting American history and the western migration.[33]

The last couple of miles before I reached the pass, the weather changed from sunny to overcast. The Bitterroot Mountains surrounded me. The temperature had dropped several degrees at the summit, and clouds turned from wispy white to threatening gray. Vehicle traffic picked up significantly descending Highway 12 into the Bitterroot

---

[33] "Devoto Grove," Idaho Historical Marker, US Highway 12, U.S. Forest Service Department of Agriculture, Clearwater National Forest, June 11, 2019

Valley, heading east to Lolo. The distinct sound of cars whizzing past me heightened my sense of awareness.

A "Welcome to Montana" sign depicted a black bear—a message to be aware of my setting now that I had crossed into the Treasure State. I had been anticipating the ride through Montana's wide-open plains, a gateway to a rocky buttress of the Bitterroot and the Rocky Mountains. The three states I'd visualized riding through the most were Montana, Wyoming, and Kansas. Pedaling through the uninhabitable wilderness beneath the big Montana sky was a magnet that pulled me to Astoria.

My hands gripped the handlebars as I descended through the Nez Perce National Forest. Meandering along Highway 12, the scenery was ever changing due to the shadows cast by the mountains. I whizzed by a "Moose Crossing" sign. I chuckled when I thought of the TV program *The Adventures of Rocky and Bullwinkle and Friends*, a show I watched religiously when I was a kid. A real moose is not so gentle, and it's best to stay clear. A single mule deer grazed in the open field. Inside a café on Highway 12 near Lolo Hot Springs, I laughed aloud as I read about the differences between black and grizzly bears on a poster inside the café. *Does it matter whether a grizzly or black bear mauled me?* I pondered. *It is a lousy ending either way!* The barren mountain range on the south side of Highway 12 from Lolo Pass (elevation 5,235 feet) to Lolo, Montana (elevation around 3,300 feet), appeared to have been destroyed by a massive forest fire. Charred, toothpick-like trees littered the countryside. Later that day, I searched online and read about lumber management practices, known as the Checkerboard Legacy, which explained why sections of forested land looked different. Some areas are owned by the Forest Service, while the Plum Creek Timber Company owns other plots of the mountainous region—the charred sector due to natural fire and lumber management practices.

On June 11, 2019, at 5:00 p.m., resting at the Lolo Super Stop at the intersection of Highway 12 and SR 93 in Lolo, Montana, I had a decision to make. *Do I ride ten miles off route to Missoula and surprise Emma when they open for business in the morning?* Doing so would set me back a full day. The clock didn't stop because I wanted to take a side trip. There were no pauses, no stages, not like the Tour de France. It was me against the clock. As much as I wanted to meet Emma, I couldn't afford to add a whole day to my time, so I continued to Hamilton, Montana, about 30 miles south of Lolo.

My brother Dan sent me a text. "I saw Harry moving at 60 mph when I checked the leader board earlier."

What a relief, I thought. Harry had found someone to transport him to a bike shop—the plausible explanation for moving at such a clip. Harry is a strong cyclist, but he's not a superman.

"Harry's pedal and crank arm connection were unsafe and needed repair. He must have found someone to transport him to a bike store," I replied. Harry would rejoin the chase, leaving White Bird a day later.

Traveler's Rest State Park, located 1.5 miles southwest of the Lolo Super Stop, was home to the only archaeologically verified Lewis and Clark Expedition campsite, their last stop before beginning their journey across the treacherous Bitterroot Mountains and over Lolo Pass in September 1805.[34] The 30-mile ride to Hamilton along the Lewis and Clark Bicycle Trail was flat as a pancake—but the *wind*, my friend. When I looked south to the Sapphire Mountains, a name taken from commercial gems mined on its eastern slopes, that big, blue Montana sky just fell into my lap when I was least expecting it. *Big sky in all its glory*, I wrote in my journal later that night.

Some state nicknames like Missouri's (the Show Me State) or New Jersey's (the Garden State) don't seem to make sense from an outsider's viewpoint. But for others, like Florida (the Sunshine State) and Montana (Big Sky Country), it's easy to see where they get their nicknames. Trees, buildings, and hills close to highways block much of the skyline in vast swaths of the eastern United States. There is no contrast between the plains and the skyline in Montana, making it more difficult to judge

---

[34] "Travelers' Rest State Park," Montana, Fish, Wildlife & Parks, accessed July 12, 2022, https://fwp.mt.gov/stateparks/travelers-rest/

scale and distance. *Are those Rocky Mountains I see in the distance five miles or one hundred miles away?* Without looking at a map, it was impossible to tell.

The University of Montana's Department of Geography describes the Montana landscape this way:

> Colorado is high, having more peaks within its borders than any other state. Wyoming is wide, with the breadth of the plains between the Bighorns and the Grand Tetons. California is handsome, with a splendor of success. It takes all three adjectives to describe Montana.[35]

When I settled into my room at the Super 8 on Hamilton's north side, I closed the chapter on map section #3. "Twenty-five percent done! Cell service is back, and Montana is really cool to ride through," I told Kelley during our first phone call in 36 hours.

I ate at a KFC next to the Super 8 motel. After filling my belly with eight pieces of Colonel Sanders's most delicious dark meat, I leaned back against the booth to straighten my torso, trying to relieve the pressure of my bloated stomach. *Two states down, eight to go!* I thought. *I've conquered the Cascades. Next up, the Bitterroots.*

My tanned, filthy face was now hidden by a scraggly, salt-and-pepper beard, and blood dripping from my chapped lips reflected the formidable nature of the journey I was on. After sharing my daily affirmation on Facebook, I laid my head on the pillow and quickly fell asleep with a deep sense of satisfaction. Somehow, I'd managed to reach Hamilton 12 days ahead of my 54-day goal.

---

[35] Rick and Susie Graetz, "Montana Remains 'High, Wide, and Handsome,'" *This is Montana*, University of Montana, accessed July 12, 2022, https://www.umt.edu/this-is-montana/columns/stories/high-wide-handsome.php

12 Days Ahead of Goal
Hamilton, Montana
June 12, 2019

David Letterman's doppelgänger was in the hotel lobby when I checked out the following day. Walter, from Australia, had been riding solo on the TransAmerica Bike Trail, traveling east to west. The resemblance between him and Letterman was uncanny. I found the strength to engage in a brief conversation, even though my eyes still held remnants of morning crust. Walter had 1,800 miles to go. His 120-pound loaded bike reminded me of an Abrams M1A1 Tank compared to my much lighter WWII M4 Sherman Tank. I tried not to dwell on the fact that I still had 2,400 miles before the finish.

I swung by the local post office, the sixth one I'd stopped at since leaving Astoria, to ship nonessential items home. Each shipment home cost between $15 to $20—not cheap. After the first shipment I made in Corvallis, Oregon, the reduced weight led to a smoother riding experience. The other four shipments supplied a mental boost more than anything, for completing one more task on my ride across America.

This time, I sent my dad a Father's Day card. I held on to my bulky, cold-weather gear, my Showers Pass 100-percent nylon trousers, and my red Showers Pass 100-percent nylon top. I wouldn't consider shipping these valuable clothing items home until after scaling the Rockies. The storm that dropped several inches of snow in Yellowstone days earlier stranded racers and forced others to find shelter, including one who, out of sheer desperation, spent hours inside a porta-potty near a construction site. A summer snowstorm in the Rockies was entirely possible.

In Albertsons, I restocked on chamois cream, an antibacterial, viscous substance that helps cut friction between skin and clothing. My fear of developing saddle sores troubled me more than anything else. I cleaned my body and washed my cycling shorts every night, some nights better than others. Each morning, I lathered my riding shorts and butt with globs of greasy chamois cream, covering the largest surface possible, mindful that an infected saddle sore could become a showstopper. I applied chamois cream the same way I ingested Motrin or Advil—if 200 mg helps reduce inflammation and knee pain, 400 mg must be better! Residual cream wound up on the outside of my cycling shorts. Streaks of the white substance drew the curiosity of some when I walked into a gas station store. According to legend, racers in the days before chamois cream would use a slab of steak to help prevent sores and then eat it that night after it had been tenderized during the ride.[36] Advancements had come by 2019.

The ride out of Hamilton, cushioned between the Bitterroot Valley—which was under 1,000 feet of water during the Pleistocene Epoch[37]—and Sapphire Mountains, was serene and free from agitation, physically and mentally. At 9:58 a.m., I reached the outskirts of Darby (population 733), the site of the historic Chief Joseph Ranch and John Dutton's home

---

[36] Fred Matheny, "How to Solve Saddle Sores," *Road Bike Rider*, accessed July 12, 2022, https://www.roadbikerider.com/how-to-solve-saddle-sores-2/

[37] "Glacial Lake Missoula and the Ice Age Floods," Glacial Lake Missoula, accessed July 12, 2022, https://www.glaciallakemissoula.org

(who was played by Kevin Costner in the television series *Yellowstone*). Many buildings lined the main street, including the Marshal's Office, which was made from logs.

Riding alone through the country's fourth-most-extensive but forty-third-least-populated state[38] conjured happiness, excitement, hope, inspiration, anticipation, longing, and satisfaction. About 10 miles south of Hamilton, I glanced west at the recently traversed snowcapped peaks of the Bitterroot Mountains. I stopped to soak in my surroundings when I rode by a road marker directing hikers to turn left to connect with the Nee Mee Poo (Nez Perce) Trail. Just outside of Sula (population 37), the Nez Perce used the trail to flee the US Army during the Nez Perce War of 1877.[39] In White Bird, Barbara explained that when the US Army forced the Nez Perce from their homeland, they entered Montana near Lolo Pass, wandered through the Bitterroot Valley, and crossed the Continental Divide near Chief Joseph Pass (7,241 feet)—12 miles from my current location—before settling near Bear Paw Mountains, 40 miles from the Canadian border.

Riding for 100 miles at an elevation between 3,000 and 4,000 feet was not as difficult as I thought it would be. I wondered if I would experience altitude sickness. The nagging headaches had often caused me distress when visiting Denver, the mile-high city, on business trips. However, I didn't experience the ill effects on the saddle, acclimating well to the gradual climbing.

Halfway up the mountain, I removed two outer layers, finishing the 10-mile, 3,000-foot climb to Chief Joseph Pass wearing my bright-yellow, short-sleeve cycling shirt. Pedaling hard and sweating profusely, I unzipped my shirt, exposing the upper half of my chest to the air.

---

[38] "Montana Population," PopulationU.com, accessed July 12, 2022, https://www.populationu.com/us/montana-population

[39] "About the Trail," Nez Perce (Nee-Me-Poo) National Historic Trail, Forest Service: Caring For the Land and Serving People, accessed July 12, 2022, https://www.fs.usda.gov/main/npnht/about-trail

The air cooled my body as I pushed to reach the summit. The sky was a monochrome shade of gray, but there was no threat of snow, and for that, I was grateful. West of the Continental Divide, I reached the Lost Trail Pass (7,014 feet). In 1805, Lewis and Clark crossed the divide one mile northwest of my position.

I would always get psyched up before a big climb. I loved the adrenaline rush and the feeling of legs working overtime. The repetition of the process always brought the same result. The euphoria of reaching the crest fueled my desire to do the same for the next. A residual amount of snow had been visible when I arrived at the top, in spots concealed by large rocks and away from direct sunlight. The temperature felt more like the sixties but had dropped to the upper forties when I stopped.

Seventeen miles east of Chief Joseph Pass on State Route 43, I stopped at the Big Hole Battlefield National Monument, a Nez Perce National Historical Park section managed by the US Department of the Interior. In 1877, nontreaty Nez Perce had settled into this territory, 10 miles west of Wisdom, Montana. The iconic Lewis and Clark National Scenic Trail's triangle-shaped sign hung next to a much larger Big Hole Battlefield National Monument sign, a reminder of the intertwined history of the Corps of Discovery's western migration and the centuries-old conflicts between settlers and Indian tribes.

It was effortless to appreciate riding through sections of the country that were ground zero for fundamental aspects of American history, areas of the country I had romanticized visiting as a child when watching my favorite cowboy and Indian television shows.

Riding on the smoothly paved asphalt and narrow shoulder of Highway 43, from Big Hole to Wisdom (population 119), rivaled the Texas desert and the never-ending Highway 90 between Van Horn, Texas, and Marfa, Texas. Seeing the Rockies reach for the sky to touch the clouds and wondering when they will be in the rearview mirror was comparable to the gut-punch feeling I'd had each time I'd reached a phantom hillcrest on my journey through Texas eight months before.

I entered Wisdom at 4:30 p.m. A colorful road sign welcomed me to this small, rural, old western community: "Welcome to Wisdom & The Big Hole Valley—Land of 10,000 Haystacks." A roadside marker described the area, which was first settled in the 1880s but was traversed by Lewis and Clark decades before.

Sacajawea, the Shoshone guide, had recognized the area she had traveled during her childhood and informed Clark that it was the great resort of the Shoshones.[40] Clark confirmed the "wisdom" of the Shoshone tradition and further christened the basin Hotspring Valley, naming it for a hot spring near present-day Jackson, my home for the night. The name Hotspring Valley was eventually changed to Wisdom, based on the Wisdom River that passes through town (now known as the Big Hole River).[41]

Three hours of daylight remained when I entered Wisdom. My determination to exceed 100 miles a day influenced my decision to swing south on State Route 278 and push 18 more miles to Jackson, Montana. I knew of the challenging headwinds between Wisdom and Jackson in the Big Hole Valley and next to Big Hole River. Even with the advanced knowledge and time to prepare, the two-and-a-half-hour ride was trying, one of the most grueling stretches of the entire 4,200-mile journey. I lowered my head, gripped the handlebars, and powered through relentless headwinds.

Next to the highway, white, cone-shaped, black-tipped structures protruded a couple of feet out of the ground. I thought I'd stumbled upon missile silos. But actually, the cones (or beacons) mark runways for pilots who fly in the Western Montana backcountry. The runway surface made from clumped grass—not gravel, sand, or dirt—makes up most airstrips in the bush.

---

[40]   Ambrose, *Undaunted Courage*, 255, 261–262

[41]   Rick and Susie Graetz, "Bit of Montana Wisdom (Part 2 of 5)," *This is Montana*, University of Montana, accessed July 12, 2022, https://www.umt.edu/this-is-montana/columns/stories/montana-wisdom-2.php

A storm was approaching. I could see dark, angry clouds slowly filling the sky. It was a race against time trying to reach Jackson before the skies opened. Three miles from town, a blue pickup truck going north on State Route 278 toward Wisdom decelerated from 60 miles per hour to a dead stop in the opposite lane of the two-lane highway. The driver, a man, leaned his head out of the window and asked if I planned to continue or stop in Jackson. I told him I hadn't decided yet but most likely would stop. He said, "If you stop, you can stay at my hotel. It's immediately on the right side when you enter Jackson." It was an invitation I wasn't expecting and one I couldn't ignore.

The Bunkhouse Hotel, one of the few buildings in this sleepy getaway town of Jackson (population 38), was unlocked when I arrived at 7:00 p.m. No one greeted me, nor was anybody working to collect money—the honor system on full display. I chose a private room with a cozy bed. A "Welcome Cyclists! Ice Cold Budweiser Here!" sign in front was the only clue I hadn't entered a time machine to the mid-1800s. The man who stopped me on the highway catered to cross-country cyclists. After settling into my room, I walked 100 feet to the mercantile next to the hotel. The owner, Maria, had recently renovated the building. She cooked a large cheese pizza and joined me outside the hotel for a much-appreciated conversation. The storm reached Jackson at 7:30 p.m., dumping buckets of rain for an hour straight. I watched the mean-looking clouds skirt through town with the determination of Olympic sprinters. *What a brilliant decision to stop in Jackson*, I thought, as I was now sheltered rather than exposed to wind, rain, and darkness on State Route 278 in the middle of Montana.

Nobody was in the lobby (or anywhere else in town) when I left the hotel at 7:18 a.m. I signed the hotel logbook, scribbled my credit card number on a piece of paper, and wrote the owners, Rick and Tammy, a thank-you note.

They left me a cordial note as well. "Hi, Larry, thanks for staying with us here at the Bunkhouse. Sorry, we couldn't check you in and show you around like we always do, but our meeting took longer, and you already went to bed." The mercantile (circa 1889), the Hot Springs Lodge, and the Bunkhouse Hotel made up all of Jackson.

The Big Hole Valley is one of the state's most popular recreation attractions, making a name for itself as a winter sports destination. People come all the way from Norway and Sweden to compete in the annual Montana Snowkite Rodeo, the Northwest's premier snowkiting competition.[42] (Snowkiting is an extreme sport in the same category as ultradistance bike racing, combining snowboarding and kitesurfing.)

Big sky, big mountains, big trucks, big trouser belts, and big ranches go hand in hand with many tiny Montana towns—with a lot of nothing in between. Maria shared that the nearest Walmart or Costco is a two- to three-hour drive. Once a month, several families meet for a day trip to buy nonperishable goods. Yes, a unique way of life. My brief stay in Jackson was one of the top 10 most treasured places I rode through on my race across America.

[42] Noah Poritz, "Snowkiting Montana: It can't get any better!," *Distinctly Montana*, December 12, 2014, https://www.distinctlymontana.com/snowkiting-montana

Chapter 14
JACKSON–VIRGINIA CITY, MONTANA (105 MILES)

June 13, 2019

Abdullah's lead had grown considerably, and now only 1,200 miles separated him from the finish. Online chatter had grown, discussing if he would break the solo record of 16 days, 20 minutes, and 41 seconds set by Peter Anderson in the 2018 TABR.

Racer 61, Larry Walsh, had 3,107 miles to go. I was pleased to average a century each day, but I wanted more. After 11 days on the saddle, I had fully embraced the notion that I could do better than I ever thought possible. Barring an unexpected injury, weather event, or mechanical issue, I felt confident in my riding ability. My perception of what good looked like evolved. The mind's extraordinary power to will an idea to reality took hold. An aha moment on steroids. My mind entirely focused on finishing this damn race in less than 40 days, but I also knew it would be tough to achieve because harrowing days awaited me farther east.

I reached the outskirts of Jackson at 7:30 a.m., riding on Country Road 278. At the summit of Big Hole Pass (7,360 feet) and the eastern entrance to Big Hole Valley, I gazed out at a series of dull, slope-backed pastures that rose to meet foothills crowded with tangled vegetation.

In a string of fortunate events, when the Corp of Discovery traveled westward in the summer of 1805, Lewis came upon Shoshone warriors at a nearby encampment on the Beaverhead River. Sacajawea recognized the Shoshone chief, Cameahwait, as her brother, which assured the explorers a friendly reception. They stayed at Camp Fortunate, established close to present-day Dillon, Montana, before continuing their trek west.[43]

"Sacajawea was a white flag and peace dividend traveling with her son—not a war party."[44]

At 9:25 a.m., about 15 miles east of Big Hole Pass on Country Road 278, I met two men cycling the Great Divide Mountain Bike Route, "the longest off-pavement route in the world."[45] Both Canadians were well-tanned from the sun's rays beating down all day. They gave off upbeat spirits, as if they didn't have a worry in the world, so it seemed. One sported a groomed silver beard and a big smile. The other also beamed, although his black, patchy, matted beard conveyed a ruggedness that matched the land of high mountains, deep valleys, and horizontal sweeps of inhospitable rangeland. Stretching from Canada to Mexico, the 3,000-mile route follows the spine of the Rocky Mountains. Segments of the trail, including this area north of Bannack, Grasshopper Creek, and Hangman's Gulch, traverse highway arteries, which tie one off-road section to another. As we compared notes on wildlife sightings, they said they had seen elk, deer, and bears, but no big cats. I had seen mule

---

[43]   Ambrose, *Undaunted Courage*, 277

[44]   *Lewis & Clark: The Journey of the Corps of Discovery*, directed by Ken Burns, aired November 4, 1997, on PBS, https://www.pbs.org/kenburns/lewis-clark/

[45]   "Great Divide Mountain Bike Route," Adventure Cycling Association, accessed July 12, 2022, https://www.adventurecycling.org/routes-and-maps/adventure-cycling-route-network/great-divide-mountain-bike-route/

deer and cattle but nothing else. I rode away, thinking off-road riding is better for viewing wildlife.

Country Road 278 passed 12 miles north of Bannack, where a big gold strike happened in 1862. Like many towns during the gold rush, Bannack's population grew virtually overnight. It was a rough-and-tumble town. Organized law never seemed to keep up with new towns popping up on the frontier. The lawlessness was perfect for thieves to roam with plenty of gold to steal. Citizens turned into vigilantes. Their method of dealing with the thieves was a quick hanging after a straightforward trial.[46]

A scratching noise had started coming from the crankset when I'd left Hamilton, despite wiping away the excess grease, grime, and dirt on the chain and crankset every morning (and sometimes at night). The Adventure Cycling Map section #4 showed a bike shop on Rife Street in Dillon (population 4,219). "Limited hours, call ahead" it stated—a request I didn't heed. Two miles off the main street, I turned left onto Rife. Cars were parked on both sides of the neighborly road. When I reached the address, I stopped and listened to silence that suggested folks hadn't begun their day yet. And sure enough, the bike shop was closed for business.

I returned to the town center. Like many I had ridden through, downtown Dillon was condensed. A postage-stamp town in an open prairie and surrounded by expansive ranches. A woman and three kids stood outside their van in the parking lot of the Atlantic Street Mercantile on South Atlantic Street. The building facade drew me closer; beneath a prominent sign on the top of the building, I saw the word "Huckleberry." My stomach churned at once, as though to say, "Feed me!" I rode into the parking lot, hopped off Tank, and lifted my 70-pound travel machine up two steps to a narrow wooden deck that stretched the length of the building. I leaned Tank next to a wall outside the store. Before pulling

---

[46] "Montana Vigilantes," Legends of America, updated April 2022, https://www.legendsofamerica.com/montana-vigilantes/

the front entrance door open, I glanced once more at the woman and noticed she wore a University of Utah women's basketball jersey. "What's the connection to Utah basketball?" I asked. She told me she'd played there. I bragged about my daughters, Tara and Jaclyn, once again, both of whom were excellent high school basketball players.

I strolled into the mercantile and at once felt at home in the hospitable and welcoming environment. I sat down at the bar. The shelf in front of me was full of jars of wild huckleberry jam. I wasn't thinking about eating huckleberries, but I craved pancakes. I devoured a full stack smothered with maple syrup, several strips of thick bacon, and several cups of coffee. A patron who had seen me enter the store and noticed my colorful cycling kit approached me. He inquired about the race and shared information about the roads leading out of Dillon. An avid cyclist, he was familiar with the TransAmerica Bike Trail and offered good insight into the roads east of Dillon. "More of the same," he said simply, implying paved roads and limited services between towns separated by many miles.

I sought human interaction less frequently, but inside the mercantile, I drew much needed energy from the combination of pancakes and conversation. My traipse to the exit to get back on my bike was visibly slower than when I entered the store an hour before. Knowing I didn't have a game plan was unnerving. *Maybe I'll turn around and stay in Dillon*, I thought. Could I find a place in Twin Bridges, 24 miles away? Or should I try Virginia City, closer to 50 miles farther east, hoping for the same comfortable feel I experienced in Dillon? I opted for the latter.

Once again, I spotted a tangle of storm clouds roiling along the horizon, promising the imminent start of harsh weather. Blankets of rain fell in the distance, descending from the furious-eyed sky. To my alarm, a gigantic, funnel-shaped nimbus moved across the plains like a bad omen, which was known for yielding unpredictably high winds and capable of generating violent supercell storms, tornadoes, and deadly wind shears. I shifted to the highest gear, gripped the handlebars, and realized that, for this not to deter me, I would have to move faster than the storm.

The angry supercell reached thousands of feet into the atmosphere. If the storm continued on its current path, I could continue riding.

I looked straight ahead, only looking to the left every couple of seconds to gauge the storm's path. About five minutes after looking at the violent column of air, the supercell changed direction. It was pivoting southeast and coming right at me. Realizing this, I began to search for shelter. On the right, about a quarter of a mile ahead, I saw a solitary home perched on a hilltop about 200 yards off Highway 41. It was a race against time. I pedaled hard and turned onto a dirt trail that led to the property. I turned right and onto the 200-foot-long, paved driveway leading to the ranch-style home. A pickup truck was parked in the driveway next to the garage—the only clue the house was currently occupied. I hopped off my bike and walked Tank toward the residence's rear, roaring, "Hello! Hello?" I was not familiar with trespassing and gun laws in the state of Montana, and I didn't want to become a statistic. Two days earlier, on June 11, when I'd descended into the Bitterroot Valley on Highway 12, I'd heard the repercussion of a gunshot coming from a solitary ranch on the south side of the highway. I'd glanced right and, in the distance, observed an individual pointing a long rifle at something in the pasture. That image popped into my mind again, as I strode toward the back patio of the ranch home to seek shelter.

Hail, wind, and sleet battered my surroundings for several minutes. I hunkered down underneath the backyard portico, where I could see the interior of the home. I kept a heightened sense of awareness, on the lookout for any movement or any sign that someone was home. The storm lasted about 20 minutes. An inch of pebble-sized hail blanketed the ground after the storm blew through. With Tank by my side, I returned to the driveway, hopped on my bike, and pedaled to Highway 41, continuing to Twin Bridges (population 381).

Near where I rode, the Corps of Discovery had stopped when they reached a confluence of three rivers. Originally named Philosophy, Wisdom, and Philanthropy by the explorers —after President Jefferson's virtues—today, they are known as Big Horn River, Ruby River (or

Stinking Water), and Beaverhead River. They flow along the valley on the southern edge of the Tobacco Root mountain range, hugging the spur that runs parallel to Beaverhead River.[47]

I avoided abrupt movements for fear of slipping on the ice that remained on sections of Highway 41. I passed by Beaverhead Rock State Park and Beaverhead Rock (5,192 feet), identified by Sacajawea in 1805 as a landmark near a summer retreat of her Shoshone people.[48]

At 3:00 p.m., after two hours of intense and stressful cycling, I stopped to decide on a destination. The first place I called was the Fairweather Inn in Virginia City. "Hi, this is Larry. I'm wondering if you have any rooms tonight? I'm on a cross-country bike ride."

Wendy, who answered, returned a pleasant greeting and told me she could hold a single room. Now traveling southeast on SR 287 toward Sheridan (population 650), I sighed in relief, knowing several hours of light remained and I only had 30 miles to go to reach Virginia City. The nasty storm had rushed through the region, and the sun now shone through the limited, wispy cloud cover.

Sheridan, in the "heart of the Ruby Valley,"[49] had been ground zero during the gold rush. As was the case in many western towns, gold was the impetus that drew thousands of individuals to these early settlements. The 19-mile stretch of highway between Sheridan, Alder (population 116), present-day Nevada City, and Virginia City (population 195), known as Alder Gulch, yielded "over $40 billion of gold (today's prices)" after its discovery in 1863.[50] At its peak, 10,000 residents lived in Virginia City, which was formed as a mining sector near Alder Creek

---

[47]   Ambrose, *Undaunted Courage*, 260

[48]   Ambrose, *Undaunted Courage*, 262

[49]   Ruby Loeffelholz, "Sheridan—Heart of the Ruby Valley," *This is Montana*, Visit Southwest Montana, accessed July 12, 2022, https://southwestmt.com/specialfeatures/this-is-montana/communities/sheridan-heart-of-the-ruby-valley/

[50]   "Gold in Alder Gulch," Montana Historical Marker, US Highway 287. Montana Department of Transportation, June 13, 2019

by Bill Fairweather and Henry Edgar during the gold rush. My bike ride across America was many things, including an educational experience.

The views of the snow-covered, 8,000-foot peaks of the Ruby Range that enveloped the horizon on the road to Alder captivated me. Vehicle traffic increased closer to Virginia City, and I incorrectly assumed Virginia City would hum with activity. At a roadside marker just outside of town, I read about the Ruby River. It was initially referred to as the Passamari by the Shoshone Indians. Miners referred to the Stinking Water as the Ruby. "Gems" found along the riverbanks were garnets, not true gems. Vigilantes ruled the era. The route I traveled was known as Vigilante Trail during the periods after the gold rush. Much of the newly discovered gold in Alder Gulch financed Harvard University in the early twentieth century.[51] Today, rusted gold dredges sat idle along the path between Alder and Virginia City. A weeded-over railway track ran parallel to Highway 287. As I approached the outskirts of Virginia City, I could see that many buildings maintained the original character and condition, including one that formed Adobetown, which settlers erected from mud and grass during the gold rush. Several homes, saloons, restaurants, theaters, and a music hall make up Virginia City today.

Wendy greeted me at the front lobby counter at 7:15 p.m. I dove right in, asking Wendy questions about this old western town. My enthusiasm was evident, as I was eager to learn. Wendy shared her story. She first visited Virginia City with her son when he was in grade school. Wendy loved the community and history of Virginia City so much that she and her son moved to Virginia City, when she started working at the Fairweather Inn. She became involved with the local chamber of commerce by working as a docent, volunteering for group tours, and taking part in reenactments for school groups and other visitors' cultural activities. Eventually, her son attended the University of Montana and finished with a history degree. Montana's eighth-grade students visit Virginia City every year on a planned field trip and immerse themselves

---

[51]   Ibid.

in a history lesson about the 1860s. They learn, as I did, that Virginia City residents first heard about Lincoln's assassination three months after it happened in 1863.

I ate pizza and treated myself to a vanilla ice-cream cone at the Virginia City Creamery across the street from the Fairweather Inn. I sat by myself, thinking about the cultural divide between communities in different regions of the United States of America. I reflected on traveling to a foreign land, the favored exchange for college students. Universities tout their foreign exchange programs as a recruitment tool. Why? What about traveling to another region of the United States in order to better understand our past? I had seen firsthand hundreds of small towns, many with different lifestyles. They all blend to form the greatest nation on earth. Sitting in the creamery, I imagined many of my friends would welcome the opportunity to trade places with me and experience seeing America one mile at a time.

I asked two college-age women working at the creamery about their experience living in Virginia City. I was particularly interested in what this place was like during the winter months, when it was bone-chilling cold with several feet of snow covering the ground. They gave a straightforward response. "Not much to do in the winter." One girl shared that the Pioneer Bar, about 0.2 miles from the creamery, was the go-to place (the *only* place open) during the winter months. Residents would often come together for a day of banter and beer.

When I returned to the Fairweather Inn, I called Kelley and told her my idea to develop an exchange program. However, this plan is still in its infancy... This idea occupied my mind for several days as I thought about executing such a plan. Since returning to New Jersey, I've contacted Wendy, who introduced me to folks from the Montana Schools and Historical Society. Just like a seedling transplanted to an area where a new forest will emerge, it only takes one student interested in other cultures to bring home a better understanding of history, people, and culture of life in the nineteenth century for a new generation of curious suburban dwellers to appreciate aspects of early America not found in history books.

Chapter 15
VIRGINIA CITY, MONTANA– YELLOWSTONE, WYOMING (105 MILES)

June 14, 2019

Seeing the Yorktown Victory monument could not come fast enough. Early in the race, I resisted the impulse to think about the finish. I also struggled to focus on something other than America's four-million-square-mile landmass. With every fiber of my being, I tried to stay disciplined on thinking about anything other than the slow slog across Montana. Father's Day was two days away, so I grabbed onto the memories of over 20 Father's Day weekends from 1997 to the present, during which I flew to Seattle to join 50 like-minded, older-than-35 hoopaholics at Basketball Camp. That annual trip to Whidbey Island, north of Seattle, to play hoops with friends who shared a passion for basketball, hunger for competition, and camaraderie was on the top of my things-to-do list every year.

Teams of nine played between six and nine full-court, 32-minute games. My younger brother Dennis joined me in 2003, the first and only year he attended, coincidently beating my team in the championship game by 25 points—an ass-whooping. They handed us a beating from the opening tip. Dennis claims I fouled him hard under the basket, trying to prevent him from scoring. I could have. It sounds like something I might do in the heat of the moment.

In 2009, my team won the championship. It took me 12 years to bring home the gold. I'm still looking for a repeat! But, if the pattern repeats, 2022 is 12 years since we raised our hands in victory. Maybe this is the year? Teams played games Friday afternoon and all day on Saturday. Then it was one and done on Sunday. Most everyone was home by late afternoon on Sunday to spend Father's Day with their family. I'd drive to Sea-Tac Airport to catch the 4:00 p.m. flight home. Every year, I missed that flight and took the red-eye home, arriving at the Newark airport at about 5:30 a.m. I'd drive home from the airport, shower, and be at work by 9:00 a.m. Monday morning. So much fun and a legion of memories.

The bed at the Fairweather Inn was uncommonly comfortable. When I woke up, the down comforter covering my body felt snug. The old-style room had one table lamp that projected dim light. It wasn't worth turning it on. I didn't wish to open the door because my room was near the main lobby, where people had started to mingle for a continental breakfast and coffee. I gathered my things, swallowed a couple of breakfast bars, and put on my cycling kit. I looked at the leaders' board at 7:30 a.m. I had completed 1,192 miles, Adam 1,123 miles, Harry 1,088 miles, and Rolf, whom I met at the prerace orientation, had ridden 1,426 miles. The Lanterne Rouge, Thomas, had kept a steady pace, completing 566 miles.

The initials AZ (Abdullah Zeinab) stood out, alone and in Missouri, while the initials TC (Thomas Camaro) hovered over a town somewhere in Oregon. The bookends, Thomas and Abdullah, were separated by over 2,000 miles. All other racers' initials stretched between Thomas and Abdullah. America seemed so small to me then, as if Abdullah held a quarter-mile lead in a two-mile running race.

It was hard to leave Virginia City, an authentic town full of history. If only the streets and buildings could talk. The comfortable bed, the crisp morning air, and the burden of an imminent 1,000-foot climb along the Gravelly Range in the Tobacco Root Mountains gave me pause. But it was time to go, so I did. Wendy wasn't working the front when I walked out of the Fairweather Inn at 8:00 a.m. I rode by the Pioneer Bar and imagined the entertaining atmosphere inside that the girls described the night before. I thought about trudging through the snow in complete darkness to greet locals at the local watering hole. Citizens from Virginia City were isolated from the rest of civilization. Someday, I want to visit again with Kelley and the kids to experience the remnants of a once-thriving village of the 1860s. My blood circulated, and my body came to life once I started the big climb east of Virginia City. Clouds covered most of the morning sky directly above. In the distance, blue sky peeked through the overcast skies.

A thrilling and completely unexpected 2,000-foot drop over a 10-mile stretch down the back side of the Tobacco Root Mountains into the Madison Valley west of Ennis (population 852), Montana, immediately followed the big climb. I finally had the experience I hoped for several months before, when I'd descended the Vulture Mountains east of Wickenburg, Arizona, destination Tempe. The grand view of the snowcapped Rocky Mountains to the east and endless open plains on both sides of me was the most captivating view of the entire 4,200-mile ride. The scene was reminiscent of the 1976 American Western film *The Missouri Breaks,* starring Marlon Brando and filmed near Virginia City. Winding through the mountain road to the valley floor, I basked in the jubilant bliss that comes only from these moments in the backcountry, no matter how fleeting. God's natural kaleidoscope of snowcapped mountains, sparkling river water, green pastures, sagebrush, and soil unfurled like a map before me, changing with each passing mile.

The landmarks and geographical formations can easily describe the back country, but it's also a state of mind—a place where I found myself unbound and focused on making progress. *Up the mountain. Down the back side. Toward a greater sense of inner self.*

I felt confident I could surpass my speed records of 45.42 mph and 24.42 mph for a 10-mile segment because of the favorable conditions and the fact that Tank carried less weight, without panniers attached to the racks. I accelerated with each pedal rotation, more forceful than the one before. I wanted to reach 50 mph. Unfortunately, I could only muster the strength to reach 44 mph during a half-mile descent in this majestic, northern Rocky Mountain region. And more disappointing, I only averaged 20 mph on the 10-mile leg.

At 9:25 a.m., I reached the outskirts of Ennis and felt like I had passed through a time machine taking me back 100 years. American flags lined both sides of the broad central avenue through town, protruding from several storefronts. I imagined I was a color guard marching down the center of the city. Quickly, my nostalgia turned to unease when I looked up toward the east end of town at the mighty, snowcapped peaks of the Rocky Mountains, which gnawed on the horizon like teeth. Intimidated for the first time, I called Kelley. "I'm about to ride through the Rockies!" I told her, excited but anxious about what lay ahead.

Eleven miles south of Ennis, I stopped to talk to a female cyclist from New Zealand, who was traveling east to west on the TransAmerica Bike Trail. During our exchange, a male cyclist riding west joined our conversation. He was from Russia, and he told me he had passed Rolf the day before, adding, "I met Abdullah several days ago." By this time, Abdullah had made such a huge impact on the racers, touring cyclists, and dot watchers that he'd become a living legend.

On this morning, the cycling conditions were optimal. Motorists passed infrequently. I approached an area devasted by an earthquake in 1959. A historical marker near Cameron, Montana, described the quake, which struck the Rocky Mountains measuring 7.5 on the Richter scale, the most devastating to hit the region in modern times. Quake Lake

(Earthquake Lake) had formed after the earthquake occurred, generating an 80-million-ton landslide. The quake destroyed several homes and killed 28 people.[52]

Today, on the southern tip of Quake Lake, is Hebgen Lake, a man-made lake that expands about 15 miles from Quake Lake to the northern boundary of West Yellowstone, Montana. Beautiful log cabin homes were perched high, overlooking the lake, with the rugged, snowcapped mountains in the background. I often visualized leading a humble existence holed up in a log cabin, sipping coffee on the front porch during the morning calmness, waiting for the sun to rise and the birth of a new day. It was beyond my imagination on this day that three months after returning home to New Jersey in October 2019, Kelley and I would purchase a log cabin on Torch Lake, Michigan. Now, coffee on the porch is no longer just a dream.

I reached West Yellowstone (population 1,321) around 5:00 p.m. Many town welcoming signs had an artistic quality to them. Here, the large, bold letters "West Yellowstone" were inscribed above the words, "Destination Adventure"—a fitting welcome to an original, old western enclave. West Yellowstone seemed like an excellent place to settle for the night, but two hours of sunlight remained, so I decided to continue riding after a rest and resupply break.

I waited in line inside the crowded West Yellowstone Visitor Information Center to purchase a ticket. Nobody appeared to be in a rush, and it was a laid-back atmosphere distinct from the frantic feel I have grown accustomed to living in the Northeast. After waiting in line for 20 minutes, barely moving, I became antsy, not knowing if I would reach the campground inside the park before dark. Finally, it was my turn. I briskly walked to the main counter and greeted the visitor center employee. "A ticket to enter, and I would like to reserve a campsite at the Madison Campground," I said, keeping a calm demeanor on the

---

[52] "Welcome Earthquake Lake Geologic Area," Montana Historical Marker, US Forest Service Department of Agriculture, Gallatin National Forest, June 14, 2019

outside, but on the inside, I was a little panicky, because less than an hour remained before sunset. The guy told me the Madison Campground was 10 miles away, which put me at ease as I calculated in my mind the task ahead of me. I knew that if I pushed it, I could make it to the campsite before it got dark. I paid $8 to camp, a discounted rate for cyclists.

I then crossed the street to the Eagles Store to restock on food and drinks. The store clerk asked if I had bear spray, to which I responded, "No." He mentioned a bear sighting had been reported earlier that day and suggested that I carry a canister. *That's not what I wanted to hear!* I purchased two large "Counter Assault Bear Deterrent Spray with Holsters." Each container weighed a little over 12 ounces and cost about $90 each. (In hindsight, it was irrational to buy two; I carried an extra two pounds for the rest of the race.)

At 4:30 p.m., I entered Yellowstone National Park. A group who had stopped at the state border sign at the same time offered to take my picture. I sent the picture of me in front of the sign to my family. My face had thinned, and my facial hair had grown. I was dirty and shabby in appearance, with tired eyes. Three miles inside the park, on Highway 20, I looked in the distance and noticed several cars had stopped. The road had turned into a parking lot. About 20 people stood outside vehicles, some on top of vehicles, gazing at the wood line. I reached the crowd, stopped pedaling, and placed my legs on both sides of the bike to steady my body.

"What's everybody staring at?" I asked nobody in particular, keeping my focus in the same direction as everyone else.

In unison, I heard the word "grizzly" uttered by a handful of people.

I locked my eyes onto the body of a massive, brown bear 30 yards from the road. I snatched my iPhone and captured a few still pictures and short videos. I knew I was experiencing something unusual; even in Yellowstone, a bear sighting doesn't often happen. I will never forget that grizzly's face. It wandered to a more visible part of the brush, then turned its head to the left, appearing to study all the people watching it. Its head was huge! I had seen black bears wandering around Morris County, New Jersey, over the years. However, black bears look nothing like the menacing grizzly I saw. Grizzlies have a hump, and their face is rounder, sizeable, and depressed between the eyes and nose. A black bear's face is straight from forehead to nose, without that classic shoulder hump. The bear attack scene in *The Revenant*, starring Leonardo DiCaprio, came to my mind rather than the docile image portrayed by Smokey Bear.

I never felt in danger, even though I was the only person without vehicle protection. After a 10-minute, Wild Kingdom–like experience, I continued on, with my eyes searching and ears listening for wildlife. My safari on two wheels had gotten off to a fantastic start, and I was fortunate to be one of the few to see a grizzly in the wild. Two miles later, a family of three stood outside a vehicle stopped in a dirt parking area, staring up at a clump of about 70-foot-tall trees.

"What are you looking at?" I asked.

"A bald eagle," the man replied, pointing his arm to help me find the eagle nesting in the tree. The national bird of the United States perched with such regal dignity. Replicating the excitement of seeing a grizzly followed by a bald eagle was hard to do. When I passed elk roaming the surrounding pastures, I thought, *What's the big deal?*

I reached the Madison Campground at 6:30 p.m., with plenty of time to set up camp before the sunset. Upon arrival, I noticed that several touring cyclists had recently pitched their tents. I met three recent Tufts University graduates riding across the country before starting their professional careers. One by one, they greeted me as I walked Tank through their campsite to a vacant plot of ground about 20 feet from theirs. All three had a job waiting upon their return home. They had been tracking the race like many others I had met. A 60-year-old Japanese man staying at the campground was riding across the country as well. A mechanical engineer by training rode solo and carried his gear in panniers attached to racks he built made from wood. I thought, *That's one way to save money.* The Michelin tires were the only bike part that looked branded; everything else appeared DIY.

Daylight turned to darkness, prompting me to set up my tent quickly. I pitched it on the hard dirt ground next to a picnic table beneath a canopy of pine trees. My air mattress, an essential item, created an air pocket between my body and the cold ground. I hung a small pocket light from the tent ceiling and placed the next day's clothing by my side. That location served two purposes. Often, I combined the clothing with the small inflatable pillow to provide an extra bit of pillow cushion. Also, on some mornings, my mind wasn't clear enough to think straight when I woke up, so preparing for the next day's ride when my mind was functioning made things much easier. I stowed my cell phone, toothbrush, medication, and breakfast bars in a small pouch connected to the inside liner above my head. Sleeping on the cold ground can be an enjoyable experience if done right. I retired map section #4 and placed it with sections #1-3 in a Sea to Summit waterproof bag.

After eating Slim Jims, breakfast bars, and assorted candy for dinner, I was reminded to store all remaining food and drink items inside a bear-resistant container by posters pinned to the trees throughout the campground. The temperature was expected to drop to freezing overnight. Unlike racers who survived on as little as three to five hours of sleep per night, I looked forward to snuggling inside my sleeping bag on this crisp evening for eight hours of shut-eye. My race strategy was working—I was not about to deviate at this point. No cell service meant no daily Facebook update.

Chapter 16
YELLOWSTONE (MADISON CAMPGROUND)–HATCHET RESORT, WYOMING (100 MILES)

June 15, 2019

When my iPhone vibrated at 6:30 a.m., I sprung out of the sleeping bag without pause. *I'm one-third of the way to Yorktown,* I thought. I rarely used the alarm, but I thought it might be tempting to sleep in this chilly morning. I had a big day ahead of me, and I needed to get moving. I stood up outside my tent, stretched my arms to help with blood flow, and glanced at the college graduates who had gathered at a picnic table, preparing their breakfast. Steam rose above a boiling pot of water, presumably for their morning coffee and oatmeal. We chatted for a couple of minutes, and then at 6:58 a.m., I told them good-bye. I walked back to the parking lot on the opposite side of the welcome center, hopped back on the saddle, and began the 15-mile ride to Old Faithful.

Do I continue, or do I ride off route to Old Faithful? I considered the two choices. It was decision time when I saw a road sign pointing to Old Faithful. *To come this far and not check it out... No way.* I exited and rode down a long, winding road to visit Yellowstone's number one attraction. Old Faithful, the most renowned geyser, spews hot water and steam into the air. There are hundreds of less famous geysers throughout Yellowstone. But Old Faithful is one of the few where you can predict when an eruption occurs. Usually, it erupts and spews jets of water and steam into the air every 90 minutes, the phenomenon resulting when the underground hot spring releases pressure.

I stared at Old Faithful, waiting patiently for the impressive eruption. Steam emitted every few seconds, a sight similar to puffs of smoke emitting from a pipe. I became antsy after 10 minutes and decided to continue riding without seeing the teakettle blow its top.

I readied my GoPro when I approached a herd of buffalo grazing in the open fields on both sides of the narrow, two-lane road. I followed behind cars that had slowed to a crawl to get a good view. One buffalo stood, watching gawkers pass by. A giant geyser emitted steam a hundred feet into the sky in the distance. The prevailing winds forced the steam to move directly overhead. It was easy to distinguish between the white, puffy steam and the little cloud cover that still remained. Several months after I arrived home to New Jersey, I read a story about a bison attacking a tourist in Yellowstone. I might have rushed past the herd without taking pictures had I read a story like that before riding through the park myself. *Where else?* I thought. *Is there another place to duplicate the Yellowstone experience? Grizzly bear, bald eagle, elk, buffalo, and geysers?* During these Jurassic Park–like scenes, dinosaurs did not run wild, but Yellowstone did provide an almost complete theme park experience.

I reached peaks over 8,000 feet in elevation, climbing greater than a 10-percent grade. It surprised me how difficult it was to ride 76 miles through Yellowstone. Reaching the summit of Craig Pass (8,261 feet), in particular, was beyond difficult. I clenched my teeth, huffed and puffed with every tire revolution, and ground it out for several minutes. I moved ever so slowly, using the granny gear. My legs burned, and I felt I didn't get enough air with each breath. Like so many climbs before (and after), I focused on reaching the summit without standing or stopping. I rewarded myself with a short break at each summit. Riding with my butt on the saddle required more physical exertion, but the few times I lifted my butt, my speed slowed and I lost momentum. Climbing a steep hill on the saddle is a different technique than many who ride hills with their butt in the air and off the saddle.

Tank felt heavier, as if the rotating tires were grabbing the asphalt. When I reached the Continental Divide, I stopped near Shoshone Lake, the largest backcountry lake in "the lower 48 states."[53] After leaving the park through the south entrance, I soon entered Grand Teton National Park. I couldn't truly tell if I was looking at the prominent summits of the Cathedral Group, the most famous of the Grand Teton (13,775 feet), as I rode along the Pitchstone Plateau. Still, I had an unobstructed view of Mt. Moran (12,605 feet), Eagle's Nest Peak (11,257 feet), Ranger Peak (11,355 feet), other peaks of the Teton Range. Why the name Teton? Many theories exist, including one that early French voyagers named it with the meaning "the three nipples."[54]

I left Yellowstone at 1:14 p.m. I entered Grand Teton National Park at 2:14 p.m., and at 5:11 p.m., I exited Grand Teton National Park. It all happened so fast. When I looked at the "leaving Teton" sign, I recall thinking, *What's the big deal?* Perhaps I was a bit jaded. It took returning home to reflect on the pictures I had taken of the razor-sharp mountaintops dusted in snow as they scraped against a perfectly blue sky to properly appreciate the majesty of that iconic, rugged mountain range.

My number one priority was locating a motel or campground on the west side of Togwotee Pass (9,658 feet). I was not about to climb

---

[53] "Shoshone Lake," National Park Service, updated July 29, 2019, https://www. nps.gov/yell/learn/nature/shoshone-lake.htm

[54] "How the Tetons Got Their Name," *Wyoming Magazine*, January 30, 2017, https:// wyomingmagazine.com/tetons-got-name/

Togwotee Pass at the end of this particularly challenging riding day. I reached the Hatchet Resort on the southern end of Emma Matilda Lake and the confluence of the Snake River, Buffalo Fork, and Buffalo Valley Road. At 8:11 p.m., I stood outside the front entrance and gazed at a blanket of fluffy clouds that reached west to touch the Bitterroots. I squinted and noticed an even grander scene farther away of peaks covered in snow. Shades of yellow, orange, white, and tan created a skyscape that mimicked Ansel Adam's famous photo titled *The Grand Tetons and the Snake River, Grand Teton National Park, Wyoming, 1942*. By 9:00 p.m., the cloud cover dissipated, and the mountains were no longer visible. The bright, yellow sunset streaked across the sky, and by 9:05 p.m., the sun had dropped behind the hills. My eyes returned to the night welkin and twinkling stars directly above. It'd been an incredible day cycling through one of the nation's richest collections of natural wonders.

Referred to as the unofficial anthem of the American West, "Home on the Range," written by Dr. Higley in 1871, inspired by his surroundings near his Kansas home, could have easily been inspired by the view on my ride from Moran, Wyoming, to the Hatchet Resort on Highway 26. "Oh, give me a home where the buffalo roam. Where the deer and the antelope play. Where seldom is heard a discouraging word. And the skies are not cloudy all day." Four horses trotted toward me from about 100 yards away. *Wild or domestic?* I thought. They were all cinnamon-colored, and three had a distinct white blaze from head to nose. A lone horse possessed a regal disposition; white socks on its lower legs moved gracefully through the field.

I walked my bike and equipment up the narrow, outdoor stairs to a second-floor room that was barely big enough for me, let alone Tank and all my gear. The first thing I did was shower. I spread my legs apart and reached down with a washcloth to clean the area prone to saddle sores. I was very anxious. I wondered how my bottom would feel when the warm washcloth contacted my skin. *I hope it doesn't burn.* I felt butterflies, not knowing what to expect when I closed my eyes to focus on the next couple of seconds. What a relief! My bottom was tender to the touch but no worse than the day before. I filled the bathroom sink with warm, soapy water and scrubbed my riding shorts clean. It was the second day in a row that I'd improvised by washing my riding shorts in a bathroom sink, using a hairdryer for drying, and sleeping butt naked to aid airflow and keep the sores at bay.

At 9:15 p.m., I sat at the bar inside the crowded restaurant attached to the resort. I felt out of place—unsure if I was tired, wanted to be alone, or both. The server placed a menu in front of me and poured a me glass of water. "I'll be back in a minute," she said, juggling food orders, talking with customers, and filling drink orders at the same time.

I estimated I had dropped about 15 pounds by that point. After 1,400-miles, my legs felt strong. Overall, my body felt great. Not surprisingly, my feet and hands were tender and numb, but they were not as bad as I had expected. My neck, lower back, and knees held up well. However, saddle sores, my greatest fear, had recently developed. Sitting at the bar, I worried the sores would grow into a much bigger problem. I'd managed to ride through days of rain in Texas with saddle sores on the Southern Tier, but something felt different now. I had an uneasy feeling in the pit of my stomach.

The server returned and asked, "What can I get you?"

I surprised myself when I blurted out, "Wedge salad and a medium-cooked bacon cheeseburger, please." Oddly, I craved a salad, albeit not exactly a healthy one. I felt a rush of energy as soon as I dove into the lettuce, bacon, blue cheese, and tomato combination. Days before, in Grangeville, Idaho, I'd craved large, juicy oranges. Almost daily, I ate orange slice, sugared candy treats. But only once, at the Hatchet Resort, did I crave a salad. My body asked for some nutrition. So, I obliged.

I had been riding in Wyoming for fewer than two days, but I could already see that hills, headwinds, and solitude would make cycling through Wyoming tough going. However, despite its mountains, winds, and overall harsh riding conditions, I have tremendously fond memories of my time in Wyoming.

Week 2: 707 total miles (101 miles/day)

Chapter 17
HATCHET RESORT–LANDER, WYOMING (93 MILES)

June 16, 2019

A 2,500-foot climb awaited me 10 miles east of the Hatchet Resort. I had a great night's sleep, followed by a relaxed, sit-down breakfast at the resort, consisting of pancakes with gobs of maple syrup, bacon, a freshly baked blueberry muffin, a large glass of orange juice, and several cups of coffee. Several adults sat at a long table, taking up a large section of the restaurant. The raised voices made it almost impossible for me not to eavesdrop. I heard the words, "York, Pennsylvania." Except for a brief moment of curiosity, I didn't have any interest in engaging in conversation with this group. Whereas the year before, on the Southern Tier, I would have held court with fellow Pennsylvanians. I had completely moved on from the joy of meeting interesting people; I wanted to get going. I set out at 8:13 a.m., en route to the Togwotee Pass (9,658 feet).

When I reached the base of the mountain, I saw a large, rectangular, flashing sign blasting an ominous warning: "Bears on Road—Do Not Approach." Seeing the sign affixed to a portable trailer positioned in this temporary location, I immediately stopped. Panic-stricken, I thought: *What will I do if I see a grizzly bear?* I reached for one of the bear spray canisters and affixed it to my CamelBak's front shoulder strap. I was confident I could outrun a bear on a downhill—and perhaps flat—road, but I wouldn't have a chance on a climb. I decided I would turn around and haul ass down the mountain if I encountered a bear on my ride to the summit. The bonus miles would be well worth it!

A few times before flying to Portland, I'd watched one specific YouTube video of a cyclist encountering a bear on a backcountry road somewhere in Wyoming. He stopped 100 yards before reaching the bear on a flat highway and waited for it to cross. The cyclist remained still and quiet until the bear reached the opposite side of the road. Out of harm's way, he continued riding slowly, gingerly passing to avoid startling the bear. It was an excellent example of what to do and had stayed with me. I wondered if I would have a similar encounter. I prayed not.

It was 8:37 a.m. when I started up the mountain, initially in lower gear. After I had enough momentum, I shifted to the granny gear and pedaled hard. I counted each time my right foot completed a full rotation. One, two, three... to one hundred. I slowed for about 30 seconds and then repeated the mantra, again, and again, and again, until I reached the top. I constantly searched my surroundings, until I saw the summit appear around a curve in the road. Two hours and 18 minutes later, at 10:59 a.m., I reached the Continental Divide (9,584 feet). Eleven minutes after that, I reached Togwotee Pass. I was relieved that I had made it to the summit, but I was exhausted by the effort to get there. At the top, the temperature had dropped a few degrees. Patches of snow lurked in the sunless corners. Nonthreatening clouds monopolized the sky above. I recall thinking the leaders had passed through days earlier, when snow levels had been much higher. A man, woman, and child stood outside an RV, taking in the spectacular scene. "Sure," I responded, when the man asked if I wanted him to take a picture of me at the summit.

What followed the challenging climb was a 25-mile rush down the back side of Togwotee Pass to the valley floor. I gripped the handlebars firmly, hunched over, and let my bike roll free through the canyons, passing near Pinnacle Butte (11,516 feet), Pilot Knob (9,659 feet), and Lava Mountain (10,452 feet). The exhilarating but nerve-wracking ride brought me to the west edge of the Wind River Indian Reservation. Windy Mountain (10,460 feet) and Whiskey Mountain (11,157 feet) appeared along the north edge of the Wind River Range.

When I began my descent—until 12:55 p.m., when I reached the "Welcome to Dubois-Valley of the Warm Winds–Established 1914" sign on the west edge of town—nature gave me a slight tailwind, which enabled me to reflect rather than work. *What is it like to live in this part of the country? What was it like when settlers met members of the Shoshone tribe who had settled this area?* I was eager to better understand the complex history of cooperation and conflict of the 1800s, after the Louisiana Purchase and the Lewis and Clark Expedition paved the way for the western migration. An unexpected encounter would soon reveal the complex history that makes the United States such a fantastic place to live.

The population of Wyoming is 580,000.[55] "That's fewer than any other state, but what a lucky few."[56] The majesty of the surrounding landscape, alternating between lush prairies, stark desert, rugged mountains, and wooded hills, was mesmerizing. At a fork in the road, I veered to the right onto Highway 26 and continued south into the Wind River Valley. The area was arid. Much of Wyoming looks similar to the scene that greeted the first pioneers on their way west: sagebrush, prickly pear cactus, and panoramic views of layered red, brown, and green rock formations. The occasional reminder of the region's rich

---

[55]   "Wyoming Population," PopulationU.com, accessed July 12, 2022, https://www. populationu.com/us/wyoming-population

[56]   Richard Corrigan, "Landforms of Wyoming," *USA Today*, May 18, 2018, Travel Tips, https://traveltips.usatoday.com/landforms-wyoming-103579.html

history near Wagon Gulch Ranch is a nod to the trails that guided settlers west. Bighorn Ridge came to life on the east side of Highway 26, as I rode parallel to Wind River through the tremendous, wide-open plains. Ancestors of the Shoshone tribe inhabited the area for over 1,000 years. The Shoshone, led by Chief Washakie, cooperated with the white men and pursued peace between the two races since the arrival of the settlers. Others, such as the Sioux, remained aggressive toward the white men.

History details a conflict in 1865, when Crows, Cheyenne, and Sioux decided to slaughter the white settlers and take back their homeland. The three tribes tried to enlist the help of Chief Washakie, who refused and instead volunteered to help the US Army wipe out the Sioux. At 3:14 p.m., I rode by Crowheart (population 141), near Crowheart Butte (6,764 feet), the site of a battle between the Crow and Shoshone tribes in 1866.

Rain began to fall 30 minutes after I started my descent into Dubois. I was cold, wet, and hungry when I reached the Village Café on Rams Horn Street on the west edge of town. Sitting at a window table inside the café, I made a reservation at the Pronghorn Inn in Lander (population 7,487), 75 miles southeast of Dubois. "Nothing," the waitress responded, after I asked if there was anything between Dubois and Lander. I left the restaurant at 1:30 p.m. and knew I would have to push myself hard to reach Lander before dark. The forecast called for unsettled weather the rest of the day.

I felt confident I would not ride into a storm that had developed northeast of my location. At 2:37 p.m., I saw three cyclists wearing rain jackets riding toward Dubois. Two had pulled the headcovers over their safety helmets. We didn't stop to chat. I could see sheets of rain northeast of me. It is difficult to judge the weather direction in a vast, wide-open desert, but the cyclists riding gear gave me a good indication they had ridden through a storm in the direction I was going.

At 3:55 p.m., the sun peaked out through the diminishing cloud cover. At 5:00 p.m., I rode by and glanced at a colorful billboard: "Our Ancestors Showed Us the Way—Eat Healthy—The Shoshone Way." The sign stood next to a black-and-white picture of a Shoshone female holding long stocks of grain. I thought of the iconic ad depicting an Indian with a tear falling from his eye when a passing vehicle throws trash on the highway. Highway 287 turned into Chief Washakie Trail. At 5:04 p.m., I entered the White River Indian Reservation, home to two Native American tribes, the Northern Arapaho and the Eastern Shoshone. It's the seventh-largest reservation by area in the United States.[57] The 2017 film *Wind River*, a thriller mystery exploring the death of a young Arapaho woman on the reservation starring Jeremy Renner, came to mind. The producers wrote the film to raise awareness of the considerable number of Indigenous women raped, murdered, or both, on and off the reservation.

I imagined stampeding bison generating massive dust clouds on the horizon and Indians on horseback galloping through the spacious countryside, hunting their prey. During the gold rush in the late 1800s, when the Union Pacific Railroad laid tracks across Wyoming, a hunter named William Cody supplied work crews with buffalo meat. He later earned the name "Buffalo Bill."[58] At first, I didn't know the name of the lonely, four-legged animal walking through the sagebrush about 50 yards away. I stopped and googled information about this interesting-looking creature. It was a pronghorn, a mix between an antelope and a deer. Two distinctly narrow, flattened, foot-long bones protruded from the front part of its skull. The fastest land mammal in the Western Hemisphere, a pronghorn can reach 60 mph and leap at 20-foot bounds. The Pronghorn is the world's second-fastest mammal, beat only by the African cheetah, but it can sustain high speeds longer than a cheetah.[59] There would be

---

[57] "Wind River Indian Reservation," Wyoming's Wind River Country, accessed July 12, 2022, https://windriver.org/destinations/wind-river-indian-reservation/

[58] Ijeoma Olou, "What the True Story of Buffalo Bill Reveals About the Myth of the Wild West," *Time*, November 12, 2021, https://time.com/6114737/buffalo-bill-cody-wild-west-myth/

[59] "Pronghorn," Speed of Animals, accessed July 12, 2022, http://www.speedofanimals.com/animals/pronghorn

several more occasions when I observed a pronghorn sauntering alone in the vast wilderness of Wyoming and Colorado. Searching for complete solitude in the heart of America is not only a human desire.

At 6:43 p.m., I entered Fort Washakie (population 1,759) and saw a road sign pointing to the Sacajawea gravesite. Lander was still 16 miles away, and a storm was brewing. But seeing this sacred site was a once-in-a-lifetime experience, so I turned off Highway 287 and began my search for Sacajawea's gravesite.

I rode on Norkok Street for about half a mile. There was an uncomfortable feeling in the pit of my stomach when I realized I had no idea where to go. I waved at a car to stop while pausing at Norkok and 2nd Street. The driver rolled down his window. "Hi, can you direct me to Sacajawea's gravesite?" I asked. The driver instructed me to continue riding on 2nd Street. He said with confidence that I would see the cemetery at a fork in the road. I grew concerned again when I didn't reach a fork, a cemetery, or anything else after a couple of miles.

I waved at another car that had been traveling on 2nd Street on this Father's Day evening. This time, the driver told me to continue riding until a T in the road. "Turn onto North Fork. North Fork becomes South Fork. The cemetery is one mile ahead on the left. Can't miss it," he explained. I felt reassured when I continued riding this time. Up ahead, I turned left onto Cemetery Lane and immediately turned right into a gravel parking lot. What seemed like an eternity had only taken 20 minutes from when I detoured on Highway 287. I was very excited but acutely aware of yet another fast-approaching storm. A car pulled into the gravel lot. I turned and noticed right away that it was the driver who'd shared the accurate directions five minutes earlier. The man (and two children) exited the vehicle and walked toward me. He greeted me, saying, "Hi, I followed you to make sure you found the cemetery."

"Thanks so much. I'm Larry," I responded.

"I'm Nolan, and these are my two kids," he answered. Then he explained that they were paying their respects to his father, who was also buried at this same cemetery. His dad, a US Navy veteran, served in the

Vietnam War. I shared my interest in the history of the West, Native Americans, and the western migration, and my fascination with the story of Sacajawea helping the Corps of Discovery navigate the treacherous and unfamiliar, hostile territory.

Nolan pointed to a narrow, well-worn dirt path. "Walk that way, and you'll see the gravesite," he said. I found Sacajawea's gravestone and those of her two sons, Baptiste Charbonneau and Bazil, in the center of the modest-sized cemetery. Many of the plots were full of weeds. Other plots, including Nolan's father's, were freshly raked. A mosaic of wooden crosses, small headstones, and colorful flowers sprinkled the hillside. According to Sacajawea's tombstone, she died on April 9, 1884. The gravestone for Baptiste Charbonneau read, "Dedicated in the Memory of Baptiste Charbonneau; papoose of the Lewis and Clark Expedition 1805–1806. Son of Sacajawea. Born February 11, 1805. Died on this reservation 1885. Buried west in the Wind River Mountains." Bazil's gravestone inscription read, "Bazil, son of Sacajawea. Aged 86 years. Died 1886."

"The Corp of Discovery went as students. They came back as teachers, but we have failed the lessons they had learned. What they did so well in dealing with native Americans, people today can't do half as well in dealing with native peoples."[60]

Only a narrow sliver of sky projected light. Cloud cover concealed a yellowish, circular sun—a backdrop for the picture of Nolan and his kids standing next to his father's grave. Nolan encouraged me to revisit Fort Washakie to meet descendants of Sacajawea. "I'd love to take you up on that," I responded, stunned while internalizing the gesture. "Do you know a quicker route to the highway, so I don't have to backtrack to where I turned off Norkok Street?" I asked.

"Follow Cemetery Lane. Turn left on Trout Creek Road, and you'll run into Highway 287," he replied reassuringly.

---

[60] *Lewis & Clark: The Journey of the Corps of Discovery*, directed by Ken Burns, aired November 4, 1997, on PBS, https://www.pbs.org/kenburns/lewis-clark/

We shook hands and went our separate ways. Nolan and I stayed in contact. I shared with him my idea to create a cultural exchange program between our two communities, an idea that began the day after my stay in Virginia City, Montana. Some accounts differ as to Sacajawea's death and burial details. Some say she died in 1812 and was buried in North Dakota, where she lived before joining Lewis and Clark on their expedition.

The sun had dropped almost entirely when I reached Highway 287 at 7:30 p.m. The air whirled and hissed. I turned on one white front light and three blinking, red rear lights to begin my dash to Lander. The temperature had dropped slightly since I'd left the cemetery. The eerie quiet that followed darkness amplified the storm's impending fury. I rode by a rest stop off of Ray Lake road, about six miles before Lander, passing right by without blinking an eye. At 9:15 p.m., I reached the north end of Lander.

I walked through the lobby of the Pronghorn Inn, feeling tired and dirty but also lucky that I'd beaten the storm. A woman working the front desk told me the room fee included breakfast and that I could eat dinner at the Oxbow restaurant if I got there before it closed at 10:00 p.m. The rain started to fall when I reached my room. The downpour started immediately—there was no transition from light rain to buckets pouring from the sky. I couldn't see two inches in front of me. I watched the water flow from the sky from underneath the overhang for about 20 minutes. When the rain subsided, I walked briskly to the restaurant before the next downpour. I had the restaurant all to myself when I entered five minutes before closing. I had fried chicken, a baked potato, warm bread (soaked in butter), and a salad from the salad bar—a somewhat nutritious meal, at least for me.

The pain from the saddle sores that had developed was a grave concern. I felt a burning sensation when my butt was on the saddle. I rode off the saddle at times to reduce the friction created with each full pedal rotation. The slight side-to-side, back-and-forth motion created friction between my body and the saddle that was not conducive to healing. After dinner,

I washed my cycling shorts using the Pronghorn Inn's public washer and dryer. For the first time, I was worried saddle sores could derail my journey across the country. Each time I checked the leaders' board, I wondered who might be the next one to scratch. But tonight, something else caught my attention. I read a heartfelt post from a racer leading the pack riding through Kansas. In part, it read, "It was a sad moment to come across John Egbers's ghost bike memorial finally… so beautifully done… I feel like I'm following in the wheel tracks of giants… now it's time to pick up where he left off and get this race finished…"

The Bike Mill store opened at 7:30 a.m. At 7:15 a.m., I walked Tank to the shop across the street from the Pronghorn Inn. The mechanic told me it would take a couple of hours to complete a tune-up and longer if he found a mechanical problem. The scratching noise was still present. I assumed there was a connection between the scratching sound and the chain skipping, which also had become a problem in the lowest gear. I was eager to leave, but I had a long way to go, and I needed Tank to function correctly. The mechanic told me to stop back at 9:30 a.m. for an update. I returned to the Pronghorn Inn and sat down in the lobby to eat breakfast. Two 60-year-old-looking men sat at the table next to me; one of them noticed I was looking at a map. "Hi, are you riding the TransAmerica route?" he asked.

"Yes, I am. I'm in the Trans Am Race," I responded.

I learned their names were Greg and Steve and that they were leisurely riding the TransAmerica Bike Trail, west to east. They last saw each other 43 years ago, in 1976, when they rode across the country, Yorktown to Astoria, during the bike centennial celebration. They were now retired. Greg told me a third guy, whom they also hadn't seen in 43 years, planned to meet them in Rawlins, Wyoming (125 miles southeast of Lander). All three would then ride together to Pueblo, Colorado, at which point only Greg and Steve would continue to Yorktown. What a reunion, and how cool for me to meet them and hear such a great story!

The mechanic couldn't isolate a specific mechanical problem. He gave Tank a tune-up. I bought an air pump to replace the one I lost riding to

Dayville, Oregon. I sent Nathan a selfie before leaving Lander. A gray, scraggly beard and emaciated face gazed into the camera, expressionless and distant. Once full of life, my facial expression revealed the truth of this journey—that my eager energy and enthusiasm were beginning to wane.

(For more information on the rich history of the Eastern Shoshone Nation, turn to the Afterword in the back of the book.)

Once full of life, my facial expression
revealed the truth of this journey
Lander, Wyoming
June 17, 2019

Chapter 18
LANDER–JEFFREY CITY, WYOMING (57 MILES)

June 17, 2019

S torm clouds covered the sky west of Lander when I began riding at 10:30 a.m., heading southeast on Highway 287. After 20 miles and a 1,300-foot climb, I reached Beaver Divide (7,185 feet) and paused to view the encircling landscape.

There was clear sky to the east of me, but behind me, an angry-looking cell had formed and was moving east, heading for Jeffrey City (population 58). It sailed across the sky so quickly, it looked like a time-lapse. Now high above Lander, I saw sheets of rainfall landing in the downtown area. Blue Ridge, Onion Flats, and Red Canyon Rim surrounded me when I caught up to Steve and Greg, who left Lander an hour before me. I shouted, "I'm stopping in Jeffrey City!"

The prickly, burning sensation of my sores forced me to ride off the saddle for about half of the 19 miles between Sweetwater Station and Jeffrey City. The night before, when I slept naked, the pain was close to intolerable. I thought exposing my bottom to the air after applying baby powder to promote the healing process would limit further infection and hopefully reduce the pain. I knew that cycling off the saddle for 2,500 miles to Yorktown would not be possible. The burning sensation had turned from excruciating to unbearable when I reached Jeffrey City.

I saw abandoned, WWII-style barracks on the south side of Highway 287. *Is this some sort of Manhattan Project, where secret shit takes place in this dusty, abandoned, western town?* Jeffrey City had previously been a boomtown that went bust in 1982. In its heyday, Jeffrey City was a uranium mining city with a population of over 10,000. During the Cold War and the height of uranium demand, Jeffrey City was full of shops, schools, churches, medical clinics, and a high school with an Olympic-sized swimming pool.[61] A few weathered, abandoned buildings littered the otherwise empty landscape. It was hard to imagine thousands of people living on this plot of ground only a generation before.

I instantly shot off the highway and weaved around several small puddles when I saw the Split Rock Bar & Café sign in front of a building with a couple of pickup trucks parked in a gravel lot. A scene from the 1965 film *For a Few Dollars More,* when Clint Eastwood enters the bar, accurately depicts what it felt like walking into the café. Curiously, the Split Rock Bar & Café housed a piano like the one in the scene with Eastwood. Unlike in the film, with dozens of patrons, the Split Rock was mostly empty. There was a server who stood behind the bar and a woman with two kids who sat at a round dining table.

The unfriendly cloud formation that I'd spotted earlier had stalled. A nasty gray cloud hovered southwest of me, but the sky wasn't nearly as scary looking in Jeffrey City. I grabbed my wallet, iPhone, and map section #5 and walked inside the poorly lit bar room. Linoleum red-and-white-checkered tile blanketed the floor, reflecting the dull glow of

---

[61]   Michael A. Amundson, "Home on the Range No More: The Boom and Bust of a Wyoming Uranium Mining Town, 1957-1988," *Western Historic Quarterly* (Oxford University Press) 26, no.4 (Winter 1995): 484-505

the ceiling lights overhead. When I looked up, I realized the lights were tinted, advertising Michelob Ultra.

Greg and Steve reached the café 30 minutes later. The woman and her two children had stopped to eat on their passage through Wyoming as part of their summer vacation. I sat on a barstool, leaned my arms on top of the wooden surface, and looked at a sign that read: "All our customers bring us happiness. Some when they come. Some when they go." An eclectic cluster of banners and oddly grouped pictures adorned the wall above the row of liquor bottles. An old, corded phone sat idle next to an old-fashioned cash register. Seeing it took me back to an age when life was simple in all parts of America, not just in rural America. I stared at it and wondered if it was operational or just for display. I imaged the drawer opening with a ding as the server pressed the keys to total the cost. The cross-country cyclists, local ranchers, and automobile travelers stopping for a lunch or bathroom break helped keep the lights on.

I ordered a cheeseburger and fries and fetched a Coke from a self-serve refrigerator. *Do I stay, or do I go?* I pondered, sitting at the bar. Greg and Steve had slept in the Jeffrey City community church when they'd first crossed the country in 1976. (The map section #5 service directory instructed cyclists to inquire about church accommodations inside the Split Rock Café.) I had only completed 57 miles—well below my 100-mile daily goal. However, my body was wet, my bottom hurt, and a significant storm was forecasted to reach Jeffrey City midafternoon. I walked outside to evaluate the conditions and saw a black sky and streaks of lightning southeast of Jeffrey City.

Rawlins (population 9,259), the next closest town, was 65 miles away. Climbing the Red Hills, Ferris Mountains, and cresting the Continental Divide were the remaining obstacles between Jeffrey City and Rawlins. I would arrive well after dark, which went against my strategy to ride only during daylight. I followed my gut and stayed at the church in Jeffrey City, choosing not to test fate by riding through a barren desert after dark. As it turned out, this decision to remain in Jeffrey City was the wisest I made on the entire trip.

It was a tough decision because it was only 2:00 p.m. Greg, Steve, and I left the café at the same time and began riding south on Crooks Gap Road, located immediately outside and west of the café. The bartender had informed us the church was on a hill about a quarter mile down Crooks Gap Road. The Baptist church came into view soon after. We hopped off our bikes at a dirt path and began a 200-yard walk through the sand to the church's back entrance. I opened the door and inched my hand around a dark room to find a light switch. *How cool is this place?* I thought as soon as the room lit up. The cavernous and cold room was empty except for a ping-pong table near the front. Curiously, I noticed a basketball hoop hanging from the inside wall next to the entrance. The rim looked much higher than a 10-foot basket. A basketball lay motionless on the ground. Someone had painted a large mural of a cyclist. Opposite the painted wall, stairs led to the church's sanctuary to my left. This large room likely served as a place where children played or attended Bible school while adults worshiped upstairs. One door in the back led to a row of sleeping rooms. The second door led to a kitchen. Hundreds of names and makeshift art decorated the back wall. Pithy statements or creative logos had been plastered everywhere and without any particular pattern.

A map of the United States displayed the TransAmerica Bike Trail from Astoria to Yorktown. Others showed off their creative talent. A drawing of E.T., arms planted on a table and hands cupping its chin in a meditative state, added to the eclectic feel. An illustration of a Bart Simpson lookalike showing his oversized teeth and raised hair led me to conclude some cycling guests had way more energy to expel when they arrived than I did. It was easy to understand why this church was a sought-after way station for cross-country cyclists. I stepped into the first vacant room, blew up my air mattress, and put my sleeping gear on the ground right away. I picked up my traveling bathing towel, washrag, and soap from my Salsa frame bag and walked down the hallway to a bathroom, anticipating a shower. The hot water fell from the showerhead onto my tired, dirty, and worn body. I recall thinking that the next several hours were critical for healing and would ultimately determine whether I could complete the race.

Greg, Steve, and I gathered in the kitchen to join a few other cyclists, including Adam. On June 8, Adam left Baker City about an hour before I did. A few miles outside of town, his derailleur broke. He broadcasted a message on the group's Facebook page, asking for help. A Good Samaritan transported him to a bike shop. On his return ride to town, he passed a cyclist, who he assumed at the time was me. He knew Harry and I stayed in Baker City because he closely monitored the leader board.

Now, inside the Jeffrey City church, I met Adam for the first time. "I've been trying to catch you for the past few days!" Adam greeted me, looking exhausted from having ridden more miles than any day since leaving Astoria. He set out to crush the epic race the summer between his junior and senior year of college. I felt like a kindred spirit, both of us hailing from Pennsylvania. Adam got off to a fast start on June 2, but the mechanical problem sidelined him for a full day. He'd made up some of the lost miles. As he sat on the chair, he flat out said, "I'm gassed right now."

Earlier that day, Adam noticed my dot had not moved since 2:00 p.m. He assumed correctly that I had stopped in Jeffrey City. At that point, determined to catch me, he pushed hard to reach Jeffrey City. We formed a bond in Jeffrey City that would remain for the rest of the race. Five other cyclists sat on chairs around the two, six-foot-long tables in the kitchen. I stood, separating my legs oddly to reduce contact between my khaki shorts and skin. We went around the room, sharing our motivation and what drew us to Jeffrey City. Greg and Steve retold their reunion story. One guy quit his job to follow his dream of cycling coast-to-coast. Another guy was a graduate student from Iowa who decided to ride his bike to Seattle to visit a friend.

"Does anyone have any ideas on how to deal with saddle sores?" I asked, taking the opportunity to listen and perhaps try something new.

Adam chimed in, "Try Maximum Strength Desitin," which I knew to be diaper rash paste with zinc oxide. Adam said Desitin helped him avoid saddle sores. He grabbed a small tube of Desitin from a pouch he carried and extended his arm. "Try this. It worked for me."

The sound of silence at 8:00 p.m. was interrupted when Adam spoke up. "I'm gassed." He was the first to stand and leave the kitchen. "Good night. I'm probably going to sleep in tomorrow." The pastor, whom I did not meet, had created a haven for cyclists in the basement of this church—a safe, warm, and dry place for cyclists riding through the vast Wyoming countryside. I shook hands with the five cyclists, and before returning to my room, I signed the guest book and placed $20 into the donation box.

I felt isolated and vulnerable. My mind raced. *Am I done?* I thought. It wouldn't matter that I had completed a cross-country ride once before. I'd be a failure if my race ended in Wyoming. I'd successfully repeated the swamp phase of Ranger School after failing the first time. Would I—*could* I—return to compete in next year's race if I failed now? These thoughts created a very uncomfortable inner turmoil when I stripped down, buck naked, lathered my butt with Desitin, and doused it with baby powder. Finally, snuggled inside the sleeping bag, I placed my head on the pillow and quickly fell asleep.

Chapter 19

JEFFREY CITY–RIVERSIDE, WYOMING (127 MILES)

June 18, 2019

Like clockwork, Wyoming's early morning calmness turns to a midmorning breeze, the roadside brush moving ever so slightly, eventually leading to the whistling wind before the clock strikes noon. Maintaining forward movement on the saddle, especially during the afternoon, was taxing. Getting an earlier start to each day—something I didn't take full advantage of—had taken a back seat to the greater good of getting a full night's sleep. However, in Jeffrey City, I had a different feel when I closed the door to my room and thought about my fate.

Fatigue quickly overcame worry, and before I knew it, the alarm buzzer went off at 5:30 a.m. I opened my eyes, grabbed my iPhone, and turned it off. I froze inside my sleeping bag, staring into the room's darkness, and ruminated on the day's goal. *I've got to move. I need to go. God, I pray my butt is okay.*

My body, mind, and butt had all gone through a transition from when I left Astoria 16 days before. I was no longer a full-faced, clean-shaven bloke, but an emaciated, shaggy-looking drifter. My spirit and enthusiasm had waned, along with the descriptive language that had brought my early journal entries to life. Now, I wrote with digits only. The night I stayed in Jeffrey City, I had enough energy to jot down *57.9 miles; 2,621 feet.*

I wiggled my legs to gauge the tenderness of my butt. *Okay so far,* I thought, a good sign. I unzipped the sleeping bag, squirmed my way out, and slowly eased to a stand, trying my best not to rub my raw skin. I hoped the healing process had been quickened with my new regimen. I walked gingerly to the door, opened it, and tiptoed down the narrow hallway to the bathroom entrance, not wanting to wake the others. While brushing my teeth, I stared at my rawboned face and unkempt beard. I recall thinking, *I can do this!* I returned to the bedroom, put everything in its proper place, and prepared Tank for the day ahead. I ate two breakfast bars and a packet of peanuts and then walked down the dimly lit hallway, rolling Tank by my side. At 6:44 a.m., I exited the door I'd entered 15 hours earlier. A single glance at the gray sky immediately made me feel nervous, my stomach churning as I thought about the ride out of Jeffrey City. But it was time to stop thinking; I needed to get moving.

Fear of failure had weighed heavily on me for the past couple of days. Facebook friends must have picked up on my anxiety, because they began offering encouraging words in response to a few of my daily posts. I knew I needed to maintain a positive outlook—mind over matter—but I also realized attitude wouldn't trump a nasty infection.

When I reached Highway 287/789, I turned east and rode to Rawlins, wondering if the next pedal stroke was when the proverbial shoe would fall. The burning sensation remained, but I felt I could continue. After 20 minutes, I recall thinking I could deal with this level of pain the rest of the way. My mood improved immediately. Saddle sores no longer consumed my thinking. It seemed odd that things had improved so much in less than 24 hours. I didn't know if it was the extra time off the saddle, the Desitin, or another reason.

I arrived at Muddy Gap junction (Three Forks Crossing), 23 miles east of Jeffrey City, at 8:40 a.m. A sharp left turn onto Wyoming Highway 220 took me east to Casper, the direction I wanted to go. The TransAmerica Bike Trail directed me to remain on Highway 287, heading south toward Rawlins. I knew I was following the correct way by continuing to Rawlins, but mentally, it was tough not to continue east. With the wild plains to my left and right and the Ferris Mountains straight ahead, I thought for a moment about what an incredible experience it was to cycle through the tenth-largest and least-populated state in the country.

Riding by natural landmarks like Crooks Mountain, Whiskey Peak, Red Hills, Great Stone Face, Bills Peak, and Split Rock made the ride more enjoyable. Sweetwater River and Sweetwater Station got their names in the late 1800s when a mule stumbled while carrying a party's sugar supply during a trip on the Oregon Trail.[62] Without the benefit of highway markers to lead the way, explorers watched for natural landmarks, like Split Rock (7,182 feet), to guide them along the trail. Named a historical site back in 1876 and located 18 miles east of Jeffrey City and 10 miles off the Muddy Gap junction between Casper and Rawlins, the Split Rock mountain has a distinctive V-shaped cleft dividing its summits. This prominent landmark on the Oregon Trail had been a sought-after overland passage landmark and navigation tool through the Rocky Mountains for fur traders, gold seekers, and many others emigrating west during the nineteenth century.[63] The Pony Express Route, completed in 1860, often followed the Oregon Trail near Split Rock. Since forts had been constructed along the Oregon Trail to protect settlers, it was wise for the Pony Express to travel this way. While the

---

[62] "Sweetwater River," Wyoming State Library, accessed July 12, 2022, https://pluto. wyo.gov/awweb/awarchive?item=11139662

[63] "Split Rock," WyoHistory.org, January 24, 2015, https://www.wyohistory.org/ encyclopedia/split-rock

Pony Express is romanticized in western novels and films, it only existed for two years because the telegraph replaced it.

Vehicles infrequently passed by me. It was tough to stay alert while riding alone in the middle of Wyoming. The solitude of nature—the sort of solitude that I and many others wish for—helped clarify my thoughts, hopes, dreams, and desires. At 10:20 a.m., two hours after I had reached Muddy Gap junction, I glanced up and saw an eighteen-wheeler barreling in my direction. It moved into the southbound traffic lane to pass a slow-moving antique car traveling northbound. Any time an eighteen-wheeler barreled toward me, I gripped the handlebars tighter, preparing myself for the gust of crosswind that would follow in its wake.

Minutes later, the same antique car passed on my left in the southbound lane. I recall thinking to myself, *Isn't that the same car?* But I quickly refocused on riding. The car slowed and shifted to the shoulder about a quarter mile ahead of me. *That's weird*, I thought. As I got closer, the driver's side door opened, and a man exited the vehicle. He stood next to the car behind the open front door, gripping a bottle of Gatorade. What happened next was one of the most surprising encounters I had on that journey.

"Doug? *Doug?* What are you doing here?!" I asked, after reaching the car and realizing who the man was. Doug is originally from Minnesota and was a member of my Southern Tier cycling group. We'd ridden together the year before, and he'd tracked me down on Highway 287!

"How on earth did you find me?" I asked as we embraced. Doug had shed the bearded Santa Claus look for a distinguished, George Clooney–style beard. With a raspy voice, he told me he was in California visiting Travis, another member of the Southern Tier group. During dinner the night before, Travis told him about my ride. He had been following my daily Facebook summaries. Doug concocted a plan to detour through Wyoming on his way home to Minnesota and attempt to surprise me—and that he did!

I was stunned but thrilled to see Doug. He offered me a Gatorade, which I secured with a bungee cord on the rear bike rack. A few hours earlier, I had felt down and truly wasn't sure if I could continue. But now, I was more energized than I had been in days. I told Doug I would contact him when I returned home. Doug and I have stayed in touch since our unexpected encounter in the middle of Wyoming that summer of 2019.

While in Rawlins (population 9,259), I devoured a tasty Big Mac, large fries, and a large Coke. I retired map section #5. Thirty-eight percent of the race, or 1,619 miles of the 4,200-mile journey, was now in the past. Riverside (population 52), 60 miles south, was the closest town with available lodging. While sitting inside McDonald's, people watching, I pondered whether to stop and give my bottom extra time off the saddle or continue to Riverside. I wanted to press on, but I didn't want to open old wounds and start the burning pain that went with it. *What do I do?* Such a simple question to ask oneself. But at that moment, the answer wasn't clear to me. The 66 miles from Jeffrey City to Rawlins was short of my daily century goal. The second day of extended rest would support the healing process, but I still had way too many miles to go to finish this race. After a few minutes of mental jujitsu, I concluded that riding less than 100 miles two days in a row with over half the race to go was not prudent.

My decision to continue to Riverside turned out to be critically important. A summer snowstorm dropped a few inches of the white stuff in the Rocky Mountains three days later. Fortunately, I crested Hoosier Pass (11,500 feet) one day before the snow fell.

"There's one cabin still available," Lee Ann, the owner of the Lazy Acres Campground, shared when I called. Lee Ann regularly hosted cross-country cyclists riding through Riverside, the only place with decent services for many miles in all directions. The ingredients for a powerful weather event appeared northeast of Rawlins. I determined the storm's trajectory would remain well north of me. If I didn't make it to Riverside before dark, I could sleep in a meadow. I was willing to take the risk—and this was why I carried a tent with me, after all. I bought Desitin cream and replenished pogey bait at the Rawlins Walmart, where folks from Jackson come for a monthly shopping spree to stock up on nonperishables.

The TransAmerica Bike Trail mostly avoids interstate highways, routing cyclists through less-traveled, picturesque roads. The TransAmerica Bike Trail, a sought-after trail for cross-country riders since 1976, guaranteed an up-close view of the beauty and uniqueness of rural America. For 1,000 miles, I had experienced one-stoplight towns like never before. That was about to change.

My GPS instructed me to turn left at the mile mark on entrance ramp #221 onto Interstate 80. I initially didn't make that left turn. *Interstate 80?* I hoped not. I studied the map, confirmed the route, and then braced myself for this unwanted experience. *A short stint on Interstate 80 heading east, followed by a straight shot south on SR 30.* For 15 miles, I white-knuckled my ride on the shoulder of the interstate. I turned onto the entrance ramp and began riding a quarter-mile stretch of road before merging with fast-moving vehicles. Once I reached the shoulder, I looked east and saw a mean sky full of dark, gray, swirling clouds—the same foreboding sky I had looked at 30 minutes before. The Rocky Mountains were no longer visible; the rumbling of thunder threatened a downpour. A large traffic sign had been permanently erected 30 feet above and across both interstate lanes, blinking a warning to interstate travelers.

"Wind Gusts—40+ MPH" flashed brightly for all to see at mile marker 234. I felt my stomach sink at the sight of the sky, the sign's ominous message, and the precarious stretch of the interstate rolling out like a map before me. The wind brushed forebodingly over the landscape—the breath of nature itself. I braced myself for the worst. Eighteen-wheelers and FedEx trucks roared by. I couldn't wait to get off the interstate. This marked the first time I had been genuinely concerned for my safety. And to make matters worse, one lane was closed due to road construction. All vehicles merged into one lane, closest to me.

When I saw the "Exit #235—one mile" sign an hour later, I expelled a huge sigh of relief. I couldn't reach it fast enough. The constant, booming roar of engines whizzing by quickly morphed into the more familiar quiet of nature when I got to the end of the off-ramp.

I stopped at a Shell gas station in Walcott Junction (population 30). An overhang ran the entire length of the front entrance. I thought about sleeping outside under the overhang as I pondered the likelihood of getting caught in a downpour.

Pools of water devoured many sections of land near Rattlesnake Pass Road as I snaked my way along SR 130, which cut through Overland Flats and San Basin. It was clear a torrent of water had fallen from the sky before my arrival. The angry-looking clouds had taken a break from their unrelenting advance. I caught a slight movement about 50 yards off the highway on a flat stretch of road surrounded by vibrant vegetation: a lonely pronghorn was walking in the brush—a natural behavior for males during the summer months.

Ten minutes before the lone gas station in town closed, I reached Riverside (population 52) on the banks of the Encampment River and less than two miles north of Encampment (population 450). This area of southern Wyoming was the site of a fur trappers' rendezvous in 1851. Toward the end of the nineteenth century, mining took over and, like so many other mining towns, this town went boom to bust when it was no longer viable to mine. Much of the populace eventually moved away. Between 1902 and 1908, a 16-mile-long tramway carrying ore from the Sierra Madre Mountains to a smelter in Riverside was the longest aerial ore tram in the world.[64]

One day earlier, I had seriously thought my race might end. Now, I had ridden 127 miles—the most I'd ever ridden in one day. I walked inside the Sinclair gas station located on the corner of SR 230 and SR 70 and searched for the candy aisle. This resting place had been a sought-after way station for ranchers and wagon travelers generations before me. The store carried everything my heart desired, including orange

---

[64] Andrew Graham, "Encampment's aerial tram," History, WyoFile, May 26, 2017, https://wyofile.com/encampments-aerial-tram/

jelly candy slices covered with refined sugar, Gatorade, beef jerky, and spam! Curiously, most—if not all—of the hundreds of stores I visited carried various orange jelly candies (Brach's, Sathers, Dylan's), Hostess donuts, and beef jerky.

Less than a mile from the Sinclair, I reached the Lazy Acres Campground. The grounds, though full of RVs, were quiet at dusk. A tree towered beside the main office building, with a large bell attached at the top and a rope hanging down in front—an unspoken, universal message: ring bell for service.

Lee Ann, the owner, welcomed me to her campground. Puddles of water dotted the dirt path leading to my one-room, newly renovated log cabin located 40 feet from the fast-running waters of the Encampment River. A tremendous amount of rain and high-intensity winds had swept through Riverside three hours before I arrived. And just like daytime follows nighttime, the sun was shining following the rain.

The morning I departed Riverside, heading toward Colorado, felt like a new beginning. The silence was interrupted by the white noise from the rushing water. The renovated campground, catering to cross-country cyclists, touted several primitive campsites, a full-service laundry room, and a full bathroom with lockers. The top-notch water pressure massaged my tired and aching body at the end of a long day.

After entering Colorado, Hoosier Pass would soon follow. As much as I enjoyed the solitude and serenity provided by the endless Wyoming highways, I desired to move beyond the afternoon winds that had wreaked havoc on my psyche. I reflected on riding 435 miles through one of the most unforgiving yet rewarding sections of the TransAmerica Bike Trail.

Dot watchers and racers lit up the group Facebook page, expressing congratulations to Abdullah, who had finished the race earlier that day. He'd reached the Yorktown Victory Monument in a record 16 days, 9 hours, and 56 minutes, shattering the previous record by 11 hours. I watched a video of Abdullah sitting at the base of the monument with his mom. She had recently arrived from Australia and was beaming with pride at the momentous goal her son had achieved. She expressed gratitude to those who had followed her son on this epic journey across America. Abdullah sat, slightly hunched over, and responded, "Exhausted!" to the question, "How are you feeling?" He went on to describe his diet as "carbohydrate heavy" and shared one story about stopping at a diner early in the race. He'd walked in and ordered a dozen hash browns. The server gave him an odd look but said nothing. He reacted by asserting, "I'm in a rush," and left it at that. When the order was ready, he paid the bill and continued his journey—a dozen hash browns in hand. In this same interview, he said he lost little weight, which I found hard to imagine, as my face continued to narrow each day and my body reshaped itself. I was burning between 7,000 and 10,000 calories each day. His record 254-mile-per-day average will probably remain for years to come. The closest competitor trailed by 400 miles when Abdullah reached Yorktown.

Fifty cyclists were still barreling toward Yorktown. More than 2,000 miles separated the second leading racer from the Lanterne Rouge. It just seemed crazy to me that someone could ride a bike 4,200 miles unsupported across the country, over five mountain ranges, in 16 days. I still had half the country to conquer! Abdullah was a folk hero when he returned home to Australia. He gave TV interviews, received a government proclamation from Australia's elected officials, and read at a parliament hearing. I enjoyed listening to and watching others talk about their personal experience competing in the TABR.

The beautiful, clear, blue sky contrasted the gloomy gray skies from the morning before. The sound of trickling water greeted me when I walked outside my cabin at 7:25 a.m. and saw the Encampment River— and was initially blinded by the reflection of the blazing sun shining directly onto the sparkling running water. A previously empty RV spot directly next to my cabin was now taken by an RV with a Michigan license plate. A man and woman stood outside the RV's entrance, steam rising from the cups they each held in their hand. A five-minute chat provided me much-needed human contact and helped prepare me to begin my day.

I was about to enter Colorado, and Hoosier Pass—the highest peak on the TransAmerica Bike Trail—felt so close, I could practically taste it. I had thought I would never get here, but soon enough, I would crest that iconic summit. I would then make a beeline to Pueblo, and from there, it was a straight shot to Yorktown. I had shrunk the country down in size so that the stretch from Pueblo to Virginia no longer seemed daunting.

In the quiet confines of the modest, one-room log cabin, I tallied total miles and elevation. I was not quite halfway to Yorktown, but since Abdullah had won the race, I felt dot watchers might start shifting their focus to the rest of the pack. I had withstood the negativity that had dominated my thinking the past couple of days and nights. On this night in Riverside, I entered a new dimension. I made the commitment to myself out loud: "I will finish this race in less than forty days!" It was a goal that would have been laughable to even think about two weeks earlier.

Chapter 20
RIVERSIDE, WYOMING— HOT SULPHUR SPRINGS, COLORADO (109 MILES)

June 19, 2019

From 100 yards, I could make out the irregular ends of the "Welcome to Colorful Colorado" wooden road sign mounted by large pieces of timber. From the summit of Coyote Hill (8,229 feet), through the Platte River Wilderness, descending through the North Gate Canyon on SR 230, I entered Colorado at 10:26 a.m. I leaned Tank against a 20-foot-high log pole set in the ground supporting the brown and white border sign. I snapped a selfie that captured the occasion superbly—four states down, six to go!

At close to 8,000 feet, I began cycling through the north edge of the Rocky Mountain Front Range Corridor, a north-to-south line of peaks stretching from Wyoming to Pueblo. Small clumps of sunscreen dotted my cherry-red, peeling nose that had succumbed to unrelenting sun exposure, wind, and rain. I licked my lips constantly, desperate for moisture, which only made them split and frequently bleed. But, despite it all, my attitude had wholly changed—the pathetic-looking cyclist I had been in Lander was now a self-assured version that I knew would carry me to the finish.

To this day, I see America's enormous size through a unique lens. By the time I reached Colorado, my perspective had changed—the illusory area seemed much smaller than the actual. Changing my view of the magnitude of the distance required to reach Yorktown made it easier to maintain a positive attitude. In my mind, once I got to Pueblo, it would be a straight shot across the heartland.

The headwinds made cycling southeast on Wyoming Highway 230 extremely challenging. My attempts to pedal fast down a 7-percent grade should've been easy, but with the force of the wind against me, it felt like I was pedaling through a quagmire. The landscape shifted when I entered Colorado. The plains widened, the mountain peaks revealed their grandeur in the distance, and snow fences (barriers to minimize snowdrifts from covering roadways) peppered the Platte River Wilderness and North Gate Canyon. The disappointment I felt crossing from Oregon to Idaho due to the unremarkable "Welcome to Idaho" sign was replaced by a profound sense of achievement.

A feeling of gratitude and anticipation flowed through my blood and shocked my body into a new phase that drove me for the next 100 miles. I thought about the morning I left Astoria, when I'd pondered what it would feel like to reach Colorado. It had just seemed so far away at the time. Now, here I was—a dream had been brought to life.

At 10:57 a.m., while riding through the Colorado Rocky Mountain High Plains, I met two cross-country cyclists heading west. This stretch of high plains was flat. One of the guys, cleanly shaven and approximately 30 years of age, wore a bright-red cycling shirt with "Tennessee" on the front. Whether his smile conveyed his true feelings, I didn't know, but his calm disposition soothed my nerves. About the same age, the second guy sported a rust-colored, kempt beard. Interestingly enough, seeing their well-groomed facial hygiene stood out because most male cyclists

I passed appeared to have entered a beard-growing contest, including me. The guy with the red cycling shirt said, "The roads in Colorado are excellent, and the scenery is amazing." The high plains extended for hundreds of yards on either side of the highway, yet the snowcapped Rocky Mountains seemed closer to me. He added that the Moose Creek Café in Walden was a good place to eat.

"It's easy to find, believe me," the other guy added.

"Okay, thanks," I replied.

It was always great to chat with strangers for a few minutes. I appreciated them sharing details about the roads and services. The number of interactions with strangers had diminished substantially with each passing day, but the limited time I spent chatting with folks supplied much-needed human connection.

Stopping at post offices replaced stopping at barbershops as my go-to therapy each time I entered a town with postal services—a magnet pulling me along from one city to the next. When I entered the village of Cowdrey, Colorado, I felt the area's best days had come and gone. A few old western–style, two-story, narrow buildings stood directly off Highway 125, designed in the days when the stagecoach passed through. A sign pointing down a gravel road to a post office caught my attention. I turned Tank and began cycling toward a small, brown building on the right side of the road. There was not a single person or car this late Wednesday morning. I squinted at a small sign attached to the front entrance when I reached the brown building. "Open for Business" had been limited to select days and only specific times each week. June 19, 2019, at high noon, wasn't one of those times. I thought I would have better success in Walden (population 608), 10 miles farther south. I retraced my tracks, returned to SR 125, and continued to Walden.

Time on the saddle turned into a mindless task. I spent the next hour wondering what item of nonessential equipment I could ship home. I located the post office on the north end of Walden. I took out a pair of thick, wool socks, an extra pair of cycling gloves, and a sweat cap from the waterproof carry bag. I left Tank unattended as I entered the post office. A couple of folks were inside the building when I walked in—a quiet morning. The post office worker completed my transaction in 10 minutes. Objectively speaking, paying to reduce a few ounces of weight was not very practical; the primary effect was psychological, in that I felt satisfaction from completing a task, even if it was an inconsequential one.

This mountain getaway with small-town charm surrounded by natural beauty offered countless outdoor activities. The downtown western atmosphere was ideal for a city slicker wanting to escape the hustle and bustle of urban life. As I was told, the Moose Creek Café was easy to spot. An oversized, brown moose made of barbed wire was in front. Appropriate for the setting, since the town of Walden claims to be the "Moose Viewing Capital of Colorado."[65] After dismounting, I pulled Tank to a wooden railing next to an outdoor seating space and sat at a table underneath a patio overhang to block the sun. The sun seemed much more intense at 8,000 feet. I had traveled about 50 miles when I stopped for lunch at 1:00 p.m. The next closest town, Hot Sulphur Springs (population 663), was 60 miles away and on the opposite side of the Continental Divide and Willow Pass (9,621 feet).

After eating my cheeseburger and fries, I called the Ute Trail Motel to reserve a room. My decision to continue and ride over the Continental Divide stands out as a seminal moment for accomplishing this fantastic race across America. However, after leaving Walden, lodging options dwindled to only camping if I couldn't reach Hot Sulphur Springs. I fretted over the prospect of being caught in a Rocky Mountain snowstorm, but I carried a tent, sleeping bag, and extra winter weather gear, just in case.

After a hearty lunch and peace of mind knowing a warm bed awaited me, it was time to get on the road. While signing my name on the credit card lunch receipt, I raised my head to look at a man and woman who were staring at me as they walked by my table. I waved and said, "Hi."

---

[65] "Walden, Colorado," Uncover Colorado, accessed July 12, 2022, https://www.uncovercolorado.com/towns/walden/

They returned the greeting and stood in place. Without being prompted, I told them I was racing across the country.

The woman responded by telling me they were traveling to Rawlins to meet up with "two guys." She added, "My husband is meeting them for a cycling reunion."

I blurted out, "Greg and Steve?!"

And sure enough, the husband planned to join Greg and Steve for an extended ride from Rawlins to Pueblo.

"I met Greg and Steve in Lander a couple of days ago. They told me about the reunion!" I replied. *What a small, small world,* I thought.

Meeting this man and woman 230 miles from Lander ranked as one of the top surprises of my journey, similar to my encounter with Doug in the middle of Wyoming. I got the sense the guy was more excited to see his friends than he was to ride 340 miles from Rawlins to Pueblo.

There was a campground about four miles off route, near Granby (population 1,864) on the west side of Willow Pass—my backup plan if I couldn't make it over the Continental Divide before dark. Another town, Rand (population 6), had a campground but not much else. Both were undesirable options. Weather is unpredictable at higher elevations, especially in the late afternoon. While I was in Lander, a dot watcher had posted on Facebook the possibility of a snowstorm hitting the Rockies "in a few days."

My ride through stiff headwinds between Walden and Rand, traveling south on State Route 125, took much longer than predicted. Views of the natural beauty of the snowcapped Rockies in the distance and lush valleys with rivers carving through them helped take my mind away from the brutal riding conditions. South of Walden, I entered the vast Arapaho National Wildlife Refuge, the "highest refuge in the lower 48 states,"[66] and dealt with fierce headwinds for a 20-mile stretch that

---

[66] "Arapaho National Wildlife Refuge," U.S. Fish & Wildlife Service, accessed July 12, 2022, https://www.fws.gov/refuge/arapaho

could only be rivaled by the 18-mile gauntlet between Wisdom and Jackson, Montana.

I stopped by the Rand Store, which had an eclectic feel, with clothing and trinkets hanging from walls and stacked on tables. Travel, adventure, and local history books were for sale as well as greeting cards, picture frames and wooden barrels full of sundry items. A small corner section displayed holiday ornaments, pottery, and a mismatch of assorted inventory. A large refrigerator stocked with Gatorade and other drinks in the back room caught my attention. I walked around, absorbing the randomness of my surroundings. The public restroom was a refurbished outhouse. Very clean, but an outhouse, nonetheless. I grabbed the items I planned to buy—Gatorade and pogey bait—and waited in line at the cash register to pay. A lady waiting in line in front of me panicked when she realized she had misplaced her purse. Several of us chipped in to help search for the missing bag. Finally, after several frantic minutes, she found her purse, which she had mistakenly placed inside a bin, making it blend in with items for sale!

I hopped on the saddle, looked east, and saw the narrow, two-lane road disappear around a bend about 300 yards south of the store. I was startled by a giant fox when it ran in front of me. When I reached the bend that veered right, I immediately started to climb. I ascended about 1,100 feet over the next 10 miles, slowly making my way up through the narrow canyon. I put Tank in the granny gear and concentrated solely on pedaling. Whenever my right pedal completed a full 360 rotation, I let out a huff, repeating this sequence until I reached the pass. The surrounding area was quiet. I could hear my labored breathing but nothing else.

Suddenly, I heard rustling in the brush on my right. I looked up. About 20 feet away, I saw a moose running parallel to the road behind the brush and trees. The moose appeared to be trying to move away from me and therefore was thankfully not threatening. One of my favorite shows growing up, *The Adventures of Rocky and Bullwinkle and Friends*, featured a flying squirrel and a silly moose. When I was young, I gave little thought to a moose's true nature. They can become aggressive, especially when hungry, tired, or accompanied by their young. I shrugged off the nonencounter and continued up the mountain.

With fewer than 10 miles to Willow Pass, I was no longer concerned about riding through poor weather. I turned my sights to the next big climb, Hoosier Pass, still 70 miles away. I knew I was riding against time. I didn't want to get caught on the west side of the Rocky Mountains.

I reached Willow Creek Pass at 6:03 p.m. I stopped to rest at a sizeable Continental Divide road sign with an arrow pointing in one direction, toward the Atlantic Watershed. And another pointing in the opposite direction, toward the Illinois River descending into North Park on the north side of the divide.

When Lewis and Clark first reached the Continental Divide in 1805, they felt jubilation that they had reached the end of the Missouri River and would soon finish their trek to the Pacific Ocean. They were sadly mistaken, as history reveals. They did not know about anything west of the Missouri River at the time. I, however, knew better, and while I was relieved to have reached this point, I also knew challenging days were ahead. I weaved back and forth, descending through the canyon surrounded by several snow-covered mountain peaks, en route to the intersection of SR 125 and US 40. About one mile before reaching the junction, I stopped pedaling at a vantage point high above Highway 125, overlooking Highway 40. Rain began falling, so I donned my red rain jacket. By 6:30 p.m., the rain had turned very cold. The last four miles riding on the shoulder of Highway 40 were miserable. Traffic increased substantially, and every time a vehicle passed by, I was doused mercilessly with a shower of frigid rainwater. The Ute Trail Motel manager greeted me with complimentary hot chocolate when I walked inside the office at 7:00 p.m. I didn't mind riding in such nasty weather because a hot shower and bed were waiting upon my arrival.

Chapter 21
HOT SULPHUR SPRINGS—
FAIRPLAY, COLORADO
(97 MILES)

June 20, 2019

*T*his is the day I will ride over Hoosier Pass, I thought, when I left the Ute Trail Motel at 7:30 a.m. Harry and I had maintained contact through text messaging since White Bird, Idaho—which was 950 miles back. *How's the weather? What's the aggressive dogs situation? How are you feeling?* The check-ins were a relief from the monotony of solitary riding. The extra day off the saddle put him about 100 miles behind me. Adam was also about 100 miles behind. Rolf maintained a 300-mile lead. I set my sights on tracking Rolf's progress, like a magnet pulling me along.

The racers who scratched after the second week were seasoned cyclists or veterans of the TABR, and all had several-hundred-mile leads on me. Saddle sores, knee pain, and, interestingly, Achilles tendonitis were the most common reasons. Those, and trying to keep pace with the leaders, were the main reasons for scratching early on. It took great discipline to maintain my strategy. Had I attempted to keep pace with the leaders, I very well may have succumbed to the physical and mental stress of attempting such a blistering pace.

I felt I belonged when I first saw the 73 racers assembled in Astoria on June 1, but I had no clue what it took to race 4,200 miles unsupported across America. This cognitive dissonance stayed with me from the start all the way to Yorktown. My daily routine had become a ritual, a vital means of judging my progress and mentally preparing myself for the next day's ride. I didn't alter my strategy—however, poor planning did eventually force me to ride after dark for three nights. I averaged 12 to 13 hours on the saddle every day, except for the day in Kansas I rode 148 miles in 14 hours.

I set my sights on reaching Breckenridge, one of the best-known ski towns in the United States, about 70 miles southeast of Hot Sulphur Springs, on the way to Hoosier Pass. I was eager to reach this famous ski resort town, but I was uneasy at the same time. I left Hot Sulphur Springs with an open mind regarding my destination. I sensed twists and turns along the way and didn't want to limit options by deciding on a location so early in the morning. At 7:45 a.m., heading west on Highway 40, which bordered the Colorado River outside of Parshall (population 47), I saw a road sign: "Kremmling—12" and "Steamboat Springs—64." Steamboat Springs was a familiar name as well, one of the notable ski destinations in the country. I was less familiar with the town of Kremmling. Seeing the sign for Steamboat Springs brought me a sense of nostalgia, though I had not spent a lot of time at Colorado ski resorts. The few times I skied in Breckenridge, Vail, and Keystone, brought fond memories of family vacations.

The initial splendor of pedaling through lush, green pastures, brilliant, blue sky, and snow-crowned peaks was overshadowed by the relentless headwinds I experienced on Highway 40. For 12 miles, I swayed side to side, struggling to sustain a four-mph pace. A vibrant "Welcome to Kremmling—Untapped Untamed" road sign signaled my arrival.

The red and yellow colors of the sign provided a contrast to the green pastures, brown lower foothills, and white-capped peaks that encompassed me. The American flag flew half-staff alongside a building. I wondered, *What national news have I missed? Did someone important die?* I saw an AH-1 Cobra attack helicopter perched on a single stanchion behind a chain-link fence next to another full-staff American flag across the highway and next to the Kremmling West Grand High School. The helicopter seemed out of place next to a high school.

I passed Junction Butte (8,700 feet) and Copper Mountain (10,125 feet), riding through Lawson Ridge, until my GPS directed me to turn right onto CR 30. I began to climb the hills surrounding the Green Mountain Reservoir and entered the outskirts of the rugged mountains of the Gore Range at the heart of Eagles Nest Wilderness. The melting spring snow plunged from the hills to create countless thundering creeks that filled the pristine reservoir. Seeing this area brought me great delight, pride, and trepidation. Because I hadn't studied map details and identified landmarks to watch for, I did not know if I had entered the initial stages of my climb to Hoosier Pass. If I had studied the map more closely, I would have realized Hoosier Pass was 50 miles south of the reservoir; I could have avoided the feeling of trepidation and thoroughly enjoyed the delightful view. When the Rocky Mountains, sharp-edged ridges, deep valleys, sparkling reservoir, and blue skies came into view, I forgot about the brutal headwinds I had ridden through to reach this vista.

Earlier, when I'd crossed over the Colorado River, I'd flashed back to the day in October 2018 when I'd ridden over the Rio Grande and remembered how disappointed I had been. The same was true when I reached the opposite side of the narrow bridge over the Colorado River. A road sign next to the bridge was the only confirmation that I had reached the famous river.

I looked out over the Green Mountain Reservoir and followed the outline of Highway 9, now a distant, dark line stretching from one end of the reservoir and through the green meadow, presumably intersecting with CR 30. I could hear the muffled sound of cars on Highway 9.

From my vantage point, the vehicles traveling over 60 mph appeared to be moving at a snail's pace. The Rocky Mountain backdrop created an acoustic environment, making the cars that passed sound much closer than they actually were.

Thirteen miles after turning onto CR 30, I reentered Highway 9. I wondered if racers before me had avoided the turnoff and continued cycling on Highway 9. I reflected on my visit to the Blazin Saddles bike shop in Sisters, Oregon, where an employee told Roger and me about the more direct route to Prineville on SR 126, which would shave off about 20 miles.

My view was awe-inspiring: verdant meadows and grazing cattle, all surrounded by the Rockies in the Eagles Nest Wilderness. The hiking trails boasted skyscraping peaks and emerald valleys stirring with wildlife. The elegance of the clear water, the sun beaming down through a fluffy cast of intermittent clouds, and the pastures flanked by spearhead mountains was a view that rivaled that of Arizona's Roosevelt Lake's striking beauty, which I'd seen in September 2018, right before I rode through the Apache Reservation east of Phoenix.

Here I was, caught up in the beauty of my environment, when I reached the western edge of Silverthorne at 12:16 p.m. (population 3,887 and elevation 8,790 feet). The sky had turned gloomy. Mean-looking clouds moved quickly, a storm rapidly approaching. Traffic increased closer to Silverthorne. I rode on the less-traveled Blue River (Bike) Trail to dodge the busy Highway 9 traffic. The narrow, 10-foot-wide, paved pathway passed through the Willow Grove Open Space on the west end of town. Shortly after, I turned onto Hamilton Creek Road and turned again onto Allegra Lane.

Surrounded by jagged mountain peaks, groves of aspen trees, Blue River, Willow Creek, and plentiful lakes, I was about to enter Breckenridge, a town named after one of the original settlers searching for gold in 1860.[67] At a confluence of intersecting streets (Allegra Lane, Bald Eagle Road, and Robin Drive), I found myself riding on Blue River Circle in an off-route neighborhood. There was always a direct relationship between a town's population and riding bonus miles. The more people milling around, the higher the chance I strayed off course. It just seemed to work that way. I stopped in front of a house, which reminded me of my home in Salinas, California, where I lived from 1989 to 1991—stucco framed, terracotta tiles along the walkway, a garage at the end of a tiny, 20-foot driveway, trees between the homes pretending to give privacy. I plucked the map from my front handlebar bag. I felt I had taken a wrong turn somewhere, but I wasn't sure. I asked a guy standing in front of his garage how to get back onto the bike trail. He told me to continue riding on Blue River Circle and I'd rejoin the trail a quarter mile ahead. This guy looked about 60 years old and appeared to be in excellent physical shape. When I think of California, I think of the sun, beaches, and traffic. When I think of Florida, I think of seniors driving Cadillac sedans, noses barely over the steering wheel. And when I think of Colorado, I think of tanned, healthy-looking ski instructors. His defined forearms and tanned body led me to inquire what he did to stay in such good shape. Sure enough, he was a ski instructor.

Farther south, I reentered the Blue River Trail and continued riding next to the fast-flowing Blue River.

On a narrow bike path meandering through the quiet Willow Grove Open Space, I crossed the Blue River. A blanket of low clouds prevented me from seeing the mountain peaks, home to ski enthusiasts for generations. Five miles before Breckenridge, I saw a sign for Keystone and Arapahoe Basin. Vivid recollections of terrible headaches from altitude sickness that nearly ruined a business meeting in Keystone in 1997 sprung to mind.

---

[67] "TransAmerica Trail map # 6 field notes," Adventure Cycling Association, accessed July 12, 2022, https://www.adventurecycling.org/routes-and-maps/adventure-cycling-route-network/transamerica-trail/

When I reached the Dillon Reservoir, a large, freshwater body of water on the north edge of Frisco (population 2,683) supplying the city of Denver, the bike path became more congested with cycling and foot traffic. On one section of the trail that hugged the swift-flowing Blue River, overhanging shrubs combined with the narrow path reduced my ability to see much ahead of me. I was mindful of the shifting terrain and reduced visibility, but I didn't adjust my speed accordingly. My view obscured, I neared a sharp curve and saw a cyclist rounding the bend, heading directly at me from about 20 feet. I swerved left. He did the same. Our bikes sideswiped, but luckily, we avoided a head-on collision. I ended up in a thicket a few feet from the river. The other cyclist also stopped, about 10 feet away from where I landed in the brush. We looked at each other and gave a thumbs-up, signaling we were not injured, although my front fender was slightly damaged. I had barely avoided a race-ending crash. Less than five minutes later, I studied a group of four (a man, a woman, and two kids) walking toward me on a straight section of the same bike path. The man wasn't paying attention to his surroundings and was oblivious to me approaching on my bike. His head was raised, and his eyes were fixated on something other than me. About 30 feet away, he strode into my lane, at which moment I howled, "Hey!" and effectively startled him. I weaved left into the opposite lane to avoid striking him. Bike paths should be relaxing, nonthreatening, and easy ways to navigate. But after near head-on collisions with a cyclist and a pedestrian, I returned to the main street leading to Breckenridge. How ironic, my first *yikes* moment took place on a bike path, of all places! (I would have two more *yikes* moments before reaching the Yorktown Victory Monument.)

The area that surrounds the Dillon Reservoir is a popular tourist attraction. Arapahoe Basin, Breckenridge, Keystone, and Copper Mountain—four ski destinations—are all close to where ice fishing and snowmobiling complement the primary skiing activity among vacationers. Famous boating and racing regattas take place during the summer months. Riding on Dillon Dam Road, I had a great view of the reservoir and downtown Silverthorne. Since September 11, 2001, dams have received considerable attention and money from the FBI, adding monitoring and security measures. Fortunately, the day I rode by, the road was open to the public.

At 1:41 p.m., I entered Frisco (population 2,683), and at 2:25 p.m., I reached the outskirts of the winter haven, Breckenridge (population 4,540). The Rockies overwhelmed the quaint little town. Dark, gray clouds covered the skies. I looked north, the direction I had come from, and noticed an extra layer of ominous, gray storm clouds in the distance. They materialized high above downtown in less than five minutes.

Cresting Santiam Pass (4,800 feet), Lolo Pass (5,000 feet), Chief Joseph Pass (7,000 feet), and Willows Pass (9,000 feet) all brought a tremendous amount of personal satisfaction. They were small milestones conquered. But when I reached Breckenridge (9,600 feet), I felt anxious about what lay ahead. *Do I continue over Hoosier Pass on this late Thursday afternoon? Or do I stop and climb to the summit after a good night's sleep?* These were my only choices. I didn't know what to do when I stopped at the Loaf 'N Jug gas station and City Market on North Park Ave on the north end of town.

The snowstorm that had been forecasted was approaching, evidenced by the clouds hovering over the north end of Breckenridge, ever so slowly making its way to the peaks south of me. I hopped off Tank and leaned it against a large window of the City Market. I placed my sweatband and riding gloves inside my helmet, hung the chin strap from the handlebar, and pulled my wallet from the front handlebar bag. I retrieved my iPhone and walked inside the market to replenish protein bars, peanuts, orange jelly sugar slices, and Gatorade. After I sat on the ground next to Tank, I unpacked my goodies from the plastic bag, and separated the snack items I would eat now from those I would save for another time. I was doing menial tasks to pass the time, not ready to decide what to do next.

According to the Adventure Cycling map, Alma (population 270) and Fairplay (population 679)—towns 15 and 20 miles away, respectively, on the eastern edge of Hoosier Pass—had lodging options from which to choose. If I could secure a room in Fairplay, I would ride today. If I couldn't find a room, then I didn't know what I would do. I called the Western Inn Motel and RV Park in Fairplay and felt a burst of energy flow through me when I heard, "Yes, we have a room for you." During the conversation with the motel employee, a man walked in front of me, approaching the store entrance. The man looked very familiar. "Excuse me for a minute, I want to say hello to someone. I'll be right back," I blurted into the phone before turning my attention to the man who had already passed me.

"Hi, I recognize you—you look familiar," I said.

The man looked down at me, sitting on the ground. With a smile, he replied, "Mark McKinnon from Showtime's *The Circus* [*Inside the Greatest Political Show on Earth*] on CNN."

"Oh yeah, that's how I know you. Great to meet you," I responded.

When my conversation with the motel employee ended, I heaved an immense sigh of relief, knowing I had shelter and a shower waiting for me 21 miles from Breckenridge. The sky above downtown Breckenridge had turned darker since I'd arrived an hour before. Ominous-looking clouds hovered above, trapped between the surrounding mountains in a holding pattern. The temperature was in the low forties. While I was troubled about riding into a rainstorm, I felt reasonably sure snow would not fall. My decision to ride over Hoosier would pay off in spades. Within 24 hours, a storm would drop several inches of snow.

My attention returned to my celebrity encounter. I'm a news junky and familiar with Mark McKinnon, an entertainment personality known for wearing a full-brimmed cowboy hat during television appearances. While I readied Tank for the big climb, McKinnon exited the store and walked in front of me. I extended my arm to shake his hand.

I broke the ice. "Hi, I'm Larry. Good to meet you."

"Good to meet you, too," he replied, with a curious demeanor that prompted me to talk some more.

"Just stopping before my climb to Hoosier Pass. When I was on the phone earlier, I was making a motel reservation in Fairplay. I'm competing in the Trans Am Bike Race. We started on June 2 in Astoria, Oregon. The final destination is Yorktown, Virginia."

McKinnon had been at the Alpine Bike and Ski Sports Center, across the parking lot from the City Market.

I dove in and announced emphatically, "You should consider riding coast-to-coast. It's an incredible experience. There's nothing like seeing America on the saddle."

He said something like, "At my age…"

I waved a hand, interrupting with, "You could do this if you set your mind to it."

We exchanged a few other pleasantries. I took a selfie, both of us smiling. We shook each other's hands again, bid each other adieu, and then I put my game face back on. It was time to tackle Hoosier Pass. (On May 17, 2021, I connected with McKinnon on social media, telling him to be on the lookout for racers coming through Breckenridge in the 2021 TABR. Covid forced the cancellation of the 2020 race. He responded, "Kick it, Larry!" I chuckled when I saw it and recall thinking he was a kind, gentle, warmhearted man.)

I would soon reach Hoosier Pass (11,519 feet), a sought-after milestone for coast-to-coast enthusiasts and a crossroads through the Rockies. Cycling through Breckenridge, Colorado—one of the most talked about ski destinations in the world—inspired a warm feeling when I pedaled by the "Welcome to the Breck Connect Gondola" sign affixed to the operating equipment shuffling visitors back and forth to the top of the mountain. No skiing, just sightseeing.

Riding through Breckenridge on a bicycle just seemed so natural, like a fun ride through my hometown on a Sunday afternoon, contrasted with the anticipation I felt preparing to visit the Rockies for a family vacation when the kids were much younger.

I had seen a highly motivating video of Abdullah arriving at Hoosier Pass several days prior. A single dot watcher set up at the summit, lens on the empty road, waiting for Abdullah to reveal himself when he swung left at the last turn before reaching the summit. I too envisioned myself looking up to witness the iconic Hoosier Pass marker reveal itself around the final bend on State Route 9.

I had visualized climbing Hoosier Pass since I'd first heard about the TransAmerica Bike Trail in September 2018. Tom and Wally mentioned it at the Loma Youth Hostel in San Diego. They had recently completed the ride from Virginia to Oregon. They were in San Diego preparing for our epic ride from California to Florida a month later. The realization that I was on the cusp of such a notable milestone ushered in an aura of contentment.

When I left downtown Breckenridge and began the gradual climb up a narrow, debris-filled road on Highway 9, I ended up white-knuckling my handlebars, as rain caused the road to become slippery. It's easy for a tire to skip on a slick surface, so I pedaled carefully and tried to avoid water spray from passing cars. The full 360 view I had in Breckenridge narrowed, so I could only see a few feet in front of me. I said hello to one lonely hiker heading toward the mountain trails, walking stick by his side, carrying his gear in a backpack. I wondered if he was on a multiday hike into the wild or an afternoon excursion. The rain started to fall when I still had 2,500 feet to reach the pass. I recall thinking the temperature would likely be much colder at the higher altitude. The white road line separating the traffic lane and shoulder would be very slippery. There were too many vehicles in both directions for me to ride in the traffic lane. Wanting to avoid riding over debris, I pedaled as close to the traffic lane as possible, hoping for the best.

Highway 9 changed into a steep road with constant switchbacks and limited visibility on all sides. The 10-percent grade, 45-degree twisted turns morphed into steeper 15-percent switchbacks near the top of Hoosier Pass. I modified the viewing window on my Garmin device to track real-time elevation changes. When I reached 10,000 feet, the combination of hard pedaling and high altitude had me feeling dizzy and tired. However, the notion that I would ride over five mountain ranges (Cascades, Bitterroots, Rockies, Ozarks, and Appalachians) had a romantic appeal.

I always tackled challenges head-on. I wished for something memorable, challenging, and different. Completing the race would fit all three categories of craziness. I had trained for this moment, riding up Calais Road (a three-quarter-mile stretch of 15-percent grade) near my home in Morris County dozens of times with Hoosier Pass on my mind. However, nothing could adequately prepare me for the painful ride I experienced, especially the last 500 feet right before the summit.

Through a rift in the clouds, I could see a beautiful, blue sky, in sharp contrast to the gloomy setting leading to the top. The sun blazed down, illuminating the pristine scenery. At the 10,800-foot mark, I stopped every 200 to 300 feet to catch my breath and rest my burning thighs. At 11,300 feet, the image of Abdullah rounding the last bend before the summit sprung to mind. I pedaled harder. An adrenaline rush boosted my drive. And there it was. As I rounded the final turn, I saw the prominent, brown National Park Service sign for Hoosier Pass.

I also spotted a dirt parking lot at the top of Hoosier Pass—a resting place—which featured the iconic sign as a backdrop for countless pictures taken over the years by those who conquered the highest peak on the TransAmerica Bike Trail. At 5:51 p.m., I turned around and looked at the expanse of a dazzling display of nature's beauty. A white Ford Explorer rounded the bend and sped by in an otherwise tranquil moment marked by a blue sky dappled with white clouds and soil-colored snowcapped mountains, which framed the sprawling highlands and meadows. Hoosier Pass was the perfect vista to take in the neighboring wilderness. And so, I took it in.

One week before—in Ennis, Montana—I'd felt intimidated when I looked up at the gargantuan Rocky Mountains; riding over them had seemed unimaginable at the time. The stories of failed attempts to cross the Rockies conjured images of Lewis and Clark's successful and safe passage over this rarely before seen land. I stood in front of the Hoosier Pass and Continental Divide sign (11,539 feet) with a sense of sheer satisfaction, knowing I had conquered the Rockies. I felt hugely energized, but I at once refocused my attention on what lay ahead. I still had a long way to go.

The winds roared. The temperature had plummeted to the midthirties. My sweaty cycling gear clung to my chest, and my hands and feet chilled terribly. When the wind pierced the layers, stinging my body, I shivered uncontrollably. I leaned Tank against the Hoosier Pass sign's stone foundation, hiding away from the gusting wind. I walked to the back of the dirt parking lot and approached a man and woman who stood next to a car. The man reluctantly agreed to snap a few photos of me standing and smiling at the Hoosier Pass sign that gets its name "from the 'Hoosier state' of Indiana, where many of the area's first explorers had come from during the 1860s."[68]

Descending Hoosier Pass filled me with tension and uncertainty. Between the steep grade, Olympic bobsled–like switchbacks, and the cross-canyon wind gusts, I felt like I was in the introduction clip to the ABC's *Wide World of Sports*—"The thrill of victory and the agony of defeat." I prayed I wasn't the cyclist version of the skier who crashes and burns when the "agony of defeat" stanza plays. I gripped the brakes tight to maintain control. One unexpected gust could easily cause me to lose my balance and tumble to the ground.

A 10-minute rest break in Alma was my lifeline, because my forearms burned from the steady tension applied on the brakes. With 1,500 miles of cycling behind me, my brakes didn't grip the tires well with their threadbare disc pads. The cables had stretched a great deal. When I pulled the brake arm, designed to apply pressure on the rotor, the bike barely slowed.

It had been a day to remember—a celebrity sighting, two near-miss accidents on a bike path, and a successful climb to Hoosier Pass. I reached my pit stop, the Western Inn Motel and RV Park, at 7:30 p.m. I faced east in the parking lot and looked to the open plains. Then I looked west at the mountains, their peaks dusted in snow. Immediately, I thought about the racers who were still on the west side of Hoosier Pass and felt

---

[68] "Hoosier Pass—Alma-Breckenridge," Uncover Colorado, accessed July 12, 2022, https://www.uncovercolorado.com/activities/hoosier-pass/

thankful that I had made it to this side. The woman I'd spoken to earlier was working the front office and expecting my arrival. I'd received a grand welcome when checking into most motels in small-town USA, and this motel was no different. She offered to wash my cycling shorts and dry my wet clothes. I was grateful because I simply wanted to eat dinner, prepare my bike and GPS for the next day's ride, and hit the sack. The $55 per night rate was a bargain compared to the cost of a motel in Breckenridge. After showering and dropping my dirty clothes off at the front office, I walked 50 yards through an adjacent RV Park to a Family Dollar store and bought my dinner, plus food and Gatorade for the next day's ride.

The North Park basin, the most sparsely populated of the three high-altitude basins of the Front Range, was now behind me. The Blue River, Breckenridge, and Dillion Reservoir are part of the smallest but most populated basin, Middle Park. The largest and most southern of the three basins is the grassland flat in central Colorado, with Fairplay being the largest town in South Park. For centuries, the South Park basin was the settlement of several different tribes of Indians, including the Kiowas, Arapahos, Apaches, and Utes. Fairplay was one of the first mining towns settled after the discovery of gold in the region in 1859; the name came from the idea that every miner should have equal rights to claim and protect property.[69] Today, the population is 724, but in the gold rush days, the population topped 8,000. When the boom went bust, Fairplay had to reinvent itself to remain a relevant and viable place to live. Fairplay erected a monument to the burro, an essential part of a miner's life, and hosts the annual World Championship Pack Burro Race."[70]

---

[69] "Fairplay, Colorado," Uncover Colorado, accessed July 12, 2022, https://www.uncovercolorado.com/towns/fairplay/

[70] Antonio Olivero, "Fairplay hosts burro world championships race with altered course because of snow," *Aspen Times*, July 25, 2019, https://www.aspentimes.com/sports/fairplay-hosts-burro-race-with-altered-course/

When I retrieved my cycling clothing, the front office manager said the weather had worsened and snow would reach Fairplay by morning. It had been a couple of days since I'd heard from Harry. When I retired to my room, I texted Harry to ask how things were working out. He said that he was stuck in Walden, Colorado—110 miles north and west of Breckenridge. Snow was falling there and had started to accumulate. Harry was holed up in a motel in Walden for an untold amount of time, not knowing when the weather would improve enough for him to continue. Harry later made the tough decision to scratch and returned home to New York City. He shared with me he was proud to have made it halfway across the country. Harry found someone to transport him to the Denver airport. He put everything into perspective, sharing that he planned to come back someday to Walden and finish the ride's second half. I'm confident Harry will be back on the saddle and eventually reach the Yorktown Victory Monument. When I snuggled underneath the covers, ready for another night of sound sleep, I recall thinking, *Once I get to Pueblo, it'll be a beeline straight to Yorktown!* For the next 115 miles, I would ride south to Pueblo, before turning east and riding Tank for the 2,500-mile homestretch! I had this image in my mind that reduced the United States landmass to a board game where I moved pieces from one state to the next. Monopoly has nothing on "Pedaling Across America with Tank."

Chapter 22
FAIRPLAY–PUEBLO, COLORADO (127 MILES)
June 21, 2019

I walked outside at 7:59 a.m. and looked east at the open plains south of Reineker Ridge. It was as though a magnetic force was pulling me in that direction. A single, dark cloud obscured the sunlight from shining on this otherwise clear, tranquil morning, making it appear more like dusk than dawn. I turned around to stare at Sheep Mountain, Lamb Mountain, and Round Hill and thought about Harry, who remained hunkered down in Walden. I was saddened for him.

Assuming I continued at my current pace, I'd fall short of my ambitious goal to finish in fewer than 40 days. The race ushered in a boost of testosterone, which equipped me with the requisite grit, drive, and determination to pull me along. After 19 days and 1,900 miles, I was confident I would complete the race, barring any unforeseen accidents or mechanical issues. I had what it took to cycle to victory on the TransAmerica Bike Trail. There would be hard days ahead, but nothing would get in my way now that Hoosier Pass was in the rearview mirror.

When the sun sprung from behind the single cloud, the sunlight warmed my body. A slight tailwind propelled me along at 20 mph with limited effort. Hypnotized by the easy ride, I felt a burst of natural energy—no caffeine necessary on this morning. When the route turned due south in Hartsel, the 16-mile stretch of Highway 9 and 1,100-foot climb to Current Creek Pass proved to be surprisingly challenging—an unwelcome development. The constant headwind and undulating hills wreaked havoc on my emotions. *Will these winds ever stop?!* I thought, when I reached Current Creek Pass and stopped to rest. I had misjudged how arduous the ride out of the Rocky Mountains would be. The net 6,700-foot drop from Hoosier Pass to Pueblo was anything but a walk in the park.

At 9:30 a.m., I entered Guffey, known for being struck by a 309-kilogram meteorite in 1907, the largest ever recorded in Colorado.[71] I passed a Comanche (War) Trail sign used by the Comanche Nation to conduct raids in the mid-nineteenth century. I rode in the middle of the vehicle lane the entire 31-mile stretch of highway from Current Creek Pass to the intersection of Highway 50, near the Royal Gorge Bridge. Hemmed in by Blue Ridge and Rice Gulch to my east and Cottonwood Ridge to my west, I gripped the handlebars, hunched over, and rode in the highest gear for two hours.

Descending from the southern edge of the Front Range, I flew by the fast-moving, crystalline Currant and Cottonwood Creek. The creeks babbled pleasantly, quieted only by the rushing air hitting my face while I cruised at 40 mph, reaching a maximum speed of 45 mph. The narrow canyons obstructed direct sunlight on this chilly late morning. Riding at such speeds felt truly exhilarating. I felt free to think, without a worry in the world. I harkened back to my younger days, when I felt invincible, jumping out of airplanes and rappelling out of helicopters. The adventures I sought as a young man had come back full circle.

---

[71] "Guffey Meteorite," Cloudbait Observatory, accessed July 12, 2022, https://www.cloudbait.com/guffeymet.php

When I reached the junction of Highway 50, now less than 600 miles from the Mexican border, I pinched myself, knowing that when I'd left Astoria, the Canadian border was only 350 miles away. This east-west route of the US Highway system stretches over 3,000 miles from Sacramento, California, to Ocean City, Maryland. It's the same Highway 50 on which I rode my ten-speed Peugeot from Harrisburg, Pennsylvania, to Ocean City, Maryland, when I was 18 years old. In Nevada, a section of Highway 50 is known today as the "Loneliest Road in America."[72]

I rode on the shoulder, mindful of the large volume of traffic that sped by as I approached Canon City (population 16,400). I rode past a 50-foot-tall brontosaurus, an element of the Royal Gorge Dinosaur Experience. A popular tourist destination, with many restaurants and hotels lined up one next to the other.

In Canon City, I decided to detour because I needed a change and thought that experiencing the hustle and bustle of Canon City for a few minutes would do more good for my emotional state than the extra few miles I would gain by staying the course. Cars, pickup trucks, and larger vehicles sped by in both directions on Royal Gorge Blvd. Cars filled the stalls at a Sonic Drive-In. I stopped at McDonald's and sat in a booth next to the window, in view of Tank. I listened to the banter and watched blue- and white-collar folks enjoying their favorite Ronald McDonald meal. I was in a much more relaxed frame of mind when I returned to Highway 115, turned south, crossed over the Arkansas River, and entered the Town of Brookside (population 233). Nathan's prerace admonition, "Remember, it's just a bike ride—nothing more, nothing less," became a daily mantra as I attempted to keep a positive attitude, which I knew would impact my behavior and decision-making. How can a visit to McDonald's possibly influence a person's overall state of mind? Five-star customer service, good-tasting food, and human interaction, that's how. Had I not experienced good service or good-tasting food, and had I sat

---

[72] "Loneliest Road in America," Travel Nevada, accessed July 12, 2022, https://travelnevada.com/road-trips/loneliest-road-in-america/

next to angry, disgruntled folks, I might not have left McDonald's with renewed vigor and vitality.

I rode parallel to the Arkansas River for the next nine miles, until I reached Florence (population 3,881), where the first oil well west of Pennsylvania was developed in 1862.[73] A crossroads of stagecoach and wagon lines, today it's home to a United States penitentiary known as the Alcatraz of the Rockies.[74] Some of the most dangerous felons, including El Chapo, Terry Nichols of the Oklahoma City bombing, and Ted Kaczynski, the notorious Unabomber, are incarcerated there. I considered stopping to take pictures of the facility and surrounding scenery but decided not to. Not wanting to draw attention to myself, I continued one mile farther south before stopping to look at the vast, brown wilderness. Snow no longer covered mountain peaks. Sagebrush dotted no-man's-land.

At 4:26 p.m., I got to Wetmore and Highway 96, which led straight to Pueblo. A transition from the snowcapped Rocky Mountains to wide open plains happened in an instant, the eastern edge of the High Plains passing the baton to the western edge of the Great Plains. A "9% downhill" sign gave me pause. I stopped on the Frontier Pathways Scenic Byway, perched high above, overlooking the sweeping views of the Great Plains.

I saw a safety triangle attached to a roadside railing and two cyclists standing in a gravel parking lot. Seeing the orange and yellow outline of a safety triangle, I immediately assumed they were members of the Adventure Cycling Tour group that had started from Yorktown on May 2, 2019, the same tour I'd considered joining months before. I rode up to the man and woman, spotting a tandem bicycle lying on the ground.

---

[73] "TransAmerica Trail map # 6 field notes," Adventure Cycling Association, accessed July 12, 2022, https://www.adventurecycling.org/routes-and-maps/adventure-cycilng-route-network/transamerica-trail/

[74] Eileen AJ Connelly, "El Chapo, Unabomber safe as 'Alcatraz of the Rockies' reports no coronavirus cases," *New York Post*, April 11, 2020, https://nypost.com/2020/04/11/alcatraz-of-the-rockies-supermax-prison-reports-no-coronavirus-cases/

"Are you with the Adventure Cycling group?" I asked, hoping they were so I could swap stories about my experience on the Southern Tier.

"No," the woman said, adding that they were riding west to east on the TransAmerica Bike Trail, however, a damaged rear tire rim forced them to the side of the road. They were waiting for a vehicle to transport them to a bike shop in Pueblo. When our brief but pleasant exchange was over, I continued pedaling to Pueblo.

Whether by good fortune, proper preventative maintenance, or both, I had been fortunate to avoid mechanical issues during the first half of the race. I recall thinking at the time how a problem requiring a mechanic's help would potentially destroy any chance I had to finish in less than 40 days. I took serious, daily preventive maintenance checks and services and avoided riding over potholes and debris with the same determination and commitment I had taken on the Southern Tier.

The honking sound of a passing pickup truck startled me. I saw a face plastered against the front window and a waving hand. I smiled and nodded my head to acknowledge their gesture, their tandem bike in the pickup's belly.

I rounded the bend high above the high desert basin and immediately felt an extreme gust of wind. My bike shook. Not sure what to do, I firmly gripped the handlebars, shifted into the lowest gear, and continued pedaling. The nonthreatening, cloudy skies at 6:15 p.m. were reminiscent of the discordance I experienced while living in Southern California, when the ferocious Santa Ana winds would blow on a clear and sunny day. When Highway 96 turned north, I looked in the distance at a speck in the middle of a flat, desert landscape. I felt like Gulliver pedaling toward miniature Lilliput and it's 106,595 Lilliputians.

Pueblo, known as "Steel City,"[75] one of the largest steel-producing cities in the United States, was that speck in the high plains. The highway

---

[75] Jon Pompia, "How 'Betsy' the blast furnace helped Pueblo become the 'Steel City,'" *Pueblo Chieftain*, August 30, 2020, https://www.chieftain.com/story/news/history/2020/08/30/how-rsquobetsyrsquo-blast-furnace-helped-become-steel-cityrsquo/42346295/

narrowed, buttressed by closely cropped hills and sagebrush on both sides. When I rounded another bend, I was exposed on all sides, no longer protected by hills. A gust of wind hit me broadside, nearly knocking me off my bike. I leaned against the pressure as soon as I realized it wasn't a spontaneous gust but a prevailing wind, cornering the road like a racer, except my speed had been reduced to less than one mile per hour. Exposed to the elements without a place to shelter, I had no choice but to continue.

At 6:50 p.m., I reached Pueblo city limits. I stopped at a red light on Pueblo Blvd, no longer met with nearly gale-force winds. The day began at an elevation of 9,954 feet and ended at 4,800 feet. A drop of over 5,000 feet, but it still ended with me climbing 3,900 feet on rolling sections of Highway 9. When I'd left Fairplay 12 hours earlier, I thought the day would be a piece of cake, especially since the first several miles were so enjoyable. How wrong I was.

I'd forgotten to reserve a motel room. *No problem*, I thought. Undoubtedly one of the city's numerous motels would have a vacancy. I stopped at Main Street and 4th Street, marking the end of the sixth map section of twelve. The city center was quiet at 7:00 p.m. For a large city with a population of over 100,000, I felt underwhelmed by the energy and lack of visible outdoor activity as I made my way through downtown. Puddles were visible on many streets. I wondered if the windstorm I rode through dumped rain in the city. Threatening rain clouds moved to the east. To my distress, there was not a single vacancy at the motels I called. I stood under the overhang of the entrance to the Pueblo Dermatology Clinic, feeling increasingly uneasy, until I finally got a room at the USA Motel on 29th Street. At 7:30 p.m., I opened the door to the hotel lobby and felt a weight lift off my shoulders. I had conquered the Rockies and added almost 30 miles to my mileage bank.

I introduced myself to a man and woman behind the front counter. I'd learned several Korean words when I was stationed at Camp Stanley, Uijeongbu, the Republic of Korea, in 1987 to 1988. When I heard them speaking to each other in the language, I smiled and said,

"*Annyeonghaseyo!*" (which is "hello" in Korean). They raised their heads, nodded, and bowed—a traditional greeting. Unfortunately, that was all the Korean I remembered.

I started a load of laundry and then walked east on 29th Street underneath Interstate 25 to the Pueblo Mall. My body welcomed the 20-minute walk after 12 straight hours on the saddle. The different muscle movements made a big difference in helping to transition from cycling to sleeping. When I see the McDonald's logo, a double cheeseburger comes to mind. Seeing the colonel of the KFC logo elicits the image of a juicy, crisp, dark meat 16-piece bucket. Dairy Queen and Dunkin Donuts have similarly mouthwatering effects. On this night, when I looked up and saw a Papa John's Pizza sign, I at once thought how good a supreme meat pizza would taste. The Papa John's logo elicited a Pavlovian conditioning response. I entered the uncrowded store and ordered their $7 large pie special.

After finishing every morsel, I walked back to the motel, retrieved my laundry, and entered my room. Earlier that day, Keith Morical, 57 years old, was the second to finish the race, arriving at the Yorktown Victory Monument in 19 days, 11 hours, and 53 minutes. I visualized reaching the monument, imagining the incredible feeling of finishing this thing and seeing my family again. I had remained disciplined on the Southern Tier, only thinking about the next 10-mile segment. Up until Pueblo, I had also trained my mind to remain disciplined. But now, when my thoughts wandered to Yorktown, I became energized. I no longer felt the need to stay solely focused on what was in front of me. I thought back to the day I earned my Ranger Tab and likened finishing the race to that moment, when I felt so proud to have achieved something so physically and mentally grueling.

In the morning, I would begin riding through eastern Colorado. Map section #7 did not display an elevation profile. Over the next few days, I hoped to challenge myself to ride 200 miles in one day.

Chapter 23
PUEBLO–EADS, COLORADO (110 MILES)

June 22, 2019

How can two days be so different? At 7:19 a.m., I stood outside the room for my morning selfie. My helmet sat high on my head, angled back like a kid wearing a baseball cap cocked sideways. I changed the lithium batteries powering the Gen X SPOT tracker. The batteries had lasted two weeks longer than I thought they would. The device kept me connected to the outside world, though hundreds of miles separated me from anybody truly familiar.

Wally from my Southern Tier group entered my mind. When he texted to congratulate me on reaching Santiam Pass, I responded that I'd call him when I reached Colorado to arrange to see each other. At the time, I'd fully intended to follow through, but now, my focus was to reach the finish line as quickly as possible.

Pueblo, the unofficial halfway point on the TransAmerica Bike Trail, is located 100 miles west of Eads, Colorado, the official halfway point and my destination. A lone cyclist passed me heading west near

Boone (population 339). Thirty minutes later, on Highway 96, two other westbound cyclists crossed the road to chat. They were part of the Adventure Cycling Tour group that left Yorktown on May 2, 2019. I knew it would be a matter of time before I'd cross paths with cyclists from the group. "Hi, I rode the Southern Tier with the Adventure Cycling Association in 2018," I shared. "Who is leading your group?" I hoped these two guys might know Wally or Joyce, my tour leaders and ACA executive committee members, but they didn't. One of the guys told me the group leader was trailing a few miles behind.

Both wore helmet visors to prevent the sun from beating down on their exposed noses, ears, and lips. My lips, ears, and nose had started to blister on June 3. I had woken up each day to a bloodied lip because of the crusting and cracking from the sun and dry air. "Much of the same," was their response when I asked how the roads were farther east. One guy shared a story about meeting Abdullah. A few days earlier, while the group was staying the night at a community church in Western Kansas, someone woke from a restless sleep at about 2:00 a.m. He checked the race leaders' board and noticed Abdullah's SPOT device pinpointed his location in the same town. Others in the group woke up, too. They were about to meet the legend himself. They identified his exact location at a gas station located at one of the two intersections in town. They walked outside, crossed the street, and found Abdullah sleeping on the ground underneath the front entrance to the gas station. Abdullah was jolted awake by the slight movement of their approach. They had disrupted one of his few catnaps on his way to a record-breaking TABR finish.

Our conversation turned to my ride into Pueblo the night before. "Did you make it to Pueblo before the storm?" one guy asked. It astonished them to learn I rode through the gale force winds. "Did you know the winds reached 38 mph?" one of the guys asked.

"Nope," I replied, going on to describe how I managed to lean into the winds to stay on the bike. (The US National Weather Service defines gale force as 34–47 knots of sustained surface winds—1 knot is 1.15 mph.)

Natural beauty and not much else surrounded the flat and desolate wilderness in eastern Colorado. I entered Boone on Church Avenue. The music from *The Good, the Bad and the Ugly*—a Western film starring Clint Eastwood—whistled through my head.

When I reached the east edge of town, I stopped to look at the map, hoping to locate someplace to resupply before I entered the remote high desert for another stretch of isolation. When I read "Camping at the city park—restrooms" in the map legend next to Boone, I immediately shifted to the next closest town, Olney Springs (population 345), 20 miles farther east.

I had a nervous feeling when I read "no services" next to Olney Springs and Crowley (population 176), four miles east of Olney Springs. A motel and a public library were in Fowler (population 1,172), two miles south of Olney Springs, but I didn't want to ride two miles off route. Adding to my already queasy stomach, my eyes focused farther east and to the next town, Sugar City (population 258): "No water or restrooms."

Everywhere I went, it all looked the same: roadside markers and vacant, dilapidated buildings on remote Highway 96. Shifting my mind to something other than the monotony and boredom that had sapped my positive energy in the heart of America, numbness had replaced forward motion. Frozen in the days of old, thinking about cowboys and Indians roaming the wilderness, I was elated to see a porta-potty nestled underneath a few trees when I reached Olney Springs (population 345). Four flag poles stood 20 feet high in front of a large stone structure with the inscription: "All Who Served, Welcome Home." A billboard with the American flag in the background and a saluting soldier revealed a oneness with patriotism in this rural, eastern Colorado town. I contemplated knocking on a stranger's front door at a random home on one of the five streets that intersected Highway 96 (known as Warner Ave in Olney Springs). Then I noticed a guy standing outside a dark-yellow building about 100 yards away, across the street, waving me over.

I stopped and shook hands with the colorfully dressed, middle-aged man when I reached the stone building. "Hi, I'm Larry. I'm taking a break before continuing my ride across the country," I said, meeting his warm and friendly smile with my own. His gap-toothed grin showed signs of dental hygiene neglect. He wore a floppy hat with a dark-colored, floral, short-sleeve shirt and held a bottle of Aquafina close to his chest. His tattooed arms were a work of art. He held a blue ribbon in his left hand, reaching out to make sure I noticed. There was a sign directly above him at the building's entrance: "Veterans Art Museum." The sign was accompanied by a photograph of the American flag taped to the interior of the front door, with the words, "God Bless America!" A semipermanent "Vet's Pavilion" shelter next to the museum, underneath shady trees and two picnic tables, revealed a gathering place for visitors. A 15-foot kayak leaned against the building's outside wall, the Arkansas River not far away. He told me he recently won the blue ribbon in a state-run veteran's art competition. His artwork was on display inside.

"Where are you originally from?" I asked.

"Pittsburgh, Pennsylvania," he responded, his accent indicating he was not a native. After serving in the Vietnam War, he settled down in Olney Springs. I didn't dig deeper into why he'd chosen Olney Springs.

I said, "Thanks, but I need to keep going," when this jolly fellow invited me inside to see the art collection. Given my personality, I knew it would be hard to disconnect once I entered the building and began touring the gallery. He had a thousand stories and would want to tell them all! I sensed his disappointment at my response, but he said he understood my desire to continue riding. I thanked him for the water and rode away from Olney Springs.

One of my favorite TV shows was the western sitcom *F Troop*, set at Fort Courage, an outpost in the Old West in the late 1860s. I often wondered how all the actors could be so clean when the log buildings and dusty wilderness suggested that people who lived out west in the late 1800s did not have the luxury of a daily shower. Another TV favorite, *The Lone Ranger*, was about a Texas Ranger who fought outlaws in the Old West with his Native American friend, Tonto. The less-traveled roads on my cross-country treks brought me closer to the places old western shows romanticized.

On the side of Highway 96, with the world all to myself, I stopped at the Olney Cattle Fields on the eastern edge of Olney Springs and watched thousands of cattle grazing. The sea of black coats stood out in an area where private farms produce corn, wheat, hay, and soybeans. Every few minutes, a car whooshed past me. I could feel the wind and hear the distinct *vroom* sound quickly approaching from behind. They were gone in an instant. Otherwise, the sound of silence grew louder as I rode closer to the Kansas border.

I frequently stopped to take pictures. Cresting Hoosier Pass had come and gone, but it was a memory that would last a lifetime. I was now in the prairies, experiencing what settlers migrating west in the late 1800s had experienced. My Surly Disc Trucker replaced prairie schooners. Telephone poles lined up on both sides of Highway 96. Four layers of wires that powered buildings, homes, and provided telephone conductivity had replaced Morse code, the Pony Express, and the telegraph.

Another thought came into my mind—that of the two incidents in which a car struck and killed a cyclist on Kansas State Route 96 in 2017 and 2018. Highway 96 was a smoothly paved, asphalt road with clearly marked yellow lines that separated two lanes going in opposite directions. A white-painted shoulder line followed the never-ending highway on each side of the road—six inches separating the driving lane from the shoulder. I chose to ride in the driving lane because I was confident that I could hear an approaching vehicle from behind. I tilted the small handlebar mirror to ensure I could see oncoming traffic from a distance. Had there been more traffic during the day, I would have felt unsafe riding on Highway 96, isolated in the plains of eastern Colorado. Forget riding in the dark! Riding on a narrow road with little to no shoulder had its drawbacks. The more considerable concern for me was drivers turning into zombies after driving for hours without a change of scenery. As far as this landscape is concerned, there is nothing to engage your mind; it's easy for your mind to wander—and for a car to drift.

In Haswell (population 67), a deserted, white, concrete building hemmed in by overgrown weeds grabbed my attention. It seemed out of place. An American flag was proudly displayed in the large picture window of the once-upon-a-time house. An eighteen-wheeler trailer was parked next to the abandoned building. I wondered if the trailer was a permanent fixture or a parking spot for a local truck driver. Unlike the weeds surrounding the abandoned building, the proximate area around the trailer had been kept free from overgrowth. Reportedly, Haswell is the site of the "Nation's smallest jail," which is 12 x 14 feet.[76]

At 7:00 p.m., I reached the west end of Eads (population 609) and looked up at a water tower and grain elevator going high into the sky. I thought about the damage a tornado would do to the exposed structure. Several days before, during the challenging mountain climbs, I recall thinking I would make up for the lower mile days when I reached the flat roads in eastern Colorado and Kansas. My body still felt good, and I wanted to continue riding with at least an hour of daylight remaining. According to the map, Tribune (population 741) was the nearest town with services, 58 miles east of Eads. I weighed the risks of riding after dark on Highway 96. The sun quickly dropped, and I saw storm clouds forming to the southwest. The mountains and plains are notorious for developing bad storms with little warning. The wise decision to stay in Eads would soon pay off.

I rode slowly down the main street, scanning for a vacancy sign. When I reached the east end of town and the vacant parking lot of the Traveler's Lodge, I became concerned. The building facade and the weeds growing from the empty gravel parking lot indicated it was no longer open for business. I turned my bike and repeated the process of looking left and right, returning to the middle of town. Perhaps I'd

---

[76] "Haswell, Colorado: Nation's Smallest Jail," RoadsideAmerica.com, accessed July 12, 2022, https://www.roadsideamerica.com/tip/55456

missed something earlier. I stopped at the intersection of Lowell Street and saw a newly constructed building, which I assumed was a motel, nestled behind a few miscellaneous stores. The outward appearance of the Cobblestone Inn & Suites gave me a good vibe. I quickly rode to the entrance, stepped off Tank, and leaned it against the side of the inn underneath an overhang with an unimpeded view of the lobby.

The interior reminded me of a motel one might see in a modest-sized town, not one with a populace of 592. A few people mingled in the lobby.

The front desk clerk looked up and said, "Hello," to which I responded, "Hi, do you have a room vacancy?" I had a nervous feeling in the pit of my stomach as I waited for her response. On the days I did not reserve a room in advance, I was taking a chance showing up late in the day. With a nasty storm approaching, there was a little more on the line. But when she said, "Yes, we have two rooms available," I could officially breathe a sigh of relief. It made for a sober ending to a misguided plan. It's the simple things in life—like a restaurant attached to the lobby of a motel and hot breakfast in the morning.

I checked into the room, showered, started a load of laundry, and then rested in the lobby. I sat at a high table next to a large picture window and witnessed storm clouds forming over the center of town; instantly, torrential rain and forceful winds swept through. Unrelenting lightning strikes lit up the sky for 30 minutes. The Weather Channel gave a tornado warning. I was beyond relieved to be inside. The thunderstorm moved through Eads with unmatched intensity.

During breakfast the following morning, the news reported a tornado had touched down a few miles east of Eads during the storm. My wish to see a tornado had almost come true. Seeing a twister (safely and from a distance) moving through the plains of eastern Colorado or western Kansas had been an irrational obsession of mine. The sensible part of my brain knew how exceedingly dangerous that would be. I had encountered Hurricane Agnes firsthand as it flooded my hometown of Camp Hill, PA, in 1972, had experienced the high winds and rain of

Hurricane Sandy in 2012, the hot, dry, fire-hazard Santa Ana winds that could reach 100 mph, the historic Laguna Beach fires of 1993, the rolling Loma Prieta (World Series) earthquake of 1989, the violent Northridge earthquake of 1994, as well as the surprisingly powerful Nisqually earthquake in Seattle in 2001. But I had never experienced a tornado. It's an odd curiosity I can't explain.

At 7:00 a.m., I called Kelley to tell her I was safe. The national news reported the previous night's tornado touching eastern Colorado, so I knew she'd likely be concerned. During our call, I reflected on how a year ago, on June 22, 2018, I'd told her about my interest in riding my bike across the country—and now, here I was, halfway through my *second* cross-country ride! I could not have imagined a more improbable path for the past nine months.

Traveling through backcountry that surprisingly few people have experienced on a bike made me appreciate this unbelievable opportunity to see America up close. There were no external pressures, no extraneous forces dictating what I should do or think. I was free from the mental gymnastics that often occurred when I took a weeks' long vacation from work. My mind would be free the first few days, and I would sleep well. And then, as the break came to an end, my mind would focus on the work I had left undone and the environment I had gladly escaped. Instead, the one valuable resource I no longer took for granted—time—allowed me to reflect on my life, the person I had become. I was content, pleased, but still not satisfied. I had a race to finish.

2,100 miles down, 2,100 to go!
Eads, Colorado
June 23, 2019

Chapter 24
EADS, COLORADO–DIGHTON, KANSAS (128 MILES)

June 23, 2019

I had averaged 99.4 miles per day during the first week and 101 miles per day in week two. When I reached Eads and the conclusion of the third week, my daily average continued to climb. Factoring in a dismal 57-mile day, I increased miles per day to 102.8 in week three. I had pedaled 2,123 miles so far. The 101-mile average was *still* not enough to put me in Yorktown in less than 40 days. Reports that the Ozark Mountains in Missouri and the Appalachians in Kentucky and Virginia were extraordinarily difficult to climb weighed heavily on my mind. In a postrace interview about the Ozarks, Abdullah shared, "The Ozarks were more challenging than the Rockies." He went on to say the constant up and down hills took a toll on him, mentally and physically. I mistakenly thought it would be a slam dunk to increase miles in the open plains of eastern Colorado and Kansas. I rode away from Eads in the right frame of mind, thinking, *I can make up ground as long as the weather conditions allow me to.*

At 7:28 a.m., fluffy, white, cotton ball clouds appeared against the backdrop of a clear, blue sky, a welcome sight for the start of a new day. A solid white line separated the vehicle lane from the six-inch shoulder, and prairie grass continued as far as the eye could see. Nature's beauty in this uninhabited wilderness greeted me when I set out on Highway 96. I counted the continuous telephone poles on both sides of the highway to pass the time, to the tune of "A hundred bottles of beer on the wall…" Occasionally, I rode past a dead critter or turtle run over by a passing vehicle, a not too subtle message to be aware of passing cars.

Every time I ate breakfast at a motel, I pocketed several of the half-ounce Smucker's assorted peanut butter and jelly packets for the road. When the sensation of weakness cried out around 2:00 to 3:00 p.m. each day, I knew I had to eat quickly. My energy level decreased, and sometimes I became light-headed. Peanut butter and jelly packets became my go-to, on-the-spot fuel supply, especially when riding through towns with little or no services.

At 8:54 a.m., I stopped pedaling. A single oil derrick stood out like a sore thumb about 50 yards off the highway, surrounded by wheat fields, various grasses, and dirt. In 2013, a new oil gusher was discovered 40 miles from the Kansas border. I looked east toward the horizon and felt the majesty of the vast high plateau of the semiarid grassland. The flat landscape and fertile ground made the region ideal for ranchers and farming. The Heart of America, this area east of the Rocky Mountains and west of the Mississippi Valley, is known as the Great Plains or simply the grasslands.[77]

A crushed Kansas box turtle lay dead on the road shoulder. It seemed wildly out of place in this dust bowl. To engage my mind, I noticed everything, scanning my surroundings. I looked at the tall grass, likely big bluestem, which can reach as high as 10 feet. Most of what I saw in the Great Plains was short grass used for pastureland and wheat fields.

---

[77] *Encyclopaedia Britannica Online*, s.v. "Dust Bowl: historic region, United States," updated May 15, 2022, https://www.britannica.com/place/Dust-Bowl

The taller, lighter shade of green grass waved in the wind. The land wasn't always this way. The term dust bowl comes from when early settlers plowed the soil and buffalo ate grass, destroying the root system.[78] There was nothing to hold the soil; when winds swept through, the soil lifted, causing great dust storms.

Near Brandon (population 21), I saw four billboards lined up next to each other. Each one told a part of the history of the Sand Creek Massacre in 1864, as this area was designated a National Historic Site. The Sand Creek Massacre (also known as the Chivington Massacre) came about when the US Cavalry attacked and killed hundreds of Cheyenne and Arapaho Indians at Sand Creek (located about 10 miles north of Brandon). A large photo of a sad-looking Chief White Antelope harkened back to the complicated history between the United States government and the Native Americans. The gold rush of the 1860s created the conditions that led the government to remove Indians from their lands to make way for settlers.

The massacre took place during the American Indian Wars. In 1864, a force of the cavalry under the command of US Army Colonel John Chivington attacked and killed an encampment of Cheyenne and Arapaho in Sand Creek. The billboard depicted Chivington as it would have been 150 years ago. Today's ghost town once consisted of 17 saloons, headquarters for a railroad line between Colorado and Kansas, and the Kingdon Hotel, described as the most magnificent in the west. The history of Chivington is instructive to much of the national dialogue that began in 2021. The raging debate about how best to teach American history has taken center stage in many parts of the country. Had these billboards not been there, I would not have stopped to read about the Sand Creek Massacre.

The effort to remove symbols of our history is beyond me, and it makes no sense. Where will it stop? I don't think it will, and that's a

---

[78] "TransAmerica Trail map # 7 field notes," Adventure Cycling Association, accessed July 12, 2022, https://www.adventurecycling.org/routes-and-maps/adventure-cycilng-route-network/transamerica-trail/

problem. The town of Chivington understood this issue well before woke politics reared its ugly head. One billboard here says it best: "Periodically, efforts have been made to petition to change the name of the town. Supporters feel that a man responsible for a massacre shouldn't be honored with a place name today. Others feel that retaining the name allows reflecting upon the past. The discussion continues about whether it is better to erase elements of history or remember and learn from them."[79]

Eastern Colorado had seen better days. Boone, Olney Springs, Crowley, Sugar City, Haswell, Eads, Brandon, and Sheridan Lake, with populations ranging from 21 to 1,080, were a shell of their past, yet the ghost of the wild, wild west lingered. When I saw the welcome to Greeley County road sign, I thought I had entered Kansas. *Where is the welcome to Kansas sign!?* I thought, wanting to capture the moment and continue the tradition of snapping a picture at every state border crossing sign. Kansas was the one state I visualized riding through more than any other, with its endless roads disappearing into the horizon.

And then I saw the outline of a small, rectangular, colorful sign, which I assumed was my Kansas greeting. Random stickers initially captured my attention—advertisements for Loyal Coffee, Emery Engineering, and Bear Zona. I saw a John Egbers postcard attached to the roadside marker. I had not connected entirely with the tragedy until I read the inscription: "Four Deadly Words—'I didn't see him'—Eyes Up!" on a sign on Highway 96 in Kansas, where the horrible accident took place. On this stretch of road notorious for cycling accidents, I wore the brightest clothes I carried and turned on three red lights attached to the rear stem, hopeful my blinking lights would cut through the blinding, clear, blue sky to be seen by motorists from hundreds of yards away.

Part of my joy in reaching Kansas was entering Wichita County and the Central Time Zone. Riding along with the wheat fields, admiring the

---

[79] "A Town Called Chivington," Colorado Historical Marker, US Highway 96., Colorado Department of Transportation, June 23, 2019

vast open landscape, I spotted an out-of-place oil derrick again that stood out like a sore thumb in the middle of the vast wheatfields. My initial impression was that Leoti (population 1,534) and Scott City (population 3,816) withstood challenging times much better than the deserted and isolated towns and buildings that made up eastern Colorado. Leoti honored hometown hero Steve Tasker, the 1993 Pro Bowl MVP. (The only special team player ever named Pro Bowl MVP.)

The 24-mile stretch of Highway 96 between Leoti and Scott City is where a car struck and killed John Egbers. The Kansas Department of Transportation dedicated a memorial honoring John near the crash site at the Heartland Mill in Marienthal (population 71). A dedication ceremony took place three days before the race began, attended by John's wife, Adventure Cycling Association members, and the Kansas Department of Transportation. I wanted to pay my respects, but unfortunately, when I rode through Marienthal, I lost focus and missed seeing the memorial. I realized my error before I reached Dighton (population 1038), 40 miles away, when I saw a giant, roadside billboard displaying: "Four Deadly Words—'I didn't see him'—Eyes Up!" The sad irony, I later learned, was that Egbers had stopped to pay his respects to Eric Fishbein, a TABR racer hit and killed by a car in the 2017 race. After paying his respects, he began cycling toward Newton. About 20 minutes later, on June 14, 2018, a car hit and killed Egbers on Highway 96 between Scott City and Leoti. Before leaving the site where Fishbein died, Egbers wrote "we are all diminished by one" on the wooden memorial post, took a picture, and continued riding. He sustained severe injuries that led to his death on July 5, 2018.[80]

There is currently an effort between the Kansas Department of Transportation and the Adventure Cycling Association to create greater

---

[80] Jordyn Brown, "Community remembers John Egbers: the cyclist, the 'soul rider,' the free-spirit," *SC Times*, October 11, 2018, https://www.sctimes.com/story/news/local/2018/10/10/cyclist-john-ebgers-remembered-trans-am-bike-race-kansas-distracted-driving/1510647002/

awareness of cyclists riding through Kansas, particularly on Highway 96. Public service announcements were broadcast on television and radio leading up to June 2, cautioning people of cyclists riding through Kansas. I was ever wary of the risks and always paid attention to my surroundings. I did not use earbuds to listen to music. I didn't listen to music at all. Riding on Kansas highways calls for constant vigilance because it is easy for drivers to become distracted.

I entered Dighton at 6:25 p.m. The sun shone bright. I still had two hours before sundown, but I had a room waiting for me at the Old Heritage Hotel on Long Street and was satisfied that I'd ridden 128 miles already that day. (In hindsight, I should have continued riding to Ness City, 30 miles east. I'm confident I would have been able to reserve a room at one of the three motels.)

The front entrance of the Old Heritage Hotel was that of an old western movie set. A strip of wooden buildings lined both sides of a smoothly paved main street—a dirt trail in the days when outlaws ran wild. When I called to inquire about room availability, a man instructed me to call when I reached town. He would send someone to the hotel. *That's an odd way to run a motel*, I thought. A car parked in front of the building, and a woman stepped out and greeted me. She opened the front door, and we both walked into an empty lobby. I stood in front of the reception desk while she fiddled to find something underneath the working side of the counter. She placed a 1970s vintage credit card swipe machine on the table and swiped the credit card I gave her. Five minutes and several swipe attempts later, she handed me my card and asked me to sign the front of the printed carbon transaction receipt. Time stood still in Dighton, Kansas—it made for a much different experience checking into a hotel compared to the hustle and bustle of big-city USA.

After showering and starting a load of laundry, I walked a quarter mile to the Kiwi Shop & Gas Station on Long Street. I sat quietly and ate by myself at a table, looking out the window, reflecting on the race. Back at the hotel an hour later, I checked the leaders' board. Garth finished the race earlier that day. He completed the race in 21 days, one day less than the 22-day goal he shared with Roger and me at the Portland bus station. He had executed his strategy flawlessly. Adam still trailed me by about 100 miles. I texted him, "Catch me, so I have someone to talk to!"

He replied, "I'm trying to!"

Competing against others was not my plan on June 2, and it still wasn't three weeks later. I had remained very disciplined in executing my strategy—ride during the day, recover with a good night's sleep, and repeat to the finish.

Many of the mental gymnastics I went through to help me through each day were practical. Others were impractical, like when I had an epiphany that I could reach Yorktown by July 4. *How cool would that be?!* I thought. Chills ran down my body when I thought about reaching Yorktown on Independence Day, but I knew that wasn't feasible at all.

Chapter 25
DIGHTON—STERLING, KANSAS (148 MILES)

June 24, 2019

Riding a bicycle across the country is not the safest activity. The requirement to obtain extreme sports insurance was a statement by itself. When the Rails-to-Trails Conservancy effort to connect Washington State to Washington DC through one continuous path is finished, cycling enthusiasts will have a safer option to complete a bucket list goal. While the project completion remains years away, several cycling organizations—such as the Adventure Cycling Association—are leading the efforts for a safer cycling experience. Noting their efforts (and others) in Kansas, the organization states, "You (we) are saving lives in Kansas! Now, we will bring this vital work to roads all over the United States."

I wondered if dot watchers would become less interested after such a spectacular finish by Abdullah. What could possibly match that excitement? Anticipating who would win was no longer a reason to rally. However, that's not what happened—quite the opposite. Dot watchers continued to post daily updates tracking the rest of the pack. Fear of failure gnawed at me and was a driving force pushing me to ride on. I did not wish to see the letters "scr" (scratch) next to my name on the track leaders' site. *If I repeat every day what I have done for three weeks, I will be fine,* I thought.

I could hear a noise from underneath the floorboards. With every step, the creaking got louder as I got closer to the open lobby. Quietly and cautiously, I walked to the exit. The lobby was dark. No windows, no light. When I opened the front door, letting in the morning light, a reflex motion immediately caused me to squint. I replaced my regular glasses with my Oakley prescription sunglasses. *How cool*, I thought, *the weather is great. Wonder if I can ride two hundred today?* I thrust my chest out; I was ready to go.

The picture I sent Nathan at 7:03 a.m. showed me beaming. My shades shielded my eyes from dirt, sand, water, and wind. This morning, the primary benefit was reducing the sun's glare, which had produced an intense need to squint and sneeze. I wiped away tears falling from my eyes.

Shortly after leaving the Old Heritage Hotel, I stopped at a Kansas Historical Marker, "Homestead of a Genius"—a tribute to George Washington Carver, an African American and one of America's leading scientists. Carver worked at the Tuskegee Institute in Alabama. However, Carver's roots began in Missouri. He moved to Ness City, Kansas (population 1,449), a town I saw on my way across the state, before settling in Alabama for 40 years.

I thought this might be the day I reached 200 miles. The flat Kansas terrain combined with the prevailing wind at my back provided the perfect opportunity to test my ability to crack the double century milestone. I knew I couldn't stop at interesting places on the route if I was to reach the 200-mile mark.

I was on Highway 96 near Bazine (population 334) when, at 10:09 a.m., I looked up and saw "Christ Pilot Me" written into the side of a ridgeline in front of three large wooden crosses lined side by side. I stopped for a couple of minutes to take pictures but quickly returned to cycling. Later that night, I read the history of the message and crosses. Reportedly, a local schoolteacher was listening to the song "Jesus, Savior, Pilot Me" one day in the 1940s, during a time when there was turmoil in the local community. The music and words inspired him to collaborate with the community and the property owners to place the message in this prominent terrain. Travelers on Highway 96 have seen the notice for over 80 years. It's a popular landmark for all who pass through on Highway 96.[81]

I zigzagged through Kansas, beginning in the center of the state near Tribune on the west end and exiting near Pittsburg, 400 miles later. Going east was a breeze, literally. Prevailing winds were my friend. I could sustain a pace of 20 mph. However, this was not the case when the route went south. The prevailing headwinds slowed my progress down to three to four mph. One minute, I was cruising at 20 mph, and the next, I was crawling at a snail's pace. Waiting for the GPS to count tenths of a mile was like watching paint dry.

I entered the Pawnee Watershed, near the Fort Larned Historic Site. At 1,567,240 acres, it's the world's largest watershed district.[82] The fort was established in 1859 to protect traffic along the Santa Fe Trail from hostile American Indians. The Pawnee River, named for the Pawnee Native American tribe that inhabited the region, runs parallel to Highway 156 and the Santa Fe Trail, an influential nineteenth-century route between Missouri and Santa Fe.

The route through Kansas traversed through the Smoky Hills section of the central Great Plains. The terrain is gently rolling. The ups and downs increased in the Smoky Hills near Ness City, and the road grade increased the closer I got to Missouri. Never let someone tell you Kansas

---

[81] "Communities throughout Ness County," Ness County, Kansas Chamber of Commerce, accessed July 12, 2022, https://www.nesscountychamber.com/communities.html

[82] "Entering Pawnee Watershed," Kansas Roadside Marker number 002714, US Highway 156, June 24, 2019

is all flat. Comparing landscapes was a favorite pastime on the saddle to keep my mind occupied. I thought about the parallels between Kansas and Texas roads. I saw more train tracks than cars in Texas but saw hardly any train tracks in Kansas. Oil derricks were a common occurrence in Kansas. Surprisingly, that was not my experience in Texas, even though Texas made up about a third of the entire ride across America in the Southern Tier. I saw more churches and trains in Texas, their whistles often shrieking in the middle of the night. This year, I saw railroad tracks for the first time on race day 23, just west of Sterling. When I arrived at the Country Inn in Sterling at 8:45 p.m., I was exhausted. Fourteen hours and 148 miles later—the most significant day yet—I was happy to be off the saddle.

After a long, hot shower, I walked 0.3 miles to Dillon's Marketplace in the south end of Sterling. I felt a stabbing pain, like a knife penetrating the meaty section on the bottom of my right foot, every time it touched the ground. The three outside toes on that foot were numb. My pain threshold is relatively high, but this numbness combined with the sharp, knifelike pain seemed unnatural and concerned me greatly. I had possibly pushed myself beyond what I was capable of with a 14-hour day. I often stopped to unclip the shoe, wiggle my toes, and shake my foot until the pain subsided. Foot numbness, which I experienced on the Southern Tier, wasn't a concern when the race began. I had grown accustomed to living with the discomfort to my extremities. But on this night, my body pushed back and told me to take it easy.

To this day, when *Forty to Finish* goes to print, my fingertips are numb when I wake up in the morning. It takes a minute before my hands can fully function. I will open and close my hands, from a fist to fingers extended, several times before I have full use. My right middle toe is still numb. When I jog, the numbness extends to a large section of the sole of my foot. The feeling is akin to a shoulder stinger in football. I often wonder if my hands and feet will return to "normal," to a preriding condition when I had 100 percent feeling of all my extremities. The discomfort is manageable. I wonder if functionality will worsen the older I get and whether other riders experience numbness long after returning home from a long-distance ride.

The proprietors of the Country Inn lived in the rear of the ranch-style building. When I returned from the walk to the downtown, a man and a teenage boy were gardening in a patch of soil next to the road. I stepped inside the lobby to inquire when breakfast was served and saw a young girl, who appeared to be a middle schooler, sitting at a table, book open, paper and pen in hand. It was nice to see a daughter and son learning the value of hard work and education from their parents, who I learned had moved to the States from India and were now living the American dream of owning their own business.

Spread out on my bed inside the inn were lunchmeat, red licorice, orange jelly candy slices, three large, juicy Sunkist oranges, and a bottle of Gatorade. I retired map section #7, retrieved section #8, and reviewed the available services east of Sterling.

Journal entry on June 24: *Trying to get as many miles in while the weather is good and the winds are favorable. One hundred and forty-eight miles down and counting.*

S   ections of the two-lane highway near the Quivira National Wildlife
    Refuge east of Sterling were underwater, the remaining runoff
caused by the biblical rains that fell recently. Had I arrived several days
earlier, I would have had to face the flooded road head-on, and I know
it wouldn't have been easy.

I started the day believing it would be another stellar day on the
saddle. If the weather was agreeable, I felt confident I would exceed 100
miles—maybe even reach 150 miles. The next couple of days would
determine whether I met my new, aggressive, less-than-40-days goal.
My scraggly beard itched incessantly. I wanted to shave, but my son,
Brian, wanted to see what Dad looked like without shaving for over a
month, so I didn't.

In Nickerson (population 1,147), I stopped and remained silent,
staring at five pronghorn antelope behind a fenced-off field on private
property. Their protruding double horns, weapons used for survival,

reminded me of a triceratops. Farther ahead, west of Buhler (population 1,331), hundreds of tiny creatures hopped on Highway 96. I thought my mind was playing tricks. I had never seen such tiny frogs. Hundreds of little, half-inch frogs scurried to the shoulder, trying to avoid being squished under the tires.

A 123-mile tributary of the Arkansas River, the Little Arkansas River snakes through the town of Buhler (population 1,111). The spring rain had caused tremendous flooding, resulting in many road closures. Fortunately, when I arrived, the floodwaters had mostly retreated to the fringes of both sides of the road. However, floodwaters reached across the street in a few lower-lying areas.

I looked to my left and saw a cyclist approaching me. We both stopped when he reached me. "Hi, I'm Terry," he began. "I tracked your location and thought I would join you for a few miles, if you don't mind?"

"Sure thing," I replied.

Terry told me downtown Buehler had been completely flooded a few days before I rode through. We stopped pedaling at a "Road Closed" sign affixed to a sawhorse road barrier about 50 yards ahead of our location.

"Terry, I've got a question," I went on, continuing to pedal. "Where is Tornado Alley?"

A smile crossed his face as he said, "We're riding through it now."

There would be no tornado sighting that day, though. A couple of days prior, a state trooper stopped a racer from Europe riding on Kansas Highway 96. In an online recounting, the racer said the trooper told him to find shelter because a tornado had touched down nearby. He didn't heed the trooper's advice and, fortunately, rode safely to the next town to wait for the storm to pass. Likely, he didn't understand the severe nature of a tornado.

Terry wished me well, turned around, and rode back to Buehler. I focused my attention on getting ready to cross over the raging water, which I estimated to be about six inches deep. Maintaining forward momentum was vital to successfully navigating a water obstacle. I put my bike in low gear and then began pedaling. The bike slowed when the tires met the water. I dropped into the granny gear and continued to move forward. I was confident the road surface was devoid of the slimy film that builds from constant running water—the road closure caused by diluvial rain weeks before that flooded the Arkansas River and nearby tributaries, turning the surrounding fields into a giant lake.

The water reached the height of my pedal on the down rotation. My shoes were soaked, but I made it across without further delay. (Rolf shared a post of his harrowing journey through a couple of days before I arrived. He carried his bike over his head and waded through about 150 yards of waist-high, flowing water.)

I arrived in Newton (population 18,847) at 11:40 a.m. While binge-watching YouTube videos leading up to the race, I saw a video that featured the Newton Bike Shop and its owners. The video portrayed the shop and its workers in such a way that drew me in. Akin to a spiritual experience for racing crazies, during the TABR, Heather and James Barringer open their doors for racers to rest, sleep, and tune up their bike any time of the day or night. A film crew captured the story of the inaugural TABR in 2014, when the Barringers opened their doors for any and all. In a feature article, Heather shared, "It was a rest, service, drop-ship point, basically whatever they needed," adding, "Each participant was filmed as they arrived, and that was put on Facebook for the world to watch." The story was turned into a documentary called *Inspired to Ride* that closely followed "the journey of a handful of the cyclists as they prepare, compete, and experience what riding 300 miles a day feels like with only a few hours of sleep."[83]

Regardless of whether Tank required maintenance, I planned to visit the Newton Bike Shop. A permanent "Welcome to Newton—TransAmerica Bike Trail" sign attached to a metal post greeted me when I reached the outskirts of town. The Barringers' central message in the

83 Wendy Nugent, "An Oasis in the Grass," *Harvey County Now*, March 4, 2015, https://harveycountynow.com/all-news/news/features/an-oasis-in-the-grass

documentary is that a vibrant cycling community would help small-town America. These small towns are invisible in a car. But on a bicycle, the buildings and people are full of stories of a better past. It's reported recreational cyclists spend "$46.9 billion on meals, transportation, lodging, gifts, and entertainment,"[84] each year traveling through small towns. The positive impact on improving the economic outlook can't be overstated. Towns like Newton understand this. The beneficial effect of small purchases, whether a slice of pizza, candy bar, or bottle of Gatorade, was always on my mind each time I entered a new town along the TransAmerica Bike Trail.

At 12:46 p.m., when I reached the Newton Bike Shop, I entered a space that was free from clutter, unlike most of the shops I'd visited since 2018, when I began long-distance cycling. Bright, painted walls were neatly merchandized with miscellaneous cycling items.

I approached a man and woman who stood behind the cash register. "Hi, I'm Larry, in the Trans Am Race," I said. They greeted me, introducing themselves as James and Heather. "I just want to let you know I was motivated to enter the race after I saw a YouTube video with you guys in it," I said with a smile. "I thought your message about cycling and small-town revitalization was on point." James and Heather were pleasant as I'd imagined they'd be. I went on, "I'm having issues with the bike. Not sure what the problem is. There is a slight wobble in the rear tire that has worsened over the past couple of days. Can you take a look at it?"

James waved for me to bring Tank to the back of the shop. I walked behind the front counter to the workstation and saw a bike already hoisted on the one bike stand. I leaned Tank against the wall and grabbed my wallet and a pair of extra socks and gloves to ship home to New Jersey, telling James I would be back in an hour. He said he would work

---

[84] Darren Flusche, "Bicycling Means Business: The Economic Benefits of Bicycle Infrastructure," Advocacy Advance, updated July 2012, https://www. advocacyadvance.org/the-economic-benefits-of-bicycle-infrastructure/

me into his schedule, emphasizing, "It should be ready to go in about an hour, unless I find some other problem."

A wall inside the bike shop was devoted to displaying memorabilia from prior Trans Am Bike Races. The cycling jersey worn by the 2016 winner, the runner-up's gloves, and other items emphasized the race's positive impact on the Newton community. There was a giant likeness of Mike Hall, 2014 TABR winner, as a centerpiece, surrounded by inspiring quotes from visitors over the years.

I asked the Barringers if Abdullah had visited their store when he rode through town. James, a veteran cyclist, replied, "Yes." I then asked him to share his point of view on Abdullah's impressive racing performance. I heard a similar response to when I'd asked Nathan days earlier in Oregon. "He's in his twenties," James replied with a shrug, as though being in one's twenties was all it took to win a race of this caliber.

Tank was hoisted up and being worked on by a mechanic when I returned to the shop. He couldn't find anything wrong. He'd trued the tires, cleaned the chain, and adjusted the brake and gear cables. I paid the small charge for the work performed. Surrounded by all the memorabilia, Heather snapped a picture of me standing by Tank. On one side of me, James displayed a wide grin, pointing a dog horn at the camera with his right hand, and a less enthusiastic mechanic stood on the other side. James placed a #bemoremike and a #2588 sticker to my bike frame, the first in remembrance of Mike Hall, and the second indicating the shop's mile mark on the 4,200-mile TransAmerica Bike Trail.

It was too early to stop when I reached Cassoday (population 129) at 4:15 p.m. A storm was forecasted to touch down later that evening. My legs had been working like pistons, firing on all cylinders just to reach the Cassoday Country Store at State Route 177 and Stony Creek Road—a typical store, gas station, and a gathering place for the local citizens. I saw a park with picnic benches and a gazebo on the edge of the gravel parking lot. Inside, several older folks sat at a wooden table. The next 17 miles south on Stony Creek Road to Rosalia would be demanding because of the relentless headwinds that showed up every time I rode south. At the intersection, the route shifted east for another 23 miles to Eureka (2,483).

I followed my instincts once again. After a 30-minute break, I saddled up, knowing full well I would arrive in Eureka after dark. The $40 a night rate at The Carriage House Motel was reasonable. The Adventure Cycling Map listed the motel on their service directory, so I presumed it would pass muster. Indoor accommodations, a bed, and a hot shower for $40—how bad could it be?

So close to finishing such a meaningful journey, I still had an empty feeling that something was missing. Here I was, almost two-thirds through the world's longest unsupported bike race, almost through the seventh state, and I had become less enthusiastic about what lay ahead than any time before. The ride from Cassoday to Eureka was merciless. The Great Plains were now behind me. Rolling hills combined with a fierce headwind put me into a mental dystopia. I tried to think about my family. That didn't help. Hearing my Garmin ping at each 10-mile mark was no longer motivating. I put my head down and counted pedal rotations in my mind (and aloud), grinding at the monotonous sameness of it all. I lost interest in my surroundings. I became complacent and pedaled with one goal—*get to Eureka*. I had thoroughly checked out. I don't recall any aspect of the 17-mile ride from Cassoday to Rosalia. Finally, after three and a half hours, I reached Highway 54 and began cycling the last leg of my day's journey to Eureka. I thought, *Let's finish this damn race!*

I tried to block out the constant what-ifs that entered my mind. *What if I can't finish this race? What if my bike breaks down?* There was a nagging sense of fait accompli that something bad would happen. Negative thoughts caused me to remove myself from the present. My mind wandered as the miles accumulated. Time and distance slowed down when negative thoughts about not finishing the race entered my mind. To raise my spirits, I tried to imagine arriving at the finish line. The big picture became irrelevant. I'd lost that *spark*, that internal drive that had enabled me to keep pushing in the past. It had been intoxicating to think I was riding in one of the world's most challenging bike races. But not anymore.

Traffic had increased, but a broad shoulder, four high-quality, blinking, red rear lights and three powerful, bright, white front lights made the transition to darkness feel much safer. When I reached town, the sun had set, the streetlights providing just enough light for me to see the Carriage House on the right side of the road. The name made it sound like a decent place, but seeing the near-empty parking lot and the "office closed" sign gave me pause. "Now I know why it cost $40," I muttered out loud, pedaling into the parking lot. There were two old sedans and two boat trailers there, but besides that, it was empty. The seedy-looking motel reminded me of a place where drug deals take place and ladies of the night do their business. A motel door opened, and a young man walked outside to greet me with a dog by his side. I handed the guy $40 in exchange for the room key. He pointed to the door directly next to his and told me to let him know if everything was okay with the room. If I had more energy, I would have taken a greater interest in hearing more of this man's story. He shared that he lived at the motel and worked at the Sonic Drive-In across the street. However, I wanted to clean my body, eat, and sleep, so that was all I heard about that stranger. I walked inside the room, turned on the light, and leaned Tank against a small, round table. The closed blinds kept out any remaining night light. The ceiling light gave off the soft, butterfly glow of candlelight. I turned on the bedside table lamp. To my alarm, a cockroach scurried out from underneath the lamp and disappeared to the back of the bed behind the headrest. The room smelled stale. The air conditioner didn't work. I saw a cigarette butt in the bathroom sink. "At least I get a hot shower," I said, too exhausted to care.

I laid my sleeping bag on top of the bed and blew up the inflatable pillow. I didn't trust that the motel linens were free from lice. I showered, walked 0.2 miles to Johnson's General Store, and ate two slices of pizza. I bought beef jerky, breakfast bars, and orange jelly candy slices for the next day's ride. Back at the inn, I felt a sense of accomplishment when

I saw my initials highlighted on the track leaders' site. It showed me near the Missouri border. I looked at the outline of the United States, traced the route from Astoria to Eureka with my finger, and shook my head in disbelief. I was 2,800 miles closer to Yorktown!

Adam was close to reaching Kansas about the same time I was about to exit. Rolf was halfway through Missouri. Several racers were bunched together in Illinois and Kentucky. I continued to feel connected to others through technology. That was the third day in a row that I'd crushed the century mile mark. When I finally laid my head on the pillow in Eureka, I was 135 miles closer to Yorktown.

Chapter 27
EUREKA–PITTSBURG, KANSAS (109 MILES)

June 26, 2019

T he shift from the plains of Western Kansas to the rolling hills in the southeastern region happened in an instant. This new landscape was consistent with the hills I grew up riding through in South Central Pennsylvania, minus the cornfields. I was no longer awed by an infinite, uninhabitable wilderness that seemed to go on forever. The temperature rose to about 80 degrees when I left Eureka at 7:37 a.m. Before I reached the edge of town, I was drenched in sweat from the heat and humidity. The forecast for the next couple of days was more of the same: hot, sunny, and humid.

At 6:55 p.m., I noticed a "God Bless America" sign hanging between two front porch columns of an abandoned building. I don't recall anything about the 92 miles I rode between 7:37 a.m., when I left the roach-infested Carriage House, and 10 hours later, when I reached the north side of Girard (population 2,710). I grew tired and less attuned to my surroundings riding through the heartland which, by now, had become a lackluster routine.

About seven miles north of Girard, I looked up to the gray sky and saw lightning strikes in the distance. The boom of thunder shook my ears several seconds after each lightning strike lit up the sky. Swirling winds, an aspect of the nearing storm, caused me to work hard to maintain forward momentum. I shifted to the highest gear and pedaled hard, anxious to reach Girard before the storm arrived. There were plenty of homes and buildings to provide shelter on Highway 7, if needed. I pushed myself harder than I did on any other multimile stretches of the entire 4,200-mile ride. I reached the north end of Girard a little after 5:30 p.m. and sought out a place to shield from the storm, which I expected to hit the area soon. I pedaled underneath a protected walkway that led to a Wells Fargo bank entrance on Summit Street. This early Wednesday evening, the downtown was quiet, the workday over. A few cars sped by. I leaned Tank against a stone wall and sat down on the ground, waiting for the storm to tear through. About 30 minutes later, I peered toward the sky on the south end of town, the direction I was heading, and noticed that the sky had cleared. The storm had passed much farther west of Girard. So, I saddled up and rode 15 miles to Pittsburg (population 20,360).

On the way, a dog chased me, a halfhearted attempt to track me down, but the adrenaline rush from pedaling fast reminded me that I had yet to ride through Kentucky, and it was now time to retrieve the dog repellent I had stashed inside my handlebar bag.

After settling into my motel room, I strolled on Broadway for three quarters of a mile to the nearest Walmart, where I bought snacks for the following day's ride and replenished my Desitin. The extreme pain I endured in Wyoming had abated. On my walk back to the Super 8, I stopped to eat dinner at Applebee's Grill & Bar.

Who the heck is Wild Birdie?! I thought when I reviewed the race results later that night. I did not recognize the name until I looked at the video of Wild Birdie arriving at the Yorktown Monument. "Wild Birdie is Rylee!" I said out loud, realizing that this was the woman Roger and I met, along with Garth, at the Portland bus terminal. Rylee was a mild-mannered, delightful person who wore a big smile. She carried herself confidently and struck me as competitive, but her youthful look and average physique could have left one with a conclusion other than that she was someone capable of riding 4,200 miles in 23 days and 23 hours.

Chapter 28

PITTSBURG, KANSAS– MARSHFIELD, MISSOURI (119 MILES)

June 27, 2019

W ith the dog repellent spray clipped to the handlebar bag's small, mesh cargo compartment, I was ready to go. Twenty-four cyclists had finished, 24 were still pedaling, and 25 had scratched. The Ozarks were looming large. The map's section #9 elevation profile forewarned what lay ahead. Unlike the Rockies, where ascents and descents were gradual and prolonged, the Ozarks' spikes appeared as irregular as shards of shattered glass. I had thought conquering the Rockies would be the most challenging part of the journey. I was wrong. Elevation has little to do with climbing a mountain. Variables such as the frequency of hills, the grade, the heat, and the humidity determine the difficulty quotient.

A middle-aged man introduced himself while we both stood in line to check out the following morning. I recognized him from the night before when I checked in to the motel. The front desk manager seemed to know the guy. The way they communicated was a clue this was not their first time meeting. He was a truck driver who often stopped at the Super 8 to rest during his transport trips. He saw Tank leaning against the outside wall, packed and ready to go. "My parents are both cycling fans. Do you mind if I take a picture of your bike and send it to them?" he asked. I was mildly amused and surprised at his request but obliged.

The woman working the front desk greeted me with a pleasant smile. "Has anyone ever said you look like Lindsay Lohan?" I asked, letting my thoughts come out unfiltered.

She responded, "No, but people tell me I look like Miley Cyrus all the time."

"I guess I don't know my celebrities very well," I said, a little embarrassed.

"That's okay." Her smile compelled me to continue our conversation. While stationed at Camp Pendleton, she and her soldier husband had lived in Oceanside, California, before moving to Pittsburg. Hearing her say Camp Pendleton piqued my interest.

"I sold medications to the Camp Pendleton hospital in the early 1990s when I lived in Orange County and worked for a pharmaceutical company. We loved living in that part of the country. But the East Coast is home, so that's where we live now."

She and her husband moved to Pittsburg when he took a job working as a stagehand for the band Metallica.

At 7:39 a.m., I crossed the Missouri border. "Six states down and four to go. Adios, Kansas!" I snapped a few pictures at the state border sign on that balmy summer morning. My body had reshaped from a 230-pound frame with middle-aged love handles to a refined, chiseled physique, the result of burning thousands of calories every day for 25 days in a row. As my body thinned, my face followed suit. The picture I sent Nathan displayed a narrow, angular face with a genuine smile and a grayish beard that told a story of grit and determination.

In Missouri, I saw route markers denoting "US (bike) 76." Since 1976, when the first group of cyclists rode the TransAmerica Bike Trail,

10 states and many small towns have embraced the cycling culture and often make cyclists feel welcome.

It didn't take long to realize the challenges of riding through the Ozarks in Western Missouri. I would speed up on the downhill, hoping my momentum would propel me to the apex of the next climb. Inertia would push me about halfway up the next hill, but that was all. To reach the top, I shifted into the granny gear. This cycle repeated for about 200 miles. The elevated temperature and increased humidity added to the challenge of the constant, rolling hills. I frequently stopped and referred to the map to gauge the distance to the next town. I then focused my attention on getting there. I substituted my 10-mile-increment GPS check-in with a map game. Towns are much closer together in Missouri than in Colorado and Kansas.

At about 9:00 a.m., pedaling east on Highway 126 (US Bike Route 76), I stopped when I saw a "Kansas City" sign at Highway 126 and Highway 71. I reflected on when I'd attended the Combined Arms Staff Service School at Fort Leavenworth, Kansas, near Kansas City, in 1989. At the time, I was still contemplating making the military a career. The school intended to develop junior military officers to take on more responsibility and lead larger units of soldiers. It was a melting pot, the United States Army bringing together like-minded men and women from all service branches for several weeks of intense coursework. There was some fun mixed in as well, especially on the weekends. I met some good people and became excellent friends with an Irishman named Neil Hyland. He spent the better part of several weeks trying to set me up with his sister! After graduating, we all returned to our permanent assignments, never to see each other again. When I heard about the terrorist attack on 9/11, I scrolled through the names of those killed at the Pentagon, and when I saw LTC Stephen Neil Hyland's name, my stomach dropped. I hoped it wasn't my friend, but when I saw a picture of Neil, it hit me that this was real. Years later, my family visited the National September 11 Memorial Museum. In one gallery are pictures of those who lost their lives. I scrolled through the names and listened to Neil through a phone bank that had captured the voices of all who perished. Hyland was the planner, the organizer, always bringing people together for a good time. When I heard his voice again, I immediately thought of the weekends he arranged for about a dozen junior officers to go "downrange" to the bars in Kansas City for a weekend full of fun (and a little drinking). In 1989, that car ride from Fort Ord, California, to Fort Leavenworth, Kansas, on isolated, never-ending roads tested me. Now, to have gotten this far on a bike seemed surreal.

I noticed a red pickup truck traveling west on US Bike Route 76, also known as State Route V. It was a little after 1:00 p.m., and I was seven miles outside Ash Grove (population 1,477). The truck slowed down shortly before reaching my location. Someone leaned out of the driver's side window and asked, "Are you Larry?" I had stopped cycling and straddled my bike at this point. The truck came to a complete stop in the middle of the road.

"Yes, how'd you know?" I replied. Ray and his sidekick, Joey, were the first dot watchers (and trail angels) who met me on the road. Ray turned his truck and followed me to Pennington's Supermarket in Ash Grove. I hopped off Tank underneath an awning next to the store entrance.

Ray, a local rancher, offered me Gatorade, beef jerky, and protein bars. I appreciated the food and drink almost as much as the much-desired human communication. Joey, a seventh grader and family friend (with his pet frog), told me about meeting Lea a few days earlier. Lea, the first female to finish the race, who had completed it in a little over 21 days, asked Joey if she could take the frog with her. Joey responded, "No," adding, "I don't want to give away my new pet frog!" I imagine Lea had been joking, because she certainly wouldn't have wanted to carry the extra ounce.

Standing outside the store with Ray and Joey, I thought about the many instances in which I chose not to interact with strangers I saw. I thought about the Southern Tier. What made that ride so unique were the stories I could tell after meeting interesting people on the road. My meeting Ray and Joey impacted how I interacted with strangers for the rest of the race. From Missouri to the monument, I welcomed many more encounters with trail angels, and some of the most memorable interactions with locals occurred during the last 1,000 miles of the journey.

The human connection I had lived without as I rode through Montana, Wyoming, Colorado, and Kansas would return and fuel my soul to push on. Ray asked a couple of the most common questions I got when meeting noncyclists on the road: *How are you feeling? How has the weather been?* Ray invited me to stay at the local bike hostel. However, at 2:00 p.m., it was way too early to stop. After an enjoyable 30 minutes, Tank and I were on our way.

I set out from Ash Grove, heading for Marshfield (population 6,686), 50 miles east. I called ahead to the Marshfield RV Express 66, in the heart of the Ozarks, located off Interstate 44 between St. Louis and Joplin. Deb, the park manager, answered the phone with abundant enthusiasm. We carried on a five-minute conversation about the race, our families, and riding through the Ozarks. It was as if we were close friends catching up on old times. She had a place set aside for me to pitch my tent and told me she would keep the office open until I arrived. The people I encountered at motels and RV parks went out of their way to make cyclists feel right at home.

Two miles north of Ash Grove, I passed by the Nathan Boone Homestead State Historic Site. Nathan Boone was American pioneer Daniel Boone's youngest son and a veteran of the War of 1812. At 7:30 p.m., 30 minutes after its closing time, I reached the RV park. Deb's husband, Doug, was a jolly older man; his long, silvery beard and full face gave off a good vibe. Deb welcomed me with the same Missouri grace I had received in Ash Grove. The RV park, located next to the interstate at a busy intersection, was surrounded by stores, restaurants, and other business establishments. The unusual location was much different than the typical RV park removed from the bustle amid a more natural environment surrounded by towering trees. Cars filled the parking lot behind the RV park and near KFC. Deb told me to pitch my tent on the grassy area behind the office, next to a community pool. She gave me the access code to the laundry room and bathroom. I was curious, so I asked, "Are you the owner?"

"No, the owner is a young woman. I'm the manager," she replied. She told me the woman's dad purchased the RV park and gave control to his daughter, saying, "Here you go, it's your business now."

That's one approach to guiding your kids, I thought.

I could tell right away Deb and Doug enjoyed meeting new people. She shared a story of meeting a fellow racer a few days before. The guy hadn't carried a sleeping bag. Deb drove home to fetch a sleeping bag, returned, and gave it to the racer for the night he stayed at their RV park. Now that's five-star customer service!

My right knee was tender, which I assumed arose from the hard ride to Girard the day before. After walking back from KFC, where I'd devoured two three-piece crispy, dark meat meals, I crawled inside my tent, snuggled inside my sleeping bag, and reflected on the choices I had made since leaving Astoria. I had feared rigorous cycling on consecutive days could cause knee tendinitis. Flare-ups had caused discomfort during the first few days but had not been a problem recently. Remaining disciplined and following my race plan permitted my body to recover with proper rest every night. My butt continued to cause discomfort; it was tender to the touch and occasionally emitted a sharp, stinging sensation. I had figured out the most comfortable position for my bottom through trial and error, but on occasion, when my cycling shorts slipped, the pain intensity skyrocketed. The fact that my lower back and neck did not bring about discomfort had been a psychological booster. I had learned to adapt to constant numbness in both feet and in fingertips on both hands. When the day ended, I had climbed 5,200 feet, almost the highest single-day climb since the Rocky Mountains.

Chapter 29
MARSHFIELD–EMINENCE, MISSOURI (108 MILES)

June 28, 2019

A t 7:24 a.m., I took off from the RV park after a fantastic night's sleep, eager to start the day. The string of intense and unpredictable elevation shifts of the Ozarks—as sudden and sharp as a row of fang-like teeth—were sure to pose a tremendous challenge. After 25 miles and three hours, I reached Hartville (population 606). It was time for another post office pit stop to ship home nonessential equipment. Carrying that extra three-ounce pair of wool socks wouldn't slow me down, but that wasn't the point—I needed to complete a task. It was another notch on my way to Yorktown.

I leaned Tank next to the post office's front door and stepped inside the small lobby. The clerk entered the shipping information into the old desktop computer. She handed me the shipping invoice when the familiar printing sound ended. I stepped to my left, slid my card into my wallet, and turned to exit. As I was leaving, my eyes met those of several adults waiting in line behind me. I overheard chitchat about something "not working." The computer had stopped functioning after my transaction. Glancing at the locals as I walked to the exit, I said, "Sorry, have a great day." Those were the only words I could think of, and they sheepishly passed through my lips.

A solo cyclist heading west had stopped at the Double Eagle Convenience Store on Main Street. He complimented me on the amount of reflective tape, quality, and quantity of rear and front lights, impressed by the safety features I had rigged on Tank. I noticed a similar effort on his bike, with one noticeable difference. He had secured a neon yellow Styrofoam tube that protruded about three feet from the left side of his bike—an extra safety measure. The theory was that a motorist not paying attention would strike the tube, stunning the driver and averting them from, swerving onto the shoulder.

Missouri roads are nicely paved. However, it was a risky situation when trucks thundered past, because there was no shoulder to ride on. The locals see cyclists frequently and slow, yield to oncoming traffic, or stop to ensure a safe cycling experience. The jackhammer sound of a truck approaching from behind alerted me, giving me enough time to tighten my grip for the crosswind that would hit soon after the truck passed by.

At 1:42 p.m., near Houston (population 2,084), on SR 17, I stopped to scan the surrounding landscape. I could see green, rolling hills for miles. The elevation profile indicated I had reached the highest elevation point of the Ozarks. I felt I could reach Eminence (population 590), which was 45 miles away, before sundown. I made a reservation at the Shady Lane Cabins & Motel in Eminence, the "Canoeing Capital of the World."[85]

A road sign announcing I had entered the Ozark National Scenic Riverways should have awakened me to prepare for a roller-coaster ride through the narrow canyons on Highway 106. After a taxing climb, I let loose and increased my speed on a downhill. I had hoped my momentum would thrust me up the next incline, a rhythm I had

---

[85] "Canoeing," Visit Eminence, accessed July 12, 2022, https://visiteminence.com/area-attractions/canoeing/

attempted unsuccessfully on countless hills since I entered the Ozarks 100 miles earlier. I was swerving through twists and turns, unconcerned about oncoming vehicles. I hit 41 mph. At that speed, riding over a pothole or slipping on wet pavement would cause me to lose control and thoroughly ruin my day. But I maintained the pace because it was exhilarating to weave through the canyons, wind blowing as I sped down the mountain. As I neared a bend, I saw a small puddle of water on the asphalt surface. The overhanging trees nearby had cast a shadow that prevented me from seeing it sooner. I tried to slow down, but the damp road reduced the disc brakes efficacy. The rear tire slid to the right, and I lost control of Tank for a couple of seconds. My forearms were fatigued. Clutching the brakes was tough to do. The combination of worn pads and slippery roads created precarious riding conditions. After a harrowing few seconds (which seemed much longer), I regained control and continued riding at a much slower pace.

At 7:00 p.m., I made it to Main Street and SR 106 in Eminence. I called the Shady Lane Cabins to inquire if I should turn left or right. I knew the lodge was close by, but I didn't want to ride in the wrong direction. There were a lot of hills, and by this point, I was *done* with hills. *No bonus miles today.* I ended up guessing and made a left turn after waiting on hold for a couple of minutes without anyone answering. After I crossed a bridge over the Jacks Fork River, I saw the Shady Lane Cabin & Motel on the left side of the road.

A motel sign dangled from the side of a building, which resembled a warehouse. I spotted a placard hanging from the opposite side of the building, where cars were parked out front. "Shady Lane Cabins Office" was painted on the outside of a large, rectangular window. A smaller announcement advertised a color TV, an air conditioner, and a laundromat for guests.

I introduced myself to the front desk manager and immediately talked about the challenging ride to get to Eminence. "I'm looking forward to riding on less hilly roads east of Eminence."

She snickered and said the highways east of town would make today's ride "feel like a walk in the park!" She recommended getting an early start the next day to avoid busses carrying visitors to Fort River, the starting point for daily canoe trips.

Morning After a Restless Sleep
Eminence, Missouri
June 29, 2019

Chapter 30

EMINENCE, MISSOURI– CHESTER, ILLINOIS (134 MILES)

June 29, 2019

A fog clouded my mind when I opened my eyes and lifted my head off the pillow. I had not had a good night of sleep. A group of young adults stayed in the room next to mine. I could hear chatter through the thin walls late into the evening. Liquor played a part in all the commotion. My thoughts drifted from one thing to the other, trying to get myself focused on the day ahead. Lying in bed, I checked the leaders' board and read Facebook posts to engage my mind, hoping to eliminate the brain fog from a restless night.

I had all the encouragement I needed after reading one racer's summary after he'd finished:

I finally made it! Hardest thing I have ever attempted in my life, an absolutely crazy "over the top" adventure with so many unpredictable and incredible twists and turns. 26 days, 9 hours, 44 minutes. To all of the racers I met along the way, it is so wonderful to be part of such an amazing family! Last but not least, the dot watchers who met me on the side of the road, you are what make ultra-races worth it. To all my family, friends, and supporters who either commented on my posts or sent me private messages, you gave me the lift I needed when things were looking dire and daunting. Thank you all from the bottom of my heart.

I walked outside at 6:30 a.m. with Tank by my side, ready to start the day. Two partiers from the room next door reminded me of my college days after a night at a 10-keg fraternity party. Their slow gait and vacant facial expressions were two indications that they were in worse shape than I was—and here they were, outside early to catch a bus to the canoeing start point to put their stomachs to the test with the erratic motion they would encounter on the level-three rapids.

I left at 6:44 a.m. to beat the 7:00 a.m. buses. The first few miles were uneventful, peaceful. The morning calm was only interrupted by the occasional rustling sound from the wood line. It was foggy and muggy, and heavy dew created wet spots on the asphalt highway. The sun struggled to peep out above the blanket of fog.

At 7:17 a.m., the rising sun's haze appeared behind a coat of fog. Yellow and milky clouds created an orange halo on the outlying fringes of the rising sun. At 7:27 a.m., when I reached the top of the undulating hills of the Ozark Mountains, the bright, yellow sun peeked through in all its vibrancy behind the blanket of haze. Two streaks of sunlight pierced through the fog and brought the dawn to life. The streaks of light angled toward the ground like a stairway to heaven on my right. At 8:26 a.m., the transformation was complete—a clear, blue sky sprawled out before me. The elevated temperature (in the high seventies), humidity, and physical exertion combined to soak my body with sweat. Dead raccoons and armadillos scattered the shoulder. Occasionally, a dead snake added to the collection of roadkill on US Highway 76 in Missouri. (I saw more roadkill in Missouri than in any other state.)

Nestled in the Ozark Mountains near Centerville (population 191), I stopped at a Trail of Tears road sign. During the 1830s to 1850s, the US

Government ordered several tribes—including the Cherokee, Seminole, Chickasaw, and Choctaw—from their motherlands in Georgia, Alabama, North Carolina, and Tennessee. These forced relocations to the new Indian Territory in present-day Oklahoma became known as the Trail of Tears.[86] A 31-mile passage of the original route traverses through this area.

I reflected on our nation's history as I rode along the same places where generations of Native Americans lived. Cycling coast-to-coast was a time to test me, but it also became a time to contemplate. Events that occurred hundreds of years ago are footnotes in history. When I was young, I assumed books written by mere mortals accurately reflected past events, but I had it all backward. Instead, we should make sure books are written according to reality. What did historians do with the facts on the ground at the time? Were there two entirely different versions of reality—what we see today, and the truth that is somewhere between? It's often said victors write history. We are a collection of experiences, knowledge, and prejudices from earlier generations that have been passed down and retold again and again. And what about the stories of the past? Why should we care? Because history is bound to repeat itself. And that alone is reason to search out the past, to understand better who we are as a nation. On a bicycle, seeing these things with my own eyes, I brought back a more profound understanding of tying our past to our present.

I had crossed through many Native American lands, home to Indian tribes romanticized in TV programs and films. Whether the Shoshone, who were distinguished for their affiliation to the Lewis and Clark Expedition, the Comanches, with their notorious surprise raids in Colorado, or the many tribes who feared the Sioux, my passion for understanding this facet of our nation's past grew. The allure of the road and seeing America motivated me to continue riding for a deeper reason than finishing the race.

---

[86] "Trail of Tears," History, updated July 7, 2020, https://www.history.com/topics/native-american-history/trail-of-tears

The appeal grew the more I pedaled, and I realized I was on the cusp of finishing something very few others have been able to. On US Bike Route 76, west of Pilot Knob (population 725), I looked up and saw two cyclists pedaling toward me on the opposite side of the highway. I assumed they would stop because this section of the road was flat. I desired human communication. I slowed down, lifted my left hand, and waved at the approaching cyclists. I yelled, "Hello!" and thought it odd I didn't get a reply. Nothing surrounded us except for the blue sky and woods. I continued looking at them as they passed by me. One of the cyclists stopped and crossed the highway to greet me. The second cyclist also stopped but didn't join his friend. We shook hands. He turned his upper torso around to show me the back of his cycling jersey. "Baer and Blake Across America" was written over an image of a tire and spokes. Underneath the tire, the words "American Society for Deaf Children" revealed why he hadn't said anything. The two deaf cyclists rode across America to raise awareness and money for the American Society for Deaf Children. The only thing I could think of at the moment was to raise my right hand and express my appreciation for their endeavor with a thumbs-up gesture. I looked across the road at the second cyclist. He had witnessed my interaction with his riding buddy. I raised my arm higher and nodded my head while conveying my admiration for their journey. After I took a picture to document this moment, they continued their trek west. (As of November 18, 2019, Conrad and Albert had raised over $27,000! The Adventure Cycling Association magazine published an inspiring article about their cross-country ride in their Aug/Sept 2020 edition.)

A cyclist going in the opposite direction crossed over Highway 221 when he saw me approach a busy intersection on the west side of Farmington (population 17,203). This time, I knew right away he was a dot watcher. "Are you Larry?" he asked.

"Yes," I replied, as we shook hands. Wayne told me he'd greeted racers ever since they began barreling through town in 2014. "I haven't missed a year," he said, adding, "A local guy from Farmington scratched a few days before."

Each time I heard the news about someone dropping out of the race, a feeling of accomplishment overwhelmed me. I was still in this thing! Some racers were on their second or third attempt.

He offered for me to stay at the local bike hostel, but it was once again too early to stop. I looked at the map to figure out where to ride to before darkness set in. Chester, Illinois, 44 miles farther east, seemed doable. I also had a backup plan: a Residency Inn & Suites 0.9 mile off route in Ozora, 25 miles east of Farmington.

Wayne asked if he could ride with me out of town for a few miles. "Of course!" I replied, happy to have a riding partner, albeit for only a short distance.

Wayne made me laugh when he said, "I will try to keep pace with you."

I quipped, "I think it might be the other way around!"

Just because I'm racing doesn't mean I am a racer. One of about a dozen still pedaling to the finish, I had set out to test myself to meet this challenge. I had successfully crossed the country once. I knew what it took, physically and mentally. If I remained disciplined and focused, taking one day at a time in 10-mile increments, the thrill of victory, my success in the struggle against the odds, would possibly satisfy my appetite for adventure. I had locked into that magic number of "less than forty" and had put myself in a dominant position. Less than *forty to finish*—an unthinkable goal in Astoria—was my endgame.

When we left the hustle and bustle of downtown Farmington, I rode at a pace of 12 miles per hour. Initially, we rode side by side. "Go faster if I'm holding you back," I said, sensing he wanted to increase the pace. Before I knew it, Wayne was several hundred yards in front of me. "Told you so," I mumbled to myself. I reflected on Dayville, Oregon, when three adults reminded me that I too was in the race. Here I was, pedaling through Missouri on a Saturday afternoon, akin to a leisurely ride through my hometown of Mendham, New Jersey. Not for the first time, I reflected on the parallel universe of cycling across America.

According to Wayne, the road was a favorite of local cyclists. The paved, two-lane country road traversed well-kept homesteads. I didn't see a single vehicle pass in either direction for a several-mile stretch. He led the way for the 15 miles to the intersection of Highway B and Highway P, near River aux Vases, waiting patiently for five minutes until I arrived. When I was about 20 feet away, I grinned and yelled, "See? I was right! You had no problem keeping up with me, did you?" Wayne asked to lift my bike so he could gauge Tank's weight. I hopped off Tank and said, "Here you go. All yours!" He looked at me with a startled expression when he grabbed the bike frame and lifted it off the ground. "That's why I call it Tank," I deadpanned. "Be on the lookout for Adam. He should reach Farmington in a couple of days," I told Wayne. "He might take you up on the offer to stay at the hostel." It was close to 6:00 p.m. when Wayne turned around and headed back to Farmington. My water supply had run low. *Only six miles to Ozora*, I thought. I called the Regency Inn & Suites in Ozora. I hung up when no one answered after the phone rang several times. *Oh well. I'll call again when I get closer to town.*

Riding through the Ozarks' constant, rolling hills was the reason for poor cell service. About two miles farther east, I called the Ozora motel again. Same result—no answer. A couple of miles later, I tried again. Still no response after several rings. I reached the road junction, at which point I had a decision to make: ride off route to the Regency Inn & Suites or continue to an unknown destination. This time, I called information to confirm the number. When I heard, "Sorry, sir, the motel is no longer in business," my spirits sank.

I was almost out of water, and the next service was located 19 miles east and across the Mississippi River in Chester (population 8,480), Illinois. The time was now 7:00 p.m., and darkness loomed in the Ozarks. Day turns to night on a dime, the mountains robbing the eyes of a beautiful sunset. My proverbial antenna raised, I searched for water, riding ever so slowly. At another intersection, I stopped again to reassess my situation. I would have gladly stopped if I saw a park or other public rest stop. The only option was to reach Chester, still several miles away.

A cyclist stopped when he saw me looking at my map. "Where are you trying to get to?" he asked.

"Thanks for stopping. Is there any place to get water before Chester?" I asked, anticipating good news.

But he merely shook his head and said, "No, Chester is the next closest city with services."

Right away, I experienced anxiety akin to my time in Jeffrey City, Wyoming. My stomach churned. The elevated humidity, absence of calorie intake, being near the 100-mile marker, and hearing the word no, drained what little energy I had left.

And then, I thought about the prerace orientation meeting. Nathan had told the group that crossing the Mississippi River near Chester was not possible because of heavy spring flooding. A couple of days before I'd reached Farmington, someone had posted that the primary route over the Mississippi River into Chester, Illinois, was now passable. Reportedly, the water had subsided. I would find out soon enough if the information was accurate.

I grew tired, plodding slowly toward Chester, hardly able to bring to bear a clear-eyed assessment of my reality. It was as though the gloom of my circumstances dulled my vision. I lifted my head, which had been drooping over my handlebars, and saw an elderly lady standing on the grass underneath a tree, appearing to be doing yard work on the side of a ranch-style home. When I reached the driveway, she stopped what she was doing and stared at me. "Pardon me. Is there a place I can fill my water bottles?" I asked. "I didn't plan very well. I'm out of water."

The lady seemed reluctant to engage. After a few seconds, which seemed much longer, she pointed to the back of the house. "You can use the water spigot."

"Thank you!" I practically bellowed. A trail angel if there ever was one!

Dusk turned to darkness as I plunged through a canyon into a valley, the Ozarks now behind me. I had successfully navigated through 300 miles of rugged, never-ending hills. As I rode the 12 miles to the Mississippi River basin, I recall thinking the Ozarks were more challenging to climb than the Cascades, Bitterroots, and Rocky Mountains. But now my attention turned east and to the several reports from cyclists who had already finished who declared the Appalachian Mountains, *not* the Ozarks, were the most strenuous.

That 12-mile, flat stretch was the longest I had ridden in over 350 miles. This marshland had been entirely underwater until a few days before. A sparkle of light in the distance caught my attention as I turned north on SR 51 and began the last five-mile trek to the Mississippi River bridge crossing. Armies of bugs filled the air, battering me incessantly. Eighteen-wheelers sped by, forcing me to the shoulder. I was compelled to ride over road debris on the shoulder because I didn't feel safe swerving into the traffic lane. I hunkered down and pedaled straight ahead. Known as Horse Island on the west bank of the Mississippi River, Lewis and Clark camped in this vicinity on November 28, 1803[87] (the site of present-day Fort Kaskaskia State Historic Site).

I was genuinely concerned about being struck by a truck, even though I was lit up like a Christmas tree with my blinking, red rear lights and bright, white lights beaming from front and back. Riding through the darkness—the thing I had avoided for 27 nights—had finally presented itself. It was pitch-black when I reached the Chester Bridge over the Mississippi River and entered Chester, Illinois.

When I crossed the bridge at 9:00 p.m., I felt simultaneously satisfied and concerned to have made it to Chester, with six miles to go before reaching the Best Western Hotel on State Street. I stopped at the Segar Memorial Park and Welcome Center next to the Mississippi River. A massive, six-foot, 900-pound, lit-up, bronze statue of Popeye was the focal point in a small courtyard next to the welcome center. Chester,

---

[87] Ambrose, *Undaunted Courage*, 122

Illinois—home to Elzie C. Segar, the real-life creator of Popeye—is proud of its association with this iconic cartoon character. A white floodlight projected from the ground lit a "Welcome to Chester–Home of Popeye" sign next to an etching of Popeye holding a pouch of tobacco in his left hand, with his right extended to welcome folks to Illinois. The bottom section of the welcome sign listed the names of 12 churches, all different denominations.

My GPS directed me to swing south and off the main road to Highway 3 shortly after leaving the welcome center. I didn't want to ride farther in the darkness, so I continued on SR 150, full of lit-up buildings and streetlights. According to the Adventure Cycling map, the hotel was located on Country Farm Road at an intersection with SR 150. Following my instinct turned out to be a wise decision once again. Finally reaching the hotel, I walked through the sliding glass door with Tank by my side. The front desk manager greeted me with a friendly smile and said, "Welcome. I've been waiting for you to arrive." I was weak, disheveled, worn out, and happy to be there. My appearance didn't faze the woman at all. She had seen many cross-country cyclists riding through town; I was not a novelty like I had been when riding with four fully packed panniers in my hometown. I told the front desk manager about my GPS guiding me to Highway 3. She told me Highway 3 was still underwater and not passable by car. Even though large swaths of the Midwestern flooding had receded, water still remained on side roads.

While lying on the bed, preparing for the next day's ride, I tallied up the miles and feet I had climbed thus far: 134 miles and 8,300 feet of climbing in 13.5 hours! I crushed the Ozarks, finished riding through the seventh state, and retired map section #9. Only three states to go! After four weeks, I had ridden 3,004 miles. Before the Rockies, I knew the best chance I had to achieve my 40-day goal would be riding well through the Great Plains. The flat states were the best chance to make up for the 10 sub-century days. The number "125.8" lit up on my iPhone calculator. "Oh my God!" I had not only made up the difference, but I had achieved something that would have seemed wildly impractical just a month earlier. The first week, I averaged 99.4 miles per day, the second week 101 miles, the third week 102.8 miles, and the fourth week 125.8 miles per day to round out my first month on the saddle.

I checked the leaders' board and saw Michael's post announcing he was scratching. Roger and I met Michael on the bus ride from Portland to Astoria on May 30. He'd been so full of energy, ready to tackle a dream after training for over a year. With less than 1000 miles to go, he must have been heartbroken to share the news.

> *TABR 2019 has been awesome. I have had an amazing journey and met some amazing people and riders. I would like to thank everyone who has checked in on me. I have officially pulled from the TABR. The bruising on my side has not gone down and after being hit for the second time during this race, I do not want there to be a third. I have had an amazing journey, and I can always finish the last leg at a different time. Again, thanks for all the support and encouragement.*—Michael, June 29

Chapter 31

CHESTER–ELIZABETHTOWN, ILLINOIS (123 MILES)
June 30, 2019

I took off from the Best Western under pleasant skies. At 8:06 a.m., with Yorktown on my mind, I set out, unaware the hills in Southern Illinois would test my physical and mental toughness more than I'd ever imagined. Had I scrutinized the map elevation profile, I would have noticed the sharp peaks of the Little Ozarks. I stopped at Commercial Ave and 20th Street in Murphysboro (population 7,894) and felt sure I could reach Goreville (population 1,080), 38 miles ahead, before dark.

Other considerations were Eddyville (population 153), about 40 miles away, and Elizabethtown (population 306), on the Ohio River across from the Kentucky border, 50 miles east of Goreville. I called the River Rose Inn Bed & Breakfast in Elizabethtown to inquire about room availability as a backup plan.

Somewhere north of Goreville, the GPS instructed me to veer right at a fork instead of continuing on Crab Orchard Lake Road. I followed my gut again—only this time, I shouldn't have. I second-guessed my decision after about half a mile on a steep downhill, but at this point, there was no turning back. Two miles later, and finally at the bottom, I stopped at an intersection to gather myself. It took me a minute to realize I had made a mistake and should have followed the GPS. I relied on dead reckoning to find my way back to the primary route that would guide me to Elizabethtown. *I missed Goreville.* I began riding on a country road with waves of slopes traversing the agricultural countryside. Blind driveway warning signs for approaching vehicles dotted the road shoulder. The newly resurfaced black asphalt road absorbed direct sunlight, raising the road temperature. The freshly laid tar stuck to my tires, and my lower body felt the heat emanating from the ground. The sauna-like conditions drained my energy. Every completed tire revolution was more challenging than the previous one. The scorching heat made the road melt in some places. I was annoyed at myself, and it felt as though Tank was moving through a bed of glue.

I saw a road sign for Eddyville six miles ahead. It was 6:23 p.m. If I pressed, I could reach Elizabethtown around 9:00 p.m., 45 minutes after sunset. I had less than two hours to ride 23 miles to avoid cycling in the dark. The sun had shone all day, but rain was forecasted surrounding Elizabethtown later that night. At 8:04 p.m., when I turned north on SR 146, I saw the sun dropping behind menacing-looking clouds in the direction I was riding. An orange line appeared on the horizon, and a bright yellow and white ball sent streaks of light in all directions. Initially, I didn't see the lightning due to the cloud cover, but then I heard the long, low rumble of thunder. The thunderclap didn't follow, so I assumed the worst of the storm was miles away. At 8:20 p.m., the slight breeze turned to gusts. I glanced at my GPS. Five miles to Elizabethtown. I was relieved. Great news!

Each subsequent sound of thunder grew louder. Branches and leaves from the surrounding wood line blew across the road. I pedaled harder, trying to reach Elizabethtown before the skies opened up, all the while concerned about slipping on wet leaves, hitting a pothole, or flying debris hitting my tire spokes. My bike lights created a beacon for traffic approaching from both directions. My GPS notified me that there was only one mile to Elizabethtown. "Finally there!" I said. Then, I saw a road sign: "Elizabethtown: 6 miles." *What the heck is going on?!*

I'd spent countless hours figuring out suitable towns to start and end each day when I created the original 54-day route. I had done an excellent job selecting where and when to ride each day. I subdivided the 4,200-mile route into 54 segments using the Ride with GPS app. I played around with various start and ending towns through trial and error, ultimately feeling good about my plan. When my GPS indicated I had reached Elizabethtown in the middle of a highway in darkness, howling wind, and rain buffeting my body, I became concerned. Now stopped on Highway 146, at a random location besieged by howling winds and torrential rain, I had a sinking feeling. The following five miles would once again test my limits.

At 8:50 p.m., at the edge of town, I saw lights on inside the Family Package Store on Highway 146. A car parked outside was a sign the store was still open. The worst of the downpour had passed southeast of Elizabethtown. I leaned Tank against the store's front window and put my headband and riding gloves inside my helmet, which I hung from the handlebar. I pulled my wallet out and entered the store, walking straight for the refrigerated section, where I grabbed a packet of turkey loaf lunch meat for dinner and resupplied my pogey bait for the next day's ride. I hustled to the front counter to pay. I tried calling the Shady Rest Cabin using my iPhone, but the cell service was poor, so I asked the front counter attendant if I could use the store's landline. A woman answered; I realized it was the same person who had taken my reservation and instructed me to call when I made it to town. She told me the cabin was "down the street and around the corner," that it was "easy to find." It was pitch-black outside. The worst of the storm was no longer a threat, but the rain continued to fall. I wasn't confident in finding the cabin on my own. I wanted to shower, eat, and sleep. And indeed, I did not want to ride aimlessly searching in the dark of night.

"Hi, I'm Larry. Do you know where the Shady Rest Cabin is?" I asked a young woman who was also shopping.

"Hi, I'm Kennedy. It's just around the corner," she said, waving an arm toward the back side of the store. "I can drive by and lead you to the cabin if you want. It's not out of the way."

"Thanks, I really appreciate it," I replied. With my dinner and breakfast items tucked away inside a plastic bag, I walked outside with the young woman and waited for her to reach her car. I saw a child buckled into a car seat. I walked closer to the car and said, "Can you excuse me for a minute? I forgot something in the store." I hurried in, hoping they were still open. I walked up to the front counter and asked the clerk, "Excuse me, do you know Kennedy? I'd like to buy her baby something to express my gratitude. Any suggestions?" He shrugged his shoulders, indicating he didn't know the woman, but suggested juice boxes. *Don't all kids love juice boxes? I know my kids did*, I thought. So that's what I bought for Kennedy's child.

I trailed Kennedy's car onto Highway 146 and immediately turned onto dimly lit Main Street off the beaten path. This town of 306 had gone quiet for the night. I couldn't see anything in front of me. Kennedy stopped her car, a signal that I had reached my destination. I hopped off Tank and walked up to the driver's side window. "Thanks so much," I said with gratitude.

She pointed down a dark, dirt path and said, "The cabin should be down there a little way, on the left side."

I said goodbye and then began walking with Tank by my side until I could see the outline of a small cabin to my left. I reached up to open a box that hung on the outside wall next to the front entrance. The woman I'd talked to earlier told me I would find the key there. I grew frustrated because I couldn't figure out how to open the box that housed the key. I had this feeling that the solution to open the box was simple, but at that point, I didn't have the patience or the energetic wherewithal to deal with it. I wanted to be inside that cabin and needed help to get inside. I called the Shady Rest Cabin and was told, "I'll send someone to meet you at the door." About 10 minutes later, a man appeared in front of me, holding a flashlight. He must have lived in one of the tiny houses lined up on the dirt path near the cabin. He turned a knob. The box opened with relative ease, and he handed me the key. I was embarrassed. The brain fog I experienced made it difficult to concentrate. I had lost my ability to think clearly. I apologized for troubling him. If the man was annoyed, he certainly didn't show it. "No problem. That's why I'm here," he replied, without a bit of sarcasm in his voice.

Located on the banks of the Ohio River, the cabin didn't look like much from the outside. I opened the front door and immediately sensed the warm, cozy, and comfortable inside of a mountain setting. This cabin had a backwoods feel and the main living room was decorated with relics. A wall hanging highlighted the colorful 1920s in Southern Illinois. "The Warring Twenties in Southern Illinois" was written above an image of the Birger Gang holding tommy guns and pistols. The picture taken of the front of the cabin, known as Shady Rest, in October 1926, brought the place to life. It had all the ambiance and ingredients that gave me a view into the past. Bootlegger and gang leader Charles Birger built Shady Rest, which had operated as a fortified speakeasy.

The inside had amenities, a washer, dryer, and television. I ate the turkey loaf, did a load of laundry, and then repeated the same routine I had done for four weeks preparing for the next day's ride. Thinking it would be a breeze cycling through Illinois, I had taken this state for granted. For the first time since the night I camped at Madison Campground in Wyoming on June 14, I logged thoughts, feelings, and observations into my yellow journal. Lying on a bed inside the Shady Rest Cabin, I reflected on my time in Illinois, recording:

- *Brutal hills*
- *Illinois, heavy air—no momentum*
- *Took for granted*
- *(Drank) water all the time*
- *Bike squeaky*
- *Adventure—storm, wind, nighttime*
- *Kennedy escorted me*

- *123 miles / 6,000 ft*
- *Start day—good*
- *Muscled my way through*
- *Got lost*
- *Tar on tire*
- *Yelled at bike*

Chapter 32
ELIZABETHTOWN, ILLINOIS–FALLS OF ROUGH, KENTUCKY (134 MILES)

July 1, 2019

At 7:17 a.m., I began the short, nine-mile ride to Cave-in-Rock (population 312), where the ferry would carry me across the Ohio River to the Kentucky border. *The last mountain range, the Appalachians, and then Yorktown. Then the race will be over.* That's what I thought about on Tower Rock Road, hemmed in by the dwellers of the thicket only stirred by the rising sun. Tower Rock Road turned into Clay Street, and after a quick right onto Canal Street, the ferry dock appeared 200 yards straight ahead at the end of the sloping, asphalt road.

As I struggled up a sharp incline, out of nowhere, a small, white dog raised from a prone position and began barking incessantly, charging right at me. I had no chance to protect myself as he lunged at my right ankle and bit. I stared down and wailed, "Go home!" The dog backed away, its upper lip exposing its fangs, and growled. My cleats had remained connected to the pedals during the first attack. With no time to retrieve the dog spray, I twisted my right shoe to free the cleat from the pedal and kicked the dog with my free leg when it lunged at my ankle for a second time. I had to be aggressive at this point. The dog retreated to the owner's lawn when I reached the property boundary. The entire ordeal seemed like it lasted longer than the few seconds it actually did.

A red Toyota Rav4 with a Kentucky license plate and a white Ford 150 pickup truck were parked on the Loni Jo ferry—a 42-foot carrier run by the Illinois Department of Transportation—waiting for it to depart at 9:00 a.m. It was perfect timing, as I rode onto the ferry platform at 8:50 a.m. *Only two more states to go.* That close contact with the small dog was a wake-up call that I was about to enter the region of the country notorious for attack dogs. The free ferry service ran every 15 minutes, crossing the 300-yard width of the Ohio River. It is large enough to carry pedestrians, cyclists, and a maximum of three automobiles. I leaned Tank against a side railing and waited for the ferry to take off. I expected to see blood when I looked at my foot and ankle area, but I didn't. The dog's bite tore a small hole in the sock. I looked closer and noticed the dog had scratched away a patch of skin on my ankle bone, but that was it though. I was lucky.

I sent a text to Adam: "Hey, be on the lookout for an aggressive dog when you enter Cave-in-Rock. It surprised the hell out of me shortly after turning onto Canal Street."

Adam responded, thanking me for the heads-up. A couple of days later, when I was close to Berea (population 14,749), Adam sent a text telling me he "took care of business" and that "the dog will have second thoughts next time a cyclist rides through town." I didn't ask what he meant, but I inferred some dog repellent had worked well.

A dog bite has the potential to cause serious injury. Dogs home in on anything that rotates—ankles, pedals, tires. The prospect of stumbling off my bike—which could cause both physical and mechanical damage— weighed heavily on my mind. I was about to find out if Kentucky lived up to its reputation as the state on the TransAmerica Bike Trail with the most dog encounters. I situated the dog horn on the outside of my handlebar bag and attached one of the bear spray canisters to the CamelBak shoulder strap. Would a dog mishap, instead of a vehicle collision, cause me to scratch?

At some point soon, I would begin riding through the Appalachian Mountains. Steep grades, narrow roads, repeated ups and downs, high temperatures, and elevated humidity led to my uneasiness. Crossing the final mountain range, culminating with the climb up Mount Vesuvius—the most difficult 3-mile stretch of the entire 4,200-mile race—would test my fortitude.

The Appalachian Mountains span a considerable chunk of the eastern United States—but not the western edge of Kentucky. Had I paid closer attention to the map section #9, I would have realized the gateway to the Appalachian Mountains was still 300 miles farther east from where I entered Kentucky in Crittenden County. I rode through Marion (population 3,025), Clay (population 1,180), and Dixon (population 608) waiting to see the big mountains reveal themselves in all their glory. When I reached the top of a hill, I wondered if this was it. Had I entered the Appalachians? The picturesque, white-picket-fence homesteads dotted the Western Kentucky landscape, a far cry from the hollers that made up the eastern section of Kentucky, where the "hillbillies" lived. The fences separated multi-acre plots, where lawn mowers moved about on this quiet Monday morning, the owners sprucing their properties for the big Independence Day celebration just ahead. *Where are the mountains? And what about those aggressive dogs?* I thought, as I cycled through Western Kentucky, which started as a puzzling but enjoyable cycling experience. For whatever reason, I'd thought dogs would start attacking the moment I set foot in Kentucky.

Riding on the quiet country roads through Western Kentucky, I reclaimed my sense of adventure. For several days, all I had thought about was finishing. Visualizing Yorktown consumed my mind. Reaching a milestone had provided motivation for me to press on countless times. *A state border crossing. Conquering Montana's expansive open landscape.*

Hoosier Pass. Reaching these milestones gave me the internal desire to go on and search for the next. But that mental focus had ended days before; I was no longer interested in anything except reaching the monument. But now, in Western Kentucky, the green pastures, the rolling hills, and a favorable, pleasant breeze all changed my mindset. In hindsight, had I known what to expect in Western Kentucky, I would have enjoyed the ride that much more. Dog attacks and climbing the steep mountains wouldn't happen for another three days. On SR 120 and SR 132, cattle grazed in the fields. Smoothly paved, 100-yard, asphalt driveways led to antebellum-style plantation homes with wraparound porches.

In Sebree (population 1,596), a white placard with blue lettering stuck out of the ground in front of the First Baptist Church. The message "Sebree First Baptist Church Cross Country Cyclist Hostel" was a greeting that reflected the bike-friendly quality Kentucky projected. Frequently, I received a warm greeting inside a convenience store. The Spoke'n Hostel in Mitchell, Oregon, the Welcome to Newton sign in Kansas, and now Sebree stood out among the many American hamlets that appreciated cyclists visiting their tiny village.

I had ridden only 40 miles that day when I entered Sebree at 2:07 p.m. I had *mostly* shied away from fried food, especially after my stomach problems from eating chili weeks before. I consumed things I knew my stomach could handle, including pizza, peanut butter, and candy bars. I love fried chicken, but I feared a reoccurrence of that awful chili experience. The threat of crapping in my shorts was the reason I'd frequently made the decision to avoid greasy food. In Sebree, I walked inside the Kangaroo Express on Main Street and immediately smelled that greasy, oh-so-good scent of fried chicken that took me on a trip down memory lane. An intense desire for chicken overwhelmed me when I saw the signs for Bojangles, Popeyes, and KFC. I set my sights on the crispy and plentiful basket of chicken that had just come out of the fryer. Fried chicken for lunch.

I didn't have a destination in mind when I left Sebree at 2:30 p.m. I rode up and down small bunny hills, passing through Beech Grove (population 243) and Utica (population 400). The sweat equity required on my first day in Kentucky was less than I'd anticipated. The opposite of the day before, when I'd underestimated the difficult riding conditions in Southern Illinois.

At 7:29 p.m., I reached Fordsville (population 528). The Fordsville Volunteer Fire Department Station's electronic message board displayed "Be Kind" in vivid, red lettering. *That's interesting*, I thought. *What's the reason for the message?* I took a picture and kept going. At a Marathon gas station, I stopped to finalize my destination. I made a reservation at the Resort Inn located in the town Falls of Rough (population 1,936), about 13 miles east of Fordsville. If I pedaled hard, I could reach the inn before dark. "Excuse me. Do you know the significance of the 'Be Kind' message on the fire station's electronic billboard?" I asked the gas station attendant while paying for supplies.

"Not really," the lady replied.

I waved goodbye, walked outside, saddled up, and took off for the last 13-mile ride.

The road narrowed, and large evergreen pine trees blocked what little sunlight lingered from the setting sun. A swarm of bugs smashed against my body as I propelled Tank into the early darkness. My open mouth rapidly turned into an insect collection receptacle. I often took sips of water to moisten my lips and throat, which were dry from the air entering my mouth. The bugs were a big nuisance, but safety was the primary motivation to avoid riding in the dark.

Annoyed with myself for poor planning again, the ride to Falls of Rough was the third straight night I rode in darkness. In total blackness, I stopped to reorient myself when I reached Highway 79. It was past 9:00 p.m., and I was concerned that I'd overshot the entrance to the Resort Inn. My stomach became queasy when I realized I didn't know where I was. *Do I turn around? Do I turn left or right?* I looked to my left and saw lights in the distance. To my right and behind me, the landscape was eerily dark. The manager answered my phone call. "Hi, this is Larry. I've got a reservation at your place. I think I'm close to you, but I'm not sure which way to go," I stated, rather tersely—not my usual, pleasant greeting. I became perturbed when Josh, the manager, informed me he didn't know which way I should turn.

"What do you mean, you don't know how to navigate from the intersection?!" I said, lashing out and clearly agitated. He couldn't help me. I tried to orient him, sharing that I was stopped at the intersection and describing a prominent road marker. After a couple of minutes of getting nowhere, he agreed to walk outside and wave a flashlight. We remained on the phone together throughout the whole ordeal. I turned left and continued pedaling on Falls of Rough Road. About a quarter mile later, I saw a white light moving, coming from an arm swinging front to back. "Hey, Josh, I think I see you up ahead. Are you now walking toward the road?"

"Yes, I am," he replied.

"Can you wave your hand above your head?" I asked.

As soon as I saw the white light rise to the sky, I felt relieved and exclaimed, "I see you! I'm on my way." Josh met me at the entrance to the parking lot. I said hello, extending my hand to greet him. My very own pathfinder guided me to the landing zone. He offered me two cans of soda, a bottle of Gatorade, and breakfast bars on the house. He also offered to wash my clothes. I felt awful that I'd spoken to Josh in such a disrespectful way on the phone. I felt like an ass. I apologized for treating him poorly. The inn was in the spot the map indicated it should have been and where my GPS directed me. My nerves had just been shattered. Time on the saddle had worn me out. I'd failed this test to remain patient through adversity. I needed to break the trend of riding in the dark.

I recovered my clothes from the office after a long, hot shower. The Cascades, Bitterroots, Rockies, and Ozarks (big and little) were behind me. I laid out the next day's riding clothes on the chair next to the bed. I repacked each item—a routine I had completed for 29 straight days. I placed map section #10 on the table next to the bed. I turned on the lamp and grabbed my iPhone to check the leaders' board. Only 900 miles to the finish. Why wasn't I more excited about being so close? What had started as a grand adventure, pregnant with unlimited possibilities, had fizzled out. At the start, everything was new and cool—discovering new things and meeting new people. I was crushing the uphills with the confidence of a seasoned cyclist. However, now I felt indifferent that I had reached this point. The internal drive that guided me had left me. I knew I was on the cusp of surpassing my goal by leaps and bounds. But somehow, at this point, it didn't matter.

My Nerves Are Shot
Falls of Rough, Kentucky
July 2, 2019

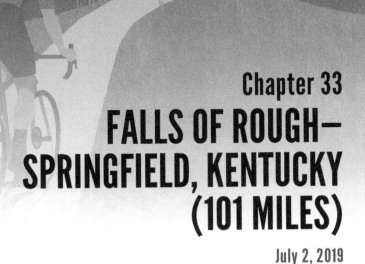

Chapter 33
FALLS OF ROUGH–SPRINGFIELD, KENTUCKY (101 MILES)

July 2, 2019

S oon after wiping the crust from my eyes, I looked over the leaders' board and the following post caught my immediate attention:

> *A busy day/night at The Monument in Yorktown. Yesterday we saw Bill Griffin complete his journey at 1:38 p.m. 'The Czechs' Jakub and Jiri arrived at 10:24 p.m., and Robert & David came at 2:54 a.m. YEAH!!!"*

> *Congratulations to you all. Job well done! And… Monument Angels were there to post a video of it all! We need to give a special shout-out to all the Monument Angels that show up at all hours of the day & night to welcome TABR riders. For almost 14 hours yesterday (including*

a ~3 a.m. arrival this morning!!!), videos from John and Tom documented racers' arrival for all the families, friends, and fans here in the USA and around the world that cannot get to Y'town. Thank you, thank you, thank you! In addition, it is so cool to see TABR riders that have completed their journey come back to the Monument to cheer on their fellow racers as they complete their trek. You guys are fantastic!

As an aside, David also rode TABR18 and wanted to beat his time from last year. And that he did! He knocked off ~8 hours from last year's ride. So double congratulations are in order! He said he would be back to ride TABR AGAIN in the future! Now get back to work dude, your family's restaurant is waiting!!!

The greatest distances covered in the last 24-hour period (7 a.m., Sun June 30 to 7 a.m., Mon July 1, EST) were:

Brad/Dan/Amy 164 miles (264 km)
Larry Walsh 137 miles (220 km)
Adam 106 miles (171 km)
Rolf 81 miles (130 km)
Kevin 80 miles (129 km)

Our Tandem Team of John and Rick had been easily covering over 100 miles a day for the last week or so. Yesterday, they broke a derailleur cable near Buchanan, VA. That knocked their distance down to 55 miles (89 km) yesterday. They have not yet gotten back on their Tandem this morning, but after taking care of that cable, they will soon have Vesuvius to tackle.

Now only 9 TABR riders left on the road... — dot watcher, July 1

The elevated temperature and high humidity stopped me dead in my tracks when I stepped outside at 7:10 a.m. I was still annoyed and disappointed in myself about the night before. My appearance channeled a concern I held about the challenging ride ahead. After 3,300 miles and 127,000 feet of climbing, my chiseled, bony, suntanned face and skinny torso would soon begin climbing the challenging Appalachian Mountains. Successfully navigating the next few hundred miles raised the stakes for a triumphant journey. I looked like a badass ready to go, wearing a white sweat beanie and wide, purple-framed Oakley sunglasses.

Heading out of Falls of Rough on SR 79 was full of rush hour traffic. I eventually turned east onto SR 84 and began a gradual climb through expansive, open farmland. I glanced ahead and saw a short, steep hill. I downshifted to prepare myself for the climb. The chain skipped. My immediate reaction to pedal harder was a bad idea. The chain came off the chainring. Due to the tremendous torque I applied with the extra pedal stroke, the chain jammed between the big chainring and back tire. "No!" I yelled. So far, I had avoided mechanical problems. An unexpected injury, accident, or mistake could render me unable to continue. The closer I got to Yorktown, the more heightened my sense of unease was that the proverbial shoe would drop.

I clipped my left shoe off the pedal and planted my foot on the ground. I swung my right leg over the frame and stood there, inspecting the extent of the jam. I bent over and laid Tank on its side in the road, unlatching the handlebar, frame, and rear rack bags and placing each on the ground. I retrieved the multitool and then began a series of unsuccessful attempts to unjam the chain. Sweat poured from my face, causing my glasses to fog. My fingers on both hands were black with chain grease. I gripped the chain near the jam with one hand while using the multitool to pry open a narrow space to release the chain from the grip. I was concerned the chain would break because I had applied so much torque and ridden 3,000 miles—1,000 more than the chain's expected life span. Negative thoughts entered my mind as I stood silent, staring at Tank, wondering what I should do. The thought that I might not make my 40-day goal after all sent me spiraling into a state of anxiety and despair. *Not now. Not when I'm so close.*

A John Deere farm tractor caught my attention. The low engine noise went silent when the tractor reached my location. A man stepped down from inside the closed-in driver's cab and said, "I saw you were having problems. I thought I would see what I could do to help."

"Thanks. I jammed the chain good. Do you have a long screwdriver?" Realizing I hadn't introduced myself, I quickly added, "I'm Larry, by the way."

The man extended his arm. "Roger."

He then turned and opened a compartment on the side of the tracker stocked with a plethora of tools. The day was still young when we met at 10:30 a.m. Roger looked like he had already completed an entire workday. His tattered jeans, covered with dirt and full of holes, conveyed a unique style of living in the Bluegrass State. He wore a Giles Farm Bureau Coop ball cap that completed the full picture of a man who worked hard all his life to keep his farm going strong but also found the desire and time to help strangers passing through Hudson, Kentucky.

For two hours, we took turns attempting to unjam the chain. There were moments when I just thought, *Screw it*, while I applied extra torque to untangle the chain from the clench of the chainring. An enormous weight fell from my shoulders when the chain finally released. I inspected the chain and chainring for any sign of damage. What-if scenarios had plagued my mind throughout the entire two-hour ordeal. But I had dodged a bullet and was relieved to get going once again. I thanked Roger and snapped a picture of him standing next to my bike with the tractor in the background.

Roger displayed a simple act of kindness—an excellent example of the "Be Kind" campaign. Property owners displayed signs on their lawns and outside police and fire departments throughout many of Kentucky's small towns. I thought a lot about the countless acts of kindness that I had experienced while on the saddle in the Bluegrass State. But I still didn't know the reason, if there was one, behind the campaign. It was not until I returned home to New Jersey in July 2019 that I read the history of the Kindness Campaign.

The "Just Be Kind" crusade began in the summer of 2018, when members of the College Heights United Methodist Church in Elizabethtown, Kentucky, began raising money for people in need. Congregants sold T-shirts and "Just Be Kind" signs, raising more than $17,000. As one adult interviewed by a local TV station said, "Kindness goes a long way. A smile goes a long way."

In 2019, inspired by the "Just Be Kind" signs they saw while driving with their parents, two preteen sisters created their own kindness movement. The girls, who lived nearby in La Rue County, dropped the "Just" and created the "Be Kind" campaign. Their message of kindness was contagious and eventually grew throughout the state. The *Today Show* interviewed the girls, and their "Be Kind" tagline was projected in Times Square for the whole world to see. One person I asked about the signs told me he thought the effort was meant to raise awareness for the opioid drug epidemic that hit rural Kentucky hard.

Kentuckians are very pleasant. People wave, whether cutting grass on a riding mower or passing in a car. I typically raised my head and exaggerated a nod if the road was busy instead of waving back. I wanted to acknowledge their gesture, but I always rode with two hands on the handlebar. Safety first!

Before reaching Springfield (population 2,519), home to our sixteenth president, Abraham Lincoln, I passed through Loretto (population 731), home of Maker's Mark Bourbon distillery. I had no idea Loretto was the home of such an iconic brand. I stopped at the junction of ST 152 and SR 49 to get my bearings before the 13-mile push to Springfield and noticed several similar enormous, black, rectangular buildings. The dozen military-style structures were cordoned off from the public by a six-foot-high chain fence. I recall thinking I had stumbled upon a secret military reservation. The mystery of Area 51 in Nevada came to mind. While the fence did not have barbed wire lining the top, I thought it was very odd I did not see a single person inside or outside the vicinity that dominated both sides of the road. My mind raced back to my childhood and the *Foundation* science fiction trilogy by Isaac Asimov, wondering if I had stumbled upon a new civilization. Immediately, I searched online and found an article titled "Loretto residents seeing black."[88] The article described the origins of the black-covered buildings. According to the report, Maker's Mark built the warehouses as part of their expansion plan. Following the warehouses' construction, a black, sooty-looking substance, a type of fungus, appeared on homes, cars, and road signs in the city. The article says an occurring fungus germinates on ethanol and makes the area around the warehouses prime breeding ground. The black soot is not unique to Loretto, it is also found in France, Scotland, and Ireland. I had solved the mystery with a quick google search.

The Springfield Inn on Lincoln Street, high above the west end of town, charged $71 for a room, with a hot breakfast included. After settling into my room, I walked outside. I was scanning the locale for a place to eat. I saw a Wendy's restaurant sign attached to a pole high up and above a strip mall. An enormous water tower reached a hundred feet into the sky. I walked across Lincoln Street, down a hill behind a Dollar Tree, and continued to the busy intersection of Triple Five Highway (SR 555). When the walk sign started blinking, I ran across the 30-foot-wide highway. It felt good to stretch my legs. At Pizza Hut, I devoured 24 dry chicken wings with blue cheese dressing for dinner—and for dessert, a small sausage pan pizza!

My legs felt strong. Muscle cramping had not happened as often as I'd anticipated. When I did cramp, usually in my calf or hamstring, it would start in the middle of the night. Suddenly, I would feel a spasm,

---

[88] Denise House, "Loretto residents seeing black: Maker's Mark's distillery warehouses are prime breeding ground for whiskey fungus," The Lebanon Enterprise, May 31, 2017, https://www.lebanonenterprise.com/content/loretto-residents-seeing-black

and then the muscle would tighten. When cramping occurred in my groin, which was often the case near the end of the race, I had no choice but to clench my teeth and endure the pain until the cramping eased. A calf cramp was easier to deal with in the limited space of my two-person Big Agnes tent. I could reach down and pull my toes toward me to release the pain instead of waiting for it to subside on its own.

Forty-one racers had finished, 27 had withdrawn, and 5, including me, remained on the road. Nathan's simple message to all of us in Astoria—"Remember, it's just a bike ride—nothing more, nothing less"—resonated with me now more than it had at any time before. I noticed the content of Facebook posts moving away from simply recognizing racers for finishing the race to reflecting on the events that had unfolded since June 2.

One, in particular, describing equipment and mechanical issues, caught my attention:

TABR 2019 review from an old bicycle mechanic. Carbon framesets, by far were the most popular. But three titanium frames passed me. One aluminum and the tandem was steel. But remember I didn't get a chance to meet every racer. Carbon wheels are reliable. The most popular tire size might be 28 mm. I saw fewer tubeless tires this year. And few mechanical problems altogether. I was aware of four derailleur cable breaks, broke spokes on the tandem and one other broken spoke. One broke derailleur hanger. I assisted in one derailleur cable replacement, one spoke replacement, several brake and derailleur adjustments. The tire pump got a lot of use. I offered cold drinks and energy bars to everyone. Took and posted dozens of pictures. Drove hundreds of miles and waited dozens of hours on the side of the road. Probably checked the tracker site hundreds of times. Met some amazing athletes. Some good people and met some for the second time. Most memorable was the two-hour bicycle repair with Boris who only knew a few words of English. I will always offer aid to every cyclist I meet and help any cyclist that asks, equally to my abilities. I did get an article into the Berea newspaper about the race and my forever request for a rest station in Berea. I tried to recruit new dot watchers and greeters to represent Berea. A few more people are aware, and I hope I can share dot stalking duties next year.—dot watcher, July 2

Chapter 34

SPRINGFIELD—MCKEE, KENTUCKY (98 MILES)

July 3, 2019

L ike horse race announcers, dot watchers gave daily updates of remaining cyclists, pointing out the leader, who's making the big moves, and splits at various points.

> *The greatest distances covered in the last 24-hour period (7 a.m., July 1 to 7 a.m. July 2, EST) were:*
>
> *John/Rick 198 miles (319 km)*
> *Brad/Dan/Amy 163 miles (262 km)*
> *Larry Walsh 141 miles (227 km)*
> *Rolf 97 miles (156 km)*
> *Adam 95 miles (153 km)*
>
> *After finishing today, our field of TABR still on the TA will be cut in half. That will leave us with only five*

*riders to follow & cheer on. Let's do just that! Come on,
Kevin, Rolf, Larry, Adam, and Tom! We still got ya!*—dot
watcher, July 2

I passed the Lincoln Homestead State Park on SR 152 (US Bike
Route 76), where President Abraham Lincoln lived until his tenth
birthday. I met Robin, who was riding across the country from Yorktown
heading west. Did Robin envy me for being so close to the finish, just
like I had envied David Letterman's doppelganger when I met him in
Hamilton, Montana, 22 days before?

I counted aloud, repeating to myself, "One, two, three…" and so
on. Then I shifted to singing out loud, "One hundred bottles of beer
on the wall, one hundred bottles of beer…" I tried anything to occupy
my mind. Four hours later, I stared at an unoccupied, run-down, white
ranch home behind a wire, chicken-coop-like fence, with several Texas
longhorns grazing in the backyard. A small, white sign displayed a bicycle
and the word "rest" underneath. There was a second sign—"cyclist only
rest stop"—and then a prominent, wooden fence sign with a welcome
message: "Bicyclist Free Water." A covered patio rest station had two
chairs arranged on the deck to sit and rest.

Inside a cooler, I found ice and different flavors of soda. Avian
water bottles also floated in the ice melting inside the white container.
There was a total of about $50 worth of goods. The property owners
had instituted their own Be Kind campaign, with the following note
written next to the cooler: "Free–Anything in cooler. Take as much
as you want. Need anything—call XXX-XXX-XXXX. Free overnight
camping–Bicyclists only. Free shower around the back of the house to
the right of an outhouse. Don't need to camp to shower!"

When I left the "cyclists only" rest stop, I reminded myself not to
lose sight of the bigger picture. What a fantastic experience I was having.
How fortunate I was to be here. When I reached Berea, the gateway to
the Appalachian Mountains, I recognized I was close to accomplishing
something extraordinary. This unlikely event, an epic race, would end

in a matter of days. Part of me felt confused. *Why did I do this twice?* I thought, while on my way to Berea (population 14,749).

My choice to step away from the job market for 18 months would surely make it more difficult to find a good-paying job upon my return. My time away from the rat race would potentially raise concerns among employers about my commitment to a professional career. It was a question I would need to face upon my return. Kelley had posed the same question when I'd first raised the idea of entering the TABR. "It will make you a more interesting person," Kelley had said when I'd debated the ride from California to Florida. "How will you explain the second one?" had been Kelley's inquiry when I'd first raised the plan of racing across America again.

I rode under Interstate 75, swung south on SR 595 (Main Street), and set my sights on reaching downtown Berea, the end point of map section #10. Just shy of 4:00 p.m., riding on a bike trail that paralleled a busy SR 595, I saw three individuals waving at me, who were standing next to a blue pickup truck 50 yards ahead. When I reached them, one guy blurted out, "We almost missed you coming through town! The tracking monitor showed you were about fifteen miles away." I immediately thought about Wayne, who'd said the same thing when we met in Farmington, Missouri.

"Others have said the same thing," I replied.

Based on the pace I had established the last few days, the three guys tracked my progress and expected me to reach Berea between 4:30 and 5:00 p.m. We shook hands, and I told them how much I appreciated their greeting me. I answered many of the same questions others had. *How are you feeling? What's it been like so far? Where are you planning to stop tonight?*

The three men worked at the same company. One of the guys told me that when they realized I had reached Berea earlier than they thought, he raced into his boss's office to ask if they could meet me on the road. "What a great boss!" I exclaimed with a smile. I set my SPOT device to ping with the satellite every 30 minutes, rather than 10 or 15 minutes. I am not sure whether the longer 30-minute interval caused the tracking problems.

There were several lodging options to choose from in Berea, including the historic Boone Tavern in the heart of town, but I had only ridden 78 miles, far short of my century goal. The next closest decently sized town, Booneville (population 112), was 49 miles farther east. I had three options: remain in Berea, ride to Booneville, or split the difference and ride to McKee, 28 miles away. Reaching Booneville didn't seem practical nor safe because that meant riding through the Appalachian range in darkness. "Is there anything in McKee?" I asked.

"Not really," one of the guys stated. "There is a big climb up the Big Hill on the outside of Berea, on the way to McKee."

I hemmed and hawed but ultimately decided to tackle the five-mile climb to the top. There, I would evaluate my situation before deciding where to stay the night.

A wide shoulder made the arduous ride to the top much safer, providing ample distance from the cars and trucks zooming by this late afternoon on July 3. When I reached the road junction, I turned on SR 421 and rode for a quarter of a mile before stopping at a Marathon gas station. By 6:00 p.m., the sun had dropped behind the mountains, significantly reducing visibility. Continuing to ride on a mountain road with limited visibility during a holiday weekend seemed like a bad idea. No one answered the phone at the only lodging option, the Town and Country Motel on SR 421, between the gas station and McKee. I googled other lodging options. The Little Turtle Lodge on the west side of McKee appeared. My stomach sank when the woman who answered told me she didn't have a vacancy. "Could I pitch my tent on your property?" I inquired, adding in a worried tone, "I want to find a safe place off the main highway. It will be dark soon, and I would like to know I've got a destination before I start riding again."

"You can stay inside a cabin my husband is building. The frame and roof are finished," she offered, picking up on my worry. "Nothing special, but at least you'll have shelter when the storm hits later," she added.

"Thanks so much!" I replied. "I'll probably arrive after dark."

She told me the cabin was on top of a hill behind their property, only accessible by a dirt road. I bought dinner and the following day's food from the Marathon convenience store, saddled up, and began the 20-mile ride to McKee.

When greeted by the shifting gray cloud cover and strong winds brought on by the approaching storm, I increased my pace. At the lodge, I located the dirt path that led me to the unfinished cabin, my shelter for the night. Pushing Tank up the short, steep path required added energy I didn't have after pedaling close to a hundred miles. I needed to lift Tank and all of my equipment to the second floor through an opening that would become the second-floor bedroom window. The dirt path was full of nails, slivers of wood, used caulking cylinders, and other construction debris. I was careful to walk Tank around the sharp objects, not over them; I sure as heck didn't want to get my first flat tire at this point. I grabbed onto the wooden frame and hoisted myself up through the opening to the second floor. I saw light fixtures and wiring installed—scattered reminders of an active construction site everywhere. Empty spools of painter's tape lay here and there. Fifteen minutes after securing my equipment inside the cabin, I watched the fierce winds and fast-moving rainstorm hit the area. Inside and away from the elements, I had once again made a wise choice to stop in McKee. I would have been caught in the middle of the torrential downpour on a narrow mountain road while contending with holiday traffic.

I heard a noise coming from outside the cabin. A man extended his arm through the would-be front door to greet me. "Hi, I'm Pete. Sharyn's husband. She told me you were staying tonight." The man's calm voice and heavy accent gave off a friendly vibe.

"Thanks so much, Pete. I'm Larry. Staying inside is a lifesaver. I didn't want to ride in the nasty rain," I replied.

Pete shared that he and his wife had recently bought the business to cater to visitors who pass through the Daniel Boone National Forest and trails nearby. They initially thought their business would primarily cater to hikers and only recently discovered that the TransAmerica Bike

Trail passed directly in front of their property. Building the cabin was part of their expansion plan to meet the growing demand from the long-distance cycling community. Sharyn and Pete could capitalize on serving the cycling community with no other indoor lodging option between Berea and Booneville. Pete ran an electrical cord from his home—about 200 feet down the hill—to the cabin so I could charge my iPhone and Garmin GPS device. The temperature fell a few degrees after the storm passed through.

I retired map section #10. A nice, cool breeze flowed through my tent in the partially built cabin. I read the field notes of map section #11: "The Appalachians may not be as tall as the Rockies, but they are much harder to cross than the mountains of the west. This is because the gentle inclines of the Rockies are not nearly as tiring as the steep, roller-coaster grades of the Appalachians." No more wondering. I would ride through the Appalachians in the morning.

The distances covered in the last 24-hour period (7 a.m., July 2 to 7 a.m. July 3, EST by our remaining five TABR racers were:

Adam 142 miles (229 km)
Rolf 94 miles (151 km)
Larry Walsh 82 miles (132 km)
Kevin 60 miles (96 km)
Thomas 37 miles (60 km)

Kevin is presently the only TABR rider in Virginia, having recently started his day on his bike somewhere between Damascus and Wytheville in the throes of the grueling Chengi Hundred. Rolf is in Kentucky with Berea in his rearview mirror. Larry is seemingly "off TABR route" but on Bike Route 76 in Springfield, KY. Adam is in Illinois approaching Cave-in-Rock to cross the ferry into Kentucky. And our Legend, Thomas, is likely bivvying, not yet into West Yellowstone, MT. Safe travels!

So, I think these are called withdrawal pains… what am I going to do for the next few days here in Central Virginia kids???—dot watcher, July 3

A cool breeze hit me when I reached the edge of the property and began cycling east at 7:45 a.m. Hot, muggy days had taken a toll on my body, so it was a pleasant change to the start of my day. The sun was beating down, but a tree canopy covered the narrow road. I saw fissures in the road, which generally occurred around a curve with a 10–15 percent grade. The cracks in the asphalt were likely due to the water runoff and lack of support at the pavement edge. Low metal railings separated the road from hundred-foot drops into the canyon.

The 26-mile ride from McKee to Booneville was full of adventurous dog encounters. I stopped keeping track of how many dogs chased me after my sixth confrontation. I sounded the horn occasionally, but most of the time, I made it past the owner's property before the dog reached me. The dogs didn't continue beyond their owners' property line. So far, my concerns regarding the dogs seemed to be real but manageable.

I thought it was cool when I arrived at Booneville (population 112), named in honor of American frontiersman Daniel Boone,[89] as one of my favorite TV shows as a boy was *Daniel Boone*. At the intersection of South Court Street, while riding on Main Street in downtown Booneville, I met a man sweeping the main street. He said, "Hi, I'm Kendall," with a pleasant smile and an equally agreeable Kentucky drawl.

---

[89] "Booneville, Kentucky," Kentucky Atlas & Gazetteer, accessed July 14, 2022, https://www.kyatlas.com/ky-booneville.html

"Great to meet you. I love this small town," I replied. "I wish I could stay longer than my typical fifteen minutes."

He turned and pointed to the building immediately in front of where we stood. "I practiced law for forty-five years in that building."

He knew Booneville was a town on the TransAmerica Bike Trail. He asked, "How have Kentuckians treated you?"

I wasn't surprised by the question, given my positive experience with many other Kentucky residents. I replied, "The folks in Kentucky have been very friendly. I've seen Be Kind signs in many towns since I entered Western Kentucky four days ago. The roads are cyclist friendly, and vehicles always give me the right of way."

He responded, "I'm pleased to hear that. I'm just a Kentucky hillbilly."

I smiled. I didn't know what else to say. We shook hands. I took a picture with Kendall to add to my collection.

"Be safe on the road, Larry," he said, and then he started sweeping again.

I saddled up and continued riding on SR 28.

A warm feeling came over me as I thought back to the last time I could recall someone referring to themselves as a "hillbilly." In 1987 to 1988, while stationed in Korea, one of my platoon sergeants from Charlie Battery, 2-61 ADA, often talked about his childhood growing up in Appalachia. Soldiers formed a strong bond out of necessity—the quintessential melting pot of American culture. Unit cohesion was a foundational guiding principle. Accepting and understanding each other's unique backgrounds and life experiences were bedrock truths. Being in close quarters for an extended time, soldiers would often share stories about growing up in their respective communities. The colorful language was an essential aspect of effective communication. Soldiers from Appalachia, the inner city, suburbia, or rural America, were each proud of their upbringing. The warrior language—referring to a second lieutenant as a butterbar, or worse, or someone from Appalachia describing themselves a hillbilly—was something you thought nothing of.

The cultural disintegration and economic hardship described in *Hillbilly Elegy* by JD Vance, a coming-of-age story that takes place in impoverished Appalachia, were present as I moved through the hollers. At one time, the Appalachia region was home to some of the finest hardwood forests in North America—trees with 10-foot diameters that rivaled the California redwoods. Certain stories mention hollow sycamores so giant that they served as homes for settlers while their cabins were being built.[90] Today, neglected, abandoned, weeded-over automobiles and trucks blend into the natural environment. An old, abandoned, eighteen-wheeler trailer underneath vines sat off the main road and next to a rickety family shanty—a roadside junkyard. Baptist churches popped up deeper into Appalachia. A medical clinic with two rusted cars in the paved parking lot stood silent.

In Buckhorn (population 154), I waved at two bearded adults outside a trailer home, with country music blaring from a boom box. Appalachia's reputation of poverty and misery was pervasive. Tank had taken me on a journey through time, akin to an amusement park ride starting in the colonial era, ending with the Jetsons flying saucer–like cars in Orbit City. However, this journey, was frozen in time from the days of Geronimo in Arizona's Apache Country to the Hatfields and McCoys in Kentucky's Appalachia region. These communities and the hundreds of others I had cycled through were part of the big American experiment.

When I left McKee, I set my sights on Hazard (population 4,724) or Hindman (population 798), 20 miles farther east of Hazard. I thought Hazard would be an excellent place to visit, as it was a frequent stop for politicians on the stump. President Clinton toured Hazard and other poverty-stricken Appalachian communities during his presidential campaigns.[91] However, more interesting to me was the lore surrounding the stars of the series, *The Dukes of Hazzard*. My favorite, Catherine Bach,

[90]   Luke Bauserman, "Giant Trees of Appalachia and the People Who Lived in Them," Medium, January 12, 2016, https://medium.com/@lukebauserman/giant-trees-of-appalachia-and-the-people-who-lived-in-them-299ea673e697

[91]   "Clinton visits the other America," All Politics, CNN, July 6, 1999, https://www.cnn.com/ALLPOLITICS/stories/1999/07/06/clinton.visit/

visited Hazard in 1981 during the Black Gold Festival.[92] Reportedly, the show's producers added an extra z to the name and filmed the series in a fictional Georgia town to evade legal issues.

As I neared Hazard, a road sign directed me to bend left, to go off route. I decided to continue riding to Hindman. A Baptist church in Hindman had hosted cross-country cyclists for many years. I called the church and left a message with the pastor, asking if I could crash inside his church. I needed a good night's sleep because I would climb Pippa Passes the next day, one of the steepest climbs in all of Appalachia.

My iPhone screen lit up. I stopped to read the text, hoping for good news. The pastor wrote he was leaving town but offered for me to stay inside the youth ministry building. He wrote, "There is a good pizza place across the street from the building." He shared that he was leaving town to attend his mother's funeral! I gave him my condolences and thanked him for responding. I didn't know what else to write. A man I had never met had recently lost his mother and still found the strength to reply to my request—that topped all other moments of generosity. Thinking about the pastor's generous spirit and the warm greetings in Berea and Booneville continued to fuel my soul. They aided me during challenging times as I entered the heart of Appalachia. My iPhone lit up again, this time about five miles west of Hindman. I assumed the message was from the pastor, but I couldn't imagine why he had reached out again. I stopped to read his words. He'd texted to warn me about a storm forecasted to strike and wanted to know if I had made it to Hindman. I thanked him for reaching out and let him know the storm was no longer a threat to me. The worst of it had passed north of my location by now. Kentucky folks are decent people. I think Kendall would have been proud of his fellow Kentuckian!

It was an unusual but understandable greeting I saw when I entered Knott County and closed in on Hindman. An unmistakable

---

[92] "Hazard, Kentucky facts for kids," Kpedia, Kiddle, accessed July 14, 2022, https://kids.kiddle.co/Hazard,_Kentucky

message plastered on a road sign that read "Entering drug dealers' worst nightmare" made me laugh, but it also got me thinking. Eastern Kentucky is reportedly one of the state's areas most affected by the fading coal business and the heightened opioid crisis. In Knott County, drug overdoses and mortality estimates are higher than the state's average.[93]

I reached the Hindman Student Ministries building at 8:49 p.m. An American flag flew outside the large, white front door and underneath a cross. I pulled Tank up the six steps to the front entrance, too tired to lift it. At the front door, I reached out my right hand to grasp the knob. Replacing "slowly I turn, step by step, inch by inch"—Moe's iconic line in the 1944 *Three Stooges Gents Without Cents* movie—with my own slow turning of the knob, centimeter by centimeter, I opened the door and saw the lobby.

My eyes eventually adjusted to the darkness. When I flipped the light switch, the illumination revealed a large, wooden floor and stage, reminiscent of a CYO gym where I played basketball in the 1970s. Stained glass windows dotted both sides from front to back. A kitchen, a washer and dryer, and a bathroom with a shower were located on the other end from the stage. I spread my sleeping bag, air mattress, and pillow on the wooden floor, so all I would have to do when I returned from eating was unzip and snuggle. I showered, dressed, slipped my water shoes on, started a load of laundry, and then walked to Paradise Pizza, located directly across the street from the youth ministries building.

One other patron entered during the one hour I sat inside the pizza place. The guy appeared to be about 30 years old and carried a pistol on his waistline. *Another state with open carry laws*, I thought. I wanted to ask the guy questions, but I didn't engage. I was hungry, tired, and ready to retire for the evening. No fireworks for me on this Independence Day.

---

[93] Mary C. Noble and Van Ingram, *2020 Overdose Fatality Report. Kentucky Office of Drug Control Policy* (Kentucky Injury Prevention and Research Center: Agent for the Kentucky Department of Public Health, May 2021), 7, https://odcp.ky.gov/Documents/2020%20KY%20ODCP%20Fatality%20Report%20%28final%29.pdf

After devouring two orders of dry chicken wings (blue cheese on the side) and a large sausage pizza, I returned to the youth ministry building. I googled open carry Kentucky laws and learned a recent Kentucky law had taken effect on June 26, 2019, which allowed concealed and open handguns and long guns. This patron had been practicing his constitutional right to open carry.

Before departing the following day, I left a donation inside a container on the kitchen table. (When I returned to New Jersey, I wrote the pastor a thank-you note for his incredible hospitality. The Hindman Baptist Church has been a way station for cross-country cyclists for 29 years.)

In the Appalachian region, Baptist churches are prevalent, as well as hollers, poverty, aggressive dogs, run-down homes, and trailers. I also saw many basketball hoops attached to poles sticking out of grass—not concrete or asphalt. I saw very few people outside. Living in the hollers is unique. Appalachia is a world unto itself.

Chapter 36
HINDMAN, KENTUCKY— HAYSI, VIRGINIA (77 MILES)

July 5, 2019

When I opened the door at 7:48 a.m., a feeling of sleepy indifference changed to one of focus and resolve. At the edge of town, I swung southeast on SR 160 and met rush hour traffic in both directions. Many families were likely getting an early start to the long holiday weekend. I saw an Exxon gas station about 200 feet ahead on the opposite side of the road. I needed to restock on water and Gatorade before ascending the sharp slope up and over Pippa Passes. I scanned my rearview mirror and lifted my left arm to alert vehicles of my intention to cross the road. When the car directly behind me stopped, I moved closer to the center lane. The approaching vehicle saw my movement and stopped as well, yielding to me. I now had the right of way, creeping closer to the middle, about to dart across the road.

I looked behind and ahead one more time. I signaled my intention by raising my left fist and giving them a thumbs-up. I sensed movement to my left, and a white van appeared out of nowhere. I swerved to the right, quickly regained my balance, and glared at the approaching van, which slammed on its brakes. I looked both ways one more time and then crossed the road, entering the safety of the parking lot. I was lucky this time. Whether I would have been injured, I'm not sure. However, Tank most likely would have been damaged, ending my race across America. I hopped off Tank, leaned it against the wall, told myself I needed to be more careful, and walked inside the store.

Saddle sores and foot pain had remained a consistent concern but no longer posed a race-ending threat. My fingertips on both hands were constantly numb, but I had grown accustomed to the daily grind and dealt with the discomfort like other ailments. Surprisingly, and for the first time on both journeys, my leg muscles tired frequently. My quadriceps had succumbed to the physical demands of riding a bike almost 4,000 miles in a little over 30 days. I paused several times to rest on each of the many steep climbs throughout all of Appalachia.

Descending the sharp, winding Appalachian mountain roads was as tricky as the ascent. Not seeing oncoming traffic due to the sharp turns and narrow mountain roads elevated my anxiety. Small potholes were commonplace, often appearing on the edge of a recently paved road. Low-hanging tree canopies limited the sun from reaching the road surface. The elevated temperature and high humidity created road moisture, increasing the chances of Tank skidding on my ride down the mountain.

At 10:45 a.m., at the bottom of Pippa Passes, I stopped at Fat Daddy's Diner in Bevinsville. The parking lot was empty on this late Friday morning in the heart of coal country. My first thought was to leave after a short rest break because the diner was closed for business. But then, close to 11:00 a.m., a car pulled into the gravel lot and parked in front of the diner. "Hi, any chance I could get a cup of coffee?" I asked the woman who exited the car, presumably there to open the diner for business.

"I'll make you a fresh pot. Just need to open up, but it shouldn't take more than a few minutes," she replied.

She knew I needed a caffeine jolt from one glance at my gnarly-looking face and weathered body. A picture of their trademark hamburger on the front entrance door made me reconsider adding food to my caffeine boost, but I shied away from the prospect of a greasy burger at only 11:00 a.m. There was a "Friends of Coal" message and a Kentucky Wildcats basketball team logo underneath the juicy burger. Jim Valvano's 1993 ESPY speech came to mind, when he told the story of using one of Vince Lombardi's motivational speeches with his Rutgers freshman basketball team, telling his men, "There are three things important to every man in this locker room. His God, his family, and the Green Bay Packers." A roar of laughter followed. I looked at the window and thought that good things come in threes in Appalachia—coal, a burger, and the Kentucky Wildcats basketball team.

The woman walked from the kitchen to the dining room carrying a freshly brewed pot of coffee. Steam rose from the carafe's small opening. That aroma presented a welcome start to a new day. "Thank you so much!" I said, right as she poured the coffee into a small, white, Styrofoam cup. I asked the woman if the coal industry had recovered since Trump became president. She replied that the larger coal market was struggling but smaller local mines had rebounded. She also told me people who lived nearby believed the coal industry would never return to normal. Efforts to refocus on expanding the tourism industry had begun. I heard similar stories riding through rural communities in the Deep South in 2018. Primary industries had disappeared. Communities struggled to reinvent themselves, which was essential for economic survival.

Appalachia is one big forest. The hills and wilderness came into view now and again at an opening in the wooded landscape. I imagined the hills and valleys exploded into a kingdom of gold, red, orange, and yellow each fall as the air got crisper and the leaves start to change. I also thought about my friend's fantastic experience walking the Appalachian Trail. When I saw a trail sign, I wondered what my buddy looked like when he walked this region. Did he have sore knees, abrasions, or poison ivy rashes—a hiker's equivalent of a cyclist's saddle sores and numb extremities?

In Elkhorn City (population 1,050), I saw a roadside marker in memory of a fallen soldier in the Confederate Army: "Name and date unknown but to God." The marker was just past Breaks Interstate Park on SR 80, near the Virginia Border. A pickup truck sped by, a giant American flag waving in the wind from the back bed. I couldn't have choreographed the scene any better.

What I hoped to feel—a sense of euphoria when I made it to the Welcome to Virginia sign—didn't happen. My emotions upon seeing a red heart and the words "Virginia Is for Lovers" at the top of an 800-foot climb fell short of expectations. I felt unfulfilled instead of an incredible rush of excitement. I had tackled a significant milestone. I was one step closer to finishing an epic race across America that only 263 people had ever completed. I didn't know why, but it just didn't seem like a big deal when I entered Virginia.

I thought about what I would do when I returned home. I had blocked any thought about what was next for me. I wondered if my cycling itch would disappear if I finished the race. From March 5, 2018, when I heard the words, "Your job has been eliminated," until July 5, 2019, when I entered Virginia, a roller coaster of emotions had tracked alongside me during that span of crossing 17 states and riding over 7,000 miles. It all seemed like a blur. I thought about paying the mortgage. I wondered how we would afford healthcare. Brian's college education, though still years away, weighed heavily on my shoulders. We had saved money that enabled me to take this time off, but it was my responsibility to earn a living, to take care of my family. At 57, I was too young to retire. I knew the day was approaching when planning for the next chapter in my life would be necessary. Standing at the Virginia border sign, I knew the parallel universe I had lived in would soon end.

Riding through the lands that shaped the United States had made this experience more than a race across America. The milestones completed brought me a sense of joy that propelled me to the next discovery. By this time, when thinking about the next achievement, my trepidation replaced my jubilation. I felt blasé, even though I was on the brink of concluding a significant, life-changing event. *For God's sake*, I thought, *why aren't I more enthusiastic?* I was exhausted, tired, spent. Riding up and over the Appalachian Mountains had proved trying.

At 5:00 p.m., I stopped at the Fas Mart Valero gas station on the north end of Haysi (population 188), having ridden 70 miles. If I continued to Rosedale, the next town with decent services, located on the downside of a steep hill 15 miles east of Haysi, it meant I would climb a treacherous mountain road after dark. I took one look at the map section #11 elevation profile and decided right away that I would stay in Haysi and tackle the big climb after a good night of sleep. The nearly 15 percent grade and 1,500-foot rise would be better to attack with fresh legs.

I walked inside the Fas Mart shop and sat on a bench with an unobstructed view of Tank, leaning against the store's window. I called the Hilltop Motel in town. The woman who answered told me there was no vacancy but asked if I wished to tent at her family-owned Thunder River Campground located three miles off the main route and on the banks of the Russell Fork River. "Sure," I replied, realizing I had limited choices, as the time neared 6:00 p.m. She set aside a primitive campsite for me—the only available spot on this holiday weekend. I had set my sights on sleeping inside, but instead, I settled on paying $12 for a plot of ground.

The ride on Splashdam Drive felt like a ride on a bosky trail. I reached the campground entrance about three miles off the main route outside downtown Haysi. The Russel Fork River bordered the campground. I saw several RVs parked along both sides of the dirt path that passed through the heart of the encampment. Kids were playing, and several people were wading in the slow-moving river. The lady I'd spoken to on the phone greeted me and pointed me to the far end, away from all the activity, where I would find a quiet place to pitch my tent.

While setting my tent up, I was startled when I heard, "Hi, do you want to join us for dinner? We've got burgers, hot dogs, and sausages."

I stopped what I was doing and shook hands with the man who had approached me. I learned he was a family member of the woman I had met a few minutes before. "Great, I'd love to join you—but I don't want to intrude. It looks like you have a large group," I said, acknowledging his generous offer.

"We'd love to have you join us," he insisted.

I said, "Thank you. I'm going to wash first, and then I will be right over." I grabbed a bar of soap, washcloth, and towel. I put my water shoes on and walked 50 feet to the river and then a few more steps into the slow-moving current. Paying particular attention to the uppermost inner thigh area affected by saddle sores, I scrubbed clean.

About 25 people gathered underneath an awning extending from the side of a 35-foot RV, making for a joyous occasion. People talked to each other. Some sat at picnic tables. All were waiting to eat the bounty on the grill. The assortment of meat, salad, and bread was one of the best tasting meals I had since the fish-and-chips meal in Astoria two nights before the race began.

Eventually, everyone gathered around a picnic table to sing "Happy Birthday." I wasn't sure whose birthday it was. The celebration included a white cake with chocolate icing served with vanilla ice cream. Two hours before, I had been resigned to the fact that I had only ridden 77 miles and disappointed that I had broken my string of consecutive century days. But now, here I was, an adopted family member for the night. I was elated to interact with folks who spoke with interesting accents!

After cake and ice cream, the kids played while the adults sat around a campfire. Aunts, uncles, and cousins took turns telling stories, in that distinctive drawl, accompanied by tremendous laughter. This family loved to dig at one another, and it was much like a Walsh family get-together. From 8:30 p.m. until 9:20 p.m., I listened to their razzing and poking fun at each other. Two 4x4 Ford trucks and an off-road dune buggy sat parked near the campfire. One guy wore a T-shirt with the words "Blood Feud" on it. Perhaps the message was meant to acknowledge a local high school football rivalry, or maybe it was a salute to the Hatfield-McCoy feud from 1860s to the 1890s that had entered American folklore. When I pulled out my iPhone to capture the fun on video, one guy quipped, "The reason you're taking videos is to capture our accent, isn't that right?"

I laughed, "That's right!" But I also appreciated the experience would be one I didn't want to forget. So, I captured the moment.

They all stopped talking when I stood up to leave, saying, "Thanks, you guys. I had so much fun spending time with your family."

There were several shouts of "Have a safe rest of your journey!" The woman I'd first met said, "Please join us for breakfast."

"Thanks," I responded, without giving a hint whether I planned to take her up on the offer.

I slipped inside my sleeping bag and considered whether I would accept their kind invitation for breakfast. The past three days, each with less than 100 miles on the saddle, had been discouraging after 12 century-plus days in a row. I made my decision and set my alarm for 3:45 a.m.

The commotion outside my tent subsided at about 9:45 p.m., after everyone retreated to their RVs. My iPhone lit up. *Who is that?* I wondered. I saw a text from Adam. His message was simply, "Are you okay?"

I answered, "Yup, all good." Less than five seconds later, my phone buzzed again.

It was Adam. "Hey, where are you?"

I replied, "How are you doing? What's going on?"

Adam informed me he had talked to his mom a few minutes before calling. His mother tracked the leaders' board and saw a Facebook post that concerned her, so she called her son. She told Adam about online chatter among dot watchers expressing concern about my safety. Adam told me that according to the satellite feed, I was in the middle of the river! I laughed and informed Adam how the day had ended with me camping *next* to the river, not *in* the river. I thanked him for letting me know about the concerns. I posted for all to see that I was okay and doing great, adding that an unexpected turn of events after a long day ended with me celebrating the holiday with new friends on the banks of the Russell Fork River.

Ummm... is this a tracker issue or is Larry Walsh really off route up some dead-end valley??? Been in one place for 1 hr. 8 minutes now.—dot watcher, July 5

Chapter 37

HAYSI–WYTHEVILLE, VIRGINIA (125 MILES)

July 6, 2019

The distances covered in the last 48-hour period (7 a.m., July 3 to 7 a.m. to July 5, EST) by our remaining five TABR racers are as follows. I have also provided the distances covered each day in brackets [Day 1/Day2] during these 2 days.

Larry Walsh 222 miles (357 km) [132 mi/90 mi]
Rolf 216 miles (348 km) [107 mi/109 mi]
Adam 172 miles (277 km) [63 mi/109 mi]
Kevin 160 miles (257 km) [89 mi/70 mi]
Thomas 47 miles (76 km) [30 mi/17 mi]

Stay safe, TABR riders. The Monument calls you all.—
dot watcher, July 5

When the alarm buzzed at 3:45 a.m., I unzipped the sleeping bag, sat up, and didn't move for a couple of seconds, trying to shake the cobwebs from my foggy brain. The last time I had gotten up this early was June 2, in Astoria. I felt driven to get an early start. I wanted to—*needed* to—make up mileage because of the short ride the day before. At 4:30 a.m., after Tank was packed and ready to go, I turned on my iPhone light and slowly walked through the grass toward the dirt road that ran through the campsite. It was quiet and dark when I passed by the party RV, the silence disrupted only by my cleats clacking against the ground.

When I reached Splashdam Road, I turned the front and rear lights on and returned to the center of Haysi. About 100 yards before turning right onto Sandlick Road, reconnecting to the main route, I stopped at an asphalt parking lot between Pizza Plus and New Peoples Bank. I waited for a couple of minutes on this predawn morning. Enough already—I wanted to escape the silence and solitude. I was energized to begin riding and wondered how many miles I could ride before the sun rose. It was time to go, and at 4:45 a.m., I turned southeast onto Sandlick Road. The cool, crisp morning air felt good against my skin as it caressed my face.

There wasn't a shoulder, so I rode in the driving lane. I stopped at the JDM Deli Mart about four miles outside of Haysi to buy Gatorade, white powdered sugar donuts, and a large cup of coffee. I needed the jolt of energy from caffeine jetting through my veins. An older man stepped down from the driver's side of a rusted Ford pickup truck and walked inside the deli. I sat alone outside, eating my sugar-filled breakfast and drinking my morning cup of joe. The nutritional value was much less than the balanced breakfast I'd passed on, but I knew if I'd accepted their offer for breakfast, I would have gotten a late start once again. Saying no to the family that had treated me so well the night before would have been uncomfortable for me. My legs felt strong when I began riding on SR 80, anticipating a big climb up Big A Mountain. The 3,694-foot peak is the highest point in Buchanan County, Virginia.[94]

I should have ridden before dawn more often. An additional two to three hours on the saddle each day could have shaved a couple of days off my time. I've reflected a lot while writing this book, debating the question in my mind as to whether I could have finished the race in fewer than 30 days if I'd executed a different strategy. Maybe I would have made it to Yorktown already by increasing daily riding time and by riding on a lower-weight carbon fiber bike.

Images of sitting around the campfire the night before occupied my mind as I rode to the base of Big A Mountain. The rising sun behind the mountains cast a rosy hue across the morning sky, bringing with it a flurry of early morning dog activity. About halfway to the top, the sound of barking dogs from behind startled me. My heart raced as my fight-or-flight response took over.

Initially, I didn't see the dogs, so I didn't know how many there were. But I knew I was the focus of their aggression. I turned my head to the right and glanced behind me. Three large German shepherds ran at me. I yelled, "Go home!" My loud shriek didn't deter them, and they continued running toward me. I grabbed the dog repellant canister I had stored in a mesh container on my handlebar. Using my left arm to control Tank, I extended my right arm and sprayed the hounds when they got to about 10 feet from me. All three dogs stopped in their tracks. *Thank God!* Several days before I climbed Big A Mountain, a dog bit a racer climbing this mountain. One of the three dogs chasing me was likely the culprit.

I dropped 800 feet over eight miles while descending Big A Mountain to Honaker (population 907). I pulled my legs close to the bike frame, hunched my torso into a tucked position, and let loose in the middle of Redbud Highway (SR 80). I pulled into the Tiger Stop gas station

---

[94] "Big A Mountain," Virginia County/City Highpoints, SummitPost.org, accessed July 14, 2022, https://www.summitpost.org/big-a-mountain/224222

at the mountain's base on the north end of town at 7:08 a.m., having ridden 27 miles.

That's thirty miles extra each day, I recall thinking. At my current pace, I *would* finish in less than 40 days, barring disaster. I thought about Michael, who had been so close to the finish line when a truck clipped his bike. After a couple of days off the saddle, he tried to come back but ultimately scratched. He'd been on pace to finish in fewer than 35 days. The unexpected can happen to anyone.

A police cruiser pulled into the parking lot while I stood outside eating donuts, a cup of coffee in hand. This cop, at the start of his shift, characterized the roads leading to Damascus (1,025) as much of the same. Damascus was one of the few towns I was familiar with, primarily due to its reputation for hosting cross-country cyclists and Appalachian Trail hiking enthusiasts.

Civil unrest and unprecedented attacks against police departments embroiled the United States in 2019. When I rode away from my brief encounter with the police officer, I remember thinking that each day he goes to work could be his last because of the rampant violence that has become a cancer in many communities. Interacting with people in nonenforcement situations to improve community relations and building relationships of mutual trust between police and the civilians in the communities they serve has become a stated priority among all stakeholders. I couldn't help but think about policing after my encounter with the man in blue.

I rode by the Elk Garden United Methodist Church in Rosedale (population 667). A "Biker's Hostel" sign was anchored in the ground next to a wooden-framed cyclist on the front lawn. According to the hostel's website, it opened in 1976 and a reservation was not required.

I crossed over Interstate 81 near Meadowview (population 967). The dark-blue interstate marker was a not-so-subtle reminder I had indeed begun the last leg of my journey. I reached Damascus (population 1,025) at 3:00 p.m. Damascus is known as Trail Town USA[95] because of the convergence of four scenic trails—the Appalachian Trail, US Bicycle Route 76, the Iron Mountain Trail, and the Virginia Creeper Trail. About 20,000 tourists converge on the town in mid-May every year to celebrate Trail Day.

My rear tire was wobbly. A bulge stuck out from the tire next to an indentation on the rim. My shifter wasn't working correctly; gears were skipping on their own, often when I pushed down hard on the pedal to climb a hill, forcing me to stop momentarily. I searched for a bike shop when I reached Damascus. The Creeper Bike Trail Rental & Shuttle shop on the south end of town seemed like a good choice.

The crowded store gave me confidence that its employees were good at their craft. Mike, the mechanic, identified the problem immediately. He thought there was a slim chance the rim would completely fail with only a few hundred miles to Yorktown, but a chance, nonetheless. "Let's replace it," I said. The mechanic walked to the back of the store and returned about 10 minutes later with bad news. The store didn't have a replacement rim for my size bike. However, Mike told me that a used bike was in the shop for repair with rims that fit Tank's frame. The store manager needed the bike owner's permission to replace my rim with his. "I can wait for a while. I'd rather try this first before taking my chances riding with a damaged rim," I said.

I waited nervously in the wings, worrying about what to do. Thirty minutes passed, which seemed like much longer, before Mike returned to tell me the bike owner agreed to sell me his rear tire rim. Now it was just a matter of time for Mike to replace the rim and add a new chain and cassette.

At 3:45 p.m., I hopped on Tank and rode along the street for a test ride, paying particular attention to any unusual noise or vibration coming from the rear. Something still didn't feel right when I shifted. It wasn't nearly as smooth as I had become accustomed to after 7,000 miles.

---

[95] "Damascus, Virginia," Trail Town, accessed July 14, 2022, http://www.trailtown.us

I asked Mike to take another look at Tank. He made adjustments to the shifter cable and checked that the back tire's rim aligned correctly. But I still had the same uncomfortable cycling experience on a second test ride. I decided perfection would not be the enemy of good enough. It was time for me to move on. I left Damascus at 4:00 p.m. and immediately began a steep climb up the Appalachian Mountains east of downtown.

Cloud cover blunted the sun's rays from reaching me as I entered the Iron Mountains, a subrange of the Blue Ridge Mountains. I searched for Appalachian Trail hikers on my climb out of Damascus. I rode through Konnarock (population unknown), Sugar Grove (population 792), and Rural Retreat (population 1,396) on my way to the Comfort Suites on the west side of Interstate 81 in Wytheville (population 7,762).

The special memories of this otherwise ordinary day were of the encounter with a police officer in Honaker and a five-minute conversation with a man and woman I met on my climb east of Damascus. Late in the day, a few miles from Wytheville, I stopped to assess my situation at an unwelcome road sign that read: "Bridge out 3 miles ahead." What did "bridge out" mean? Was the warning intended for vehicles only? Or was the road impassable? Maybe I could cross the bridge on my bicycle? All the possibilities peppered my mind. I took my chances and continued riding in the direction of the bridge. If the bridge was closed and I couldn't cross, I would camp on the side of the road. The forested area had endless places to call home for a night.

Yellow construction equipment lay idle on the bridge that Saturday evening. Cars and trucks would not have been able to get through. But on a bike, it was not a problem. It was just a matter of time before I made it to Wytheville. "Be on the lookout for bridge construction west of Wytheville," I texted Adam when I reached the other side of the bridge.

When I reached the Comfort Inn, the sky had turned to a rich orange and yellow hue, signaling the transition from day to night. I checked in, bought food from the lobby store, walked to my room on the first floor, and repeated my nightly routine. I checked Facebook and read a dot watcher's synopsis of my day on the saddle. Unknown to me, I had finished the demanding Chengi Hundred—the 100-mile length between Haysi and Wytheville has the most rise in elevation, over 14,000 feet, along the entire route. This analysis, conducted by Prashanth Chengi after he completed the 2017 TABR, describes this part of the race as the most difficult 100-mile stretch of the entire 4,200-mile trail. Following the 2017 race, dot watcher Ron Nelson dubbed it the "Chengi Hundred." The name has stuck.

Chapter 38
WYTHEVILLE–TROUTVILLE, VIRGINIA (104 MILES)

July 7, 2019

Blood continued to ooze from the cracks in my continually chapped lips, but multiple ear and nose blisters had healed. Like footprints across America, the selfies provided a snapshot of my emotions as I made my way across the land. From pride in Astoria, to uncertainty, curiosity, and concern across the heartland, eventually it was sheer determination that escorted me to the finish. Each picture portrayed my mental and physical state throughout my journey.

At 7:37 a.m., I rode underneath Interstate 81 and began the next leg on Peppers Ferry Road. When I crossed the interstate, I thought about my daughter Jaclyn, who graduated from James Madison University, located in Harrisonburg, Virginia, bisecting Interstate 81 north of Wytheville. At 10:55 a.m., shortly after entering rural Pulaski County on CR 658 near Newbern, I glanced at a white church building up ahead. A few people were walking toward the front entrance. Then I heard, "There's water for you under the pavilion in the parking lot." The shout came from a woman greeting congregants about to enter for the 11:00 a.m. service at the Mountain View United Methodist Church.

"Thanks!" I replied and at once turned right and entered the parking lot, passing by a sign that read: "Welcome Trans Am Racers! H20 Under Shelter." I coasted about a hundred feet to the covered pavilion behind the church. A few stragglers hurried to enter as the clock struck 11:00 a.m., reminding me of many Sunday mornings I had rushed to make it to Mass on time.

I reached Radford (population 15,410), home to Radford University, at 11:27 a.m. I followed CR 626 to Lee Highway, turned right onto US 11, and crossed a bridge over New River. At a busy, four-signal intersection, I stopped to look at the "See Radford Detail Map." I thought, *Here we go again.* Generally, navigating through cities was not straightforward. The Adventure Cycling Association maps provided greater detail to pedal through one-way street intersections, which are often necessary in larger communities and urban centers.

I followed US 11 along First Street to Wildwood Park. I became confused when the GPS directed me to go across the street and then circle back through a tunnel. Now inside Wildwood Park, I became disoriented. I couldn't figure out how to find the road to Christiansburg. I had no patience and became frustrated. I told myself, "Forget it," and retraced my tracks back to the busy intersection where I'd been 15 minutes before. I rode south instead of north, toward downtown. Perhaps I'd see a college student I could ask for directions. A few people gathered outside churches. When I reached Rock Road on the southernmost edge of town, I stopped again. Now really annoyed, I retraced my tracks once again, this time riding north and returning to the busy intersection. *Maybe the third time is the charm,* I thought. An older man stood outside a café, wearing his Sunday best. He'd likely attended service at the New River Valley Metaphysical Church, Valley Bible Church, Carter Street United Methodist, or one of the many other churches in Radford.

"Hi, I'm trying to find SR 787 to Christiansburg," I said.

He pointed for me to continue north on West Main Street and said, "You'll run right into it." I was relieved to hear him say it with such conviction. *Forget reading a map*, I thought. I thanked him and began riding north just like the man said. Thirteen miles later, at 1:12 p.m., I reached Christiansburg (population 21,454)—the end point for map section #11.

I received another warm welcome when I reached Christiansburg. Prominently displayed on the edge of town was a sign that read: "Welcome Cyclists!" There was even a URL listed for a site that featured resources on finding food, shelter, and showers for the night. The town was first established in the late 1600s by German, French, Scotch-Irish, and English settlers. Shawnee and other Native American people also inhabited the area near the New River, which is described as the "second oldest river in the world."[96]

At 3:00 p.m., riding on the southern slopes of the Blue Ridge Mountains, I saw storm clouds forming. It was only a matter of time before the skies opened up. I scanned the vicinity, searching for shelter. I passed by many farmhouses, but I didn't see a garage or shelter accessible from the road. A couple of miles farther, when the wind gusts increased, I saw a large, concrete structure covered with a corrugated metal roof—an ideal location to wait out the storm. I turned into a gravel parking lot and settled underneath the large storage facility. The rain started coming down slowly—*drip, drip, drip*—but the intensity picked up after a few seconds. I heard the clacking, sharp, constant noise and felt reverberations of the rain hitting the roof. The acoustics created an echo that hindered me from being able to hear the woman at the Holiday Inn in Troutville (population 431) when I called to make reservations. The rain lasted for about 30 minutes.

Finally, after the worst of the storm passed, I continued riding along Catawba Road (SR 785), which paralleled the North Fork Roanoke

---

[96] "History of the New River," New River Water Trail, accessed July 14, 2022, https://www.newriverwatertrail.com/NRWT/history-of-the-new-river/

River. A "Road Flooded" sign signaled I was nearing a water obstacle. Raging water flowed underneath a low-lying bridge. Sections of the road remained underwater.

When I reached the inn, I felt the weight of the world on my shoulders. The big climb to the top of Mount Vesuvius awaited me the next day. If the lore of Mount Vesuvius was close to the real thing, I would need a good night of sleep and a hot breakfast for sure. After settling into my room, I walked across Lee Highway and ate the new fried chicken meal at the Cracker Barrel next to Interstate 81.

And then there were four...

As I started to write this, Rolf was scaling Vesuvius and soon will be in the hands of our fabulous Blue Ridge Parkway. It looks like R.R. took a long break (~10 hrs.) in Lexington, so he might be looking to make a run for the border... errrrrr the finish line.

Larry Walsh crossed the Kentucky/Virginia border on Friday, July 5, at about 5 p.m. and is presently past Wytheville, VA, which means he has put the grueling Chengi Hundred behind him. His history shows he took a 12-hour break in Rural Retreat, maybe to rest up his legs. But he still has more climbing in VA and around 415 miles (668 km) until Y'town.

Adam awoke after what appears to have been an 11-hour rest to find himself in Kentucky for what possibly could be his last day as he is presently "only" ~100 miles from the border. But in that stretch is the infamous Pippa Passes, where the top three racers in TABR17 were bitten, possibly by the same dog!!!! OUCH!! And... I read in someone's

post that A.B. has ridden the ENTIRE TABR solo. Bravo!
Soldier on!

And the best that I can tell, Thomas is living the life
bivvying in Hatchet Campground, a National Forest
Campground near Moran, WY. A recent reviewer said,
"Biggest, Maddest, Mosquitos, ever"!!!! I hope you didn't
donate too much blood there T.C.! Roll on!

The distances covered in the last 48-hour period (7
a.m., July 5 to 7 a.m., July 7, EST) by our remaining
four TABR racers (including K.W. final numbers) are as
follows. I have also provided the distances covered each day
in brackets [Day 1/Day2] during these 2 days.

Kevin 292 miles (470 km) [164 mi/127 mi]
Rolf 235 miles (378 km) [107 mi/128 mi]
Adam 204 miles (328 km) [106 mi/99 mi]
Larry Walsh 190 miles (306 km) [89 mi/101 mi]
Thomas 90 miles (145 km) [35 mi/55 mi]

It continues to be hot and humid in Virginia. Even too
uncomfortable for the dogs during the day... but our
TABR riders pedal on! Be safe, guys!—dot watcher, July 7

Chapter 39
TROUTVILLE—WHITE HALL, VIRGINIA (112 MILES)

July 8, 2019

There were 342 miles to go when I took off at 7:22 a.m. Now, riding east on SR 640, a woman standing in the parking lot of a church caught my attention. She waved me over to a table set up in the front of the building. Sitting in a chair behind the table was another woman. The lady sitting down asked, "Coffee or donuts?"

I smiled, accepting both. "Thanks! A great way to start my big day," I said, before we got to introductions. I learned she was Sharon, the pastor of the Ebenezer United Methodist Church, which we were standing in front of.

Surprisingly, the two ladies were not aware the TransAmerica Bike Trail passed by their church!

The ladies set up a table every Monday morning to serve coffee and donuts to all passersby. I gave Pastor Sharon the contact information for the Adventure Cycling Association's map department and suggested she contact them to add the church to their next printing so future cyclists would be aware. I warned them to prepare for a deluge of folks, as their church site was a perfect location to rest before the big climb up Mount Vesuvius, 75 miles northeast of Troutville.

Pastor Sharon asked if we could all say a prayer for my safe passage to Yorktown. "Thanks so much," I replied, as the three of us bowed our heads. Orange juice, a glazed donut, and a cup of coffee helped prepare me for the ride to Lexington (population 7,042) along SR 640.

I arranged to meet my younger brother Dennis around 11:00 a.m. in Lexington. He was driving home to Northern Virginia, returning from vacation with his family. The road changed names often as it meandered through the countryside, bordering the James River to my south, Short Hills, and curiously named mountains, such as Purgatory Mountain (2,910 feet). At 10:10 a.m., I stopped at an Exxon gas station on SR F-055 to rest, rehydrate, and resupply. I met a retired police officer who was from Queens, New York, where I was born, who now lives in Atlanta, Georgia. He was traveling across the country on his Harley-Davidson motorcycle.

A US Bike Route 76 road sign directed me to cross over Interstate 81 once again. I cycled through the surrounding valley, shaded by a canopy of robust maple, pine, and poplar trees. I didn't have cell service and wondered if the trees had anything to do with it. When the signal returned, I texted Dennis to let him know I was behind schedule by about 30 minutes. After several unsuccessful attempts to reach me by phone, he'd continued driving home. I checked my satellite position and realized it was showing my location much farther away from Lexington than where I actually was. Maybe if I had adjusted my SPOT device to ping with the satellite more frequently, the Walsh family rendezvous would have occurred. My nieces, Maria, Sara, Eva, and Erin, the family trail angels, had arranged to surprise me with vanilla cream–filled donuts! My favorite! I missed out!

I rode by the Stonewall Jackson Memorial Cemetery—now named Oak Grove Cemetery—on Main Street, which is the site of General Stonewall Jackson's tomb. Everything but his arm has been laid to rest there. Apparently, his arm is buried 100 miles away in Chancellorsville. I stared at the life-size, bronze statue atop a large, concrete base.

A graduate of the US Military Academy at West Point, Jackson taught at the Virginia Military Institute in Lexington before joining the Confederate Army shortly after the attack on Fort Sumter, the first battle of the American Civil War. Over a hundred confederate soldiers are buried at the Oak Grove Cemetery. (The Lexington City Council, responding to calls from community members, voted to rename the cemetery, and on September 3, 2020, Stonewall Jackson Memorial Cemetery changed to Oak Grove Memorial Cemetery.)

Seeing Jackson's statue once again reminded me of our nation's complicated yet remarkable history. It's a history borne out of a person's desire to find freedom, independence, and self-reliance. And, like the United States and its allies defeated Nazi Germany, we as a people defeated slavery. To never repeat the past, we must learn from it.

"What's past is prologue." — Shakespeare, *The Tempest*

I rode on Main Street through the heart of the Virginia Military Institute campus and past the football stadium. Vehicle traffic increased considerably when Main Street merged with Lee Highway. The anticipation of climbing Mount Vesuvius had been building since Berea, Kentucky—the western gateway to the Appalachians. For 17 miles, I was anxious about the challenge ahead. I was about to tackle the greatest remaining barrier on this epic journey. I saw a Ford Explorer parked in a gravel lot off the road, rear latch lifted, with a man standing behind it. "Hi, Larry, I'm Dan," he introduced himself. "We've been tracking your progress. Are you ready for Vesuvius?"

Trail angels are on call whenever a racer approaches Mount Vesuvius. Whoever is closest and available grabs the moment and drives to the base of the mountain to greet the racer. Dan handed me a banana, which I ate right away. I had experienced cramping in my groin and hamstring the past several nights, so I figured ingesting a little potassium wasn't a bad idea. He handed me a bottle of Gatorade. I used a bungee cord to secure it to the rear rack. The snack bars I stuffed inside the middle frame bag.

Dan, a high school teacher and avid cyclist, shared his thoughts about Mount Vesuvius. "It's a demanding hill," he said, expressing that the route weaves through dense, lush forest on a narrow, shoulder-free road. There was a 3.5-mile climb where the grade exceeds 20 percent in some spots. Dan told me he would drive in front and stop at various places to take pictures of my progress on my way to the top.

I was ready to go. At 1:58 p.m., Dan closed the latch on his SUV and asked, "Do you want to put any of your gear in my truck to lighten the load?" I politely declined; I intended to ride every frickin' inch of the 4,200-mile race the way I had, including the grueling Mount Vesuvius. I wondered if other racers accepted similar offers from trail angels along the way. I looked so damn tired, maybe he felt I needed the help. Or maybe he felt sorry for me riding a steel frame bike!

I completed the first mile without resting, pedaling with my butt on the saddle. Except for riding through Wyoming, when excruciatingly painful saddle sores forced me to raise my butt, I found riding on the saddle the most efficient and comfortable riding position. My quadriceps burned. Around sharp curves, the slope increased, making it difficult to maintain forward momentum. Elevated humidity, limited air circulation, and a dense canopy overhead contributed to feeling like I was riding through a sauna. During the last two-mile stretch, I stopped every quarter of a mile to catch my breath and rest my legs. The road leveled off, and then I saw a bridge. I knew I was nearing the summit. I saw Dan's Ford Explorer parked on the other side of the bridge. I rode through the tunnel underneath the bridge and stopped at Highway 56 (Blue Ridge Parkway). One hour, 1,500 feet, and 3.5 miles later, I had conquered the last significant obstacle on my way to Yorktown.

Dan was standing behind his SUV, holding a carton of strawberries in one hand and a cold, wet rag in the other. It felt so good when I put the cold cloth around my neck. And then I savored each strawberry. A rush of energy came back to my body with each bite. I shook Dan's hand and continued riding along the Blue Ridge Parkway, the time now 3:12 p.m.

I did not know the difficulty of cycling on the Blue Ridge Parkway when I pedaled away from Dan. Afton was the closest town, about 25 miles away on the northernmost end of the Blue Ridge Parkway. Well-known among cross-country cyclists, Afton is famous for the Cookie Lady, June Curry. During the inaugural bike centennial ride in 1976, Curry, whose home was on the bike trail, met tired cyclists searching for food and water as they passed by her house. She started baking cookies, which earned her the nickname "Cookie Lady." For over 35 years, she offered food, lodging, water, and showers to cyclists passing through town.[97]

When I left Dan, I initially thought I could reach Charlottesville, 50 miles from the top of Vesuvius. I'd arrive after dark, but I expected it to be easy to find a motel room near the University of Virginia campus. Worst case scenario, I could crash at a frat house! Each pedal stroke required extraordinary effort. I pedaled. I coasted. Repeating that process for miles at a time, I found myself constantly pedaling to maintain a snail's pace. With each rotation, I seemed to stall. I pushed again and then delayed again. I rode into a slight headwind, but it was nothing extreme. Forward progress was a chore. I fretted. The sky above turned cloudy.

Farther ahead, the sky turned gray, and low cloud cover moved swiftly, creating an eerie feeling that I was about to enter a nasty storm. I looked north, down into the rolling forest surrounding the majestic Blue Ridge Highway. Unlike the swift-moving storms of the High Plains, the clouds could not escape the mountain range, which locked together like a bulwark. The combination of rain, extreme humidity, fog, and low cloud cover created conditions that limited my visibility. My glasses fogged. Everything at my disposal was wet, so I couldn't wipe my glasses dry to see clearly again. I stopped to don rain gear. My body was soaked

---

[97] Yvette Stafford, "Bikers' beloved Cookie Lady passes away," Blue Ridge Outdoors, August 28, 2012, https://www.blueridgeoutdoors.com/people/twice-an-angel/

to the core. The rain started slowly, but when the intensity increased, the road became very slippery, and my tires kicked up spray. My white front lights and rear red lights barely pierced through the thick fog. It was hard to know if the storm would pass through or linger for an extended period of time.

Through my fogged glasses, I saw a man standing in the rain on the side of the road. "Hi, I'm Dave. Do you plan on staying at the Cookie Lady's house tonight?" he asked, in a high-pitched voice that pierced the rhythmic tapping sound of the rain pounding the pavement. This trail angel had driven out of his way to meet me in the mountains rather than take the chance that I might not find the hostel on my own.

"I'm not sure I should stop if I want to make it to Charlottesville," I answered. At that time, my priority was escaping from the mountains and the nasty weather.

Dave talked me into getting out of the wet weather. "The storm is supposed to move through pretty quickly," he said. "I'll be waiting for you four miles ahead. The last two miles you'll be on a steep, winding downhill."

I thanked him for everything, and he then hopped into his blue sedan for the return trip to the Cookie Lady's house.

Even in the best of conditions, it would have been easy to miss the place. June Curry's story is interesting. I reached the small, nondescript home at 6:00 p.m. It had accumulated an enormous collection of photographs and other souvenirs donated by cyclists who'd passed through over the years. Postcards and pictures hung on the walls. Cycling paraphernalia scattered around the three main first-floor rooms. Family pictures from when Curry and her husband were much younger dotted the walls. An old piano and a rug typical of a bygone area provided the ambiance of a modest family.

My body was frigid from sweat and water clinging to my skin underneath my layered clothing when I hopped off Tank at the front entrance and stood in front of a stone with the inscription "In Loving Memory of June Curry, the Cookie Lady, February 8, 1921–July 16,

2012." Curry had been the subject of a Charles Kuralt *On the Road* segment of CBS Sunday Morning. According to reports, 14,000 cyclists visited Curry over the years. She suffered a stroke in 2005. Donations poured in from cyclists and cycling organizations who had learned of her health issues. Curry's serendipitous encounters with hungry and thirsty cyclists in 1976 became a lifelong passion of hers and a welcome support for the cycling community. About an hour after reaching the bike hostel, I was ready to continue. My body temperature had increased; I felt warm and comfortable after changing into a dry cycling shirt. Another cyclist staying the night took a picture of Dave and me with the American flag and a "We Love You" sign in the background.

At 6:37 p.m., I walked outside with Tank by my side and rode away from the Cookie Lady's house. It was no longer raining, but the threat loomed overhead. I decided to spend the night at the White Hall Community Center in White Hall, a small community east of Crozet (population 5,565) but 15 miles west of Charlottesville, which meant I would reach my destination before dark. The community center was isolated behind a tall hedge that bordered the road and was across the street from Wyant's Store. Farther west, I saw a couple of other buildings, but I couldn't make out what they were. I hopped off my bike, walked to the community center's front entrance, and tried to open the door, but it was locked. The back door was also closed. I wanted to shower in the worst way. I called the manager and asked where he had hidden the key. I was then told that I'd misunderstood the arrangement. My stomach sank so deep it lay in a nauseous mess at my feet. I thought he'd offered for me to stay *inside* the community center. Instead, he had given me permission to sleep on the community center grounds and use the outside hose to wash my body and clothes.

I scanned my surroundings for the best location and settled on sleeping inside a small, run-down shed located next to the hedges on the edge of the property that bordered SR 810. The wood-paneled floor was sturdy enough to withstand my large frame, and I couldn't see the light coming in from above—a good indication rain wouldn't fall on top of me should the skies open up in the middle of the night. I set up camp inside the shed and washed my body using the hose attached to the outside spigot in the backyard. I didn't see a soul around, so I stripped naked without any concern.

The Wyant's Store was closed, so I walked west toward the buildings I had seen when I first reached the community center. The Piedmont Store was also closed. The local post office next to the Piedmont Store was closed. I bought a bottle of Dr Pepper from an outside vending machine and then walked back to the community center. I called College Pizza on Main Street in Charlottesville. The first person I spoke to said he thought someone could deliver pizza to White Hall, but he needed to check with the manager. I offered to pay a hefty tip, whatever the store manager requested to make it work. I waited patiently for the employee to return to the phone. I had a sinking feeling when I heard, "Sorry, I asked my manager, and he told me not only no, but *hell* no!" After riding 112 miles and climbing nearly 8,000 feet, I needed to consume more calories than a Dr Pepper and one jelly packet provided. I searched through every section of my frame bag, handlebar bag, and weatherproof carry bag, hoping to uncover a morsel of food. No luck tonight.

Dan is on L.W... He saw him between Lexington and Vesuvius but seemed on a roll, so he didn't ask to stop. Last I texted him, he was going to wait for L.W. at the base of Vesuvius and then go to the B.R.P. to help out farther down the route! He is pulling double duty today!! I'm sure he'll have pictures to post later!—dot watcher, July 8

Resting at the Summit of Mount Vesuvius
The Last Big Climb
Vesuvius, Virginia
July 8, 2019

Chapter 40
WHITE HALL– MECHANICSVILLE, VIRGINIA (128 MILES)

July 9, 2019

By 7:20 a.m., I was ready for a hearty breakfast and to say goodbye to the sleepy town. Throughout the night, I'd woken up repeatedly to a scratching noise caused by some critter holed up beneath the floor. The Wyant's Store looked as if time had stood still since the 1880s, when the family first built it. Inside, the warm country feel was a nod to the past. Pet food, fishing supplies, automobile oil, antifreeze, candy, soda, Gatorade, Advil, cigarettes, and even Little Debbie Cakes replaced "the horse and mule collars, horseshoe nails, farm hand tools, and plugged tobacco" that had been for sale in earlier days, when wagons passed by on their way to Mechums River, a railroad shipping point.[98] Several

---

[98] Phil James, "Secrets of the Blue Ridge: The Country Store of Adam K. Wyant," *Crozet Gazette*, November 8, 2019, https://www.crozetgazette.com/2019/11/08/secrets-of-the-blue-ridge-the-country-store-of-adam-k-wyant/

white-framed pictures were on a stand in a side room. One picture of NFL officials posing on a football field raised my curiosity.

A man stood behind a counter at the back of the store. "Good morning, I'm Larry. I showed up last night after you had closed. I stayed across the street at the community center," I began, reaching out to greet my new friend.

"Good to meet you. I'm David," the older gentleman replied.

"Are you open for breakfast?" I asked.

"Yes. It will take a few minutes to prepare," he responded.

"Can I get scrambled eggs, bacon, and coffee?" I asked.

After he put the bacon on the grill and cracked open the eggs, he walked to the front of the store to wait on a young man who had entered shortly after I did.

I heard David say, "The same today?"

"Yes," the man replied.

David prepared the usual order of three slices of fresh cheese. After the guy paid and walked out of the store, David shared how this man stopped in every morning to buy fresh cheese—a practice more common in the early 1900s when, according to an article in the *Crozet Gazette*, farmers and ranchers stopped in for their daily dose of molasses, lard, coffee, salt, sugar, and flour.[99]

David recounted some of the store's past while I was there; other tidbits I learned were due to my own research after returning home. In the same *Crozet Gazette* article, Dr. Sidney Sandridge talked about growing up in a country store. "I could never figure out what children do who grow up in any other environment."

My planned 30-minute breakfast break turned into an extended stay. I learned that David was the fifth-generation owner of the oldest, continuously family-owned country store in the United States. Built in 1888, with a dance hall on the second floor, his great-great-great-grandpa's mission was to create a store for the community where people

---

[99] Ibid.

can mingle. The same attraction that drew people in the 1900s still holds today in this rebuilt and restored slice of small-town Virginia.

David was familiar with the bike race. His store had welcomed countless cyclists over the years. He told me Rolf had visited the day before, and he asked me to sign a guest book before leaving. I then asked about the picture of the NFL referees I had seen earlier. He told me he'd been an NFL referee for many years.

Okay, I thought, *I'm not going anywhere yet.* I asked him to tell me more about his background as an NFL referee.

He worked as an NFL official for 23 years; his last game had been the Super Bowl XLVIII on February 2, 2014, between the Seattle Seahawks and the Denver Broncos (Seattle won 43-8). He had since retired but still served as a senior NFL recruiting official. He was flying to Dallas later that afternoon to attend some meetings.

I dove right in, asking, "How did you become an NFL official when you're from such a small town in the middle of Virginia?"

He shared his secret to success: work hard, network, take advantage of every opportunity, and hope for a bit of luck.

"Do you know Kyle Brady?" I probed. "My youngest brother, Kevin, and Kyle were friends growing up in Pennsylvania." (Kyle played for the Penn State Nittany Lions and later for the Jets, Jaguars, and Patriots in the NFL.) He said he knew of Kyle but that was it. He didn't mind answering my onslaught of probing questions about the life of an NFL referee.

"I'd love to spend three more hours with you, but I've got to keep moving if I want to finish this race!" With that and a handshake, I signed my name in the guest book and was back on the road. *I wonder if I can catch Rolf*, I thought, the distance between us now less than 100 miles. I walked back across the street to retrieve Tank, glancing to my right and spotting a black SUV with a custom Virginia license plate: NFL SJ.

When I began my ride to Charlottesville at 8:00 a.m., I reflected on the conversation. David lived in the middle of a small Virginia town of less than 6,000, also traveling to big cities to experience the life of an NFL referee. I too found solace in the quiet surroundings of a small community after 30 years of flying from one big city to the next during my professional career.

Before the pandemic, my family visited NYC during the holiday season to attend a Broadway play, staying the night at the Marriott Marquis in Times Square. The following day, we ate at the famous Junior's Restaurant & Bakery, hoping to get a glimpse of an actor. As much fun as I had feeling the energy of NYC, after 24 hours, I couldn't wait to return to the peace and serenity of small-town Mendham.

Traffic increased by the time I reached the outskirts of Charlottesville that Tuesday morning. The route meandered through a neighborhood along Old Garth Road and Old Ivy Road, off the main artery to Charlottesville. A young lady walked her dog, and a few cars drove by. I rode by 5,000-square-foot homes on acre plots with hundred-foot-tall trees, maybe University of Virginia professors' residences, I thought. When Old Ivy Road converged with US Bus Route 250, the traffic increased. The streets were humming with activity when I entered Charlottesville at 8:49 a.m. Cars moved slowly through the intersections. Many people walked on the sidewalks.

The first time I visited Charlottesville was with my dad in 2012, when we attended a Penn State vs. Virginia football game (the Cavaliers won 17–16).

"There it is—College Pizza!" The place that refused to deliver a pizza the night before was located on University Avenue. I stopped at a roadside marker to read about the history of the university. Thomas Jefferson founded the University of Virginia in 1817. In the presence of Jefferson, Madison, and Monroe, the cornerstone of the first building was laid at this location. A few minutes later, I stopped at the junction of West Main, Ridge Street, and McIntire Road when I saw a sculpture of Lewis, Clark, and Sacajawea. (On July 10, 2021, the Charlottesville City Council voted to remove the statue that had stood since 1919 as a testament to the expedition that then-President Thomas Jefferson approved.)

I began riding through the countryside when I reached Interstate 64, east of downtown Charlottesville, and continued on SR 53—a narrow, meandering road that passed Thomas Jefferson's plantation home near Monticello. A short time later, I passed by President James Monroe's homestead. Relying on sound, not sight, I heard the low roar of a vehicle approaching from behind. I maneuvered Tank to the edge of the one-foot-wide shoulder, trying to continue straight on the thin tightrope separating pavement from grass. I thought to myself, *If I lose my balance, I will fall into the brush.* The typical roar of an engine changed rapidly, shifting to something that sounded more like a .50-caliber machine gun. Hearing the compression release brake of an eighteen-wheeler, I white-knuckled my handlebars and concentrated on maintaining my balance. I knew the truck would produce a delayed crosswind. The eighteen-wheeler sped past me. Seconds later, 50 yards ahead, it veered right and onto the shoulder of the road before quickly correcting itself. I gasped at the terrifying reality that had it done so a few seconds sooner, while it was passing me, I would've become a statistic.

The truck created a powerful crosswind that knocked me to the right, which caused me to lose my balance for a couple of seconds. Fortunately, I didn't fall. I stopped pedaling, released my cleats from the pedals, straddled Tank, and thought, *That was a close call!* Those several seconds in which the truck flew by me were nerve-wracking—more so than any other time on this race. My heart pounded as this brush against the wind almost ended my race—only the third close encounter on this race across America. The first, on the bike path in Colorado, struck me as ironic. The second, while leaving Hindman, Kentucky, during rush hour traffic, was a reminder to not take anything for granted. And now, in Virginia with less than 200 miles to go… Was I tempting fate?

The data for cyclists injured while sharing a road with motor vehicles is limited. Nathan communicated the odds were good that two race entrants would be involved in a vehicle accident. I was aware of a racer colliding with a car on day one, less than an hour after the bell rang. And weeks later, in Kentucky, a pickup truck's side-view mirror clipped

Michael, which resulted in bike damage and personal injury. Nathan wasn't kidding.

I rode by a billboard extolling the Patrick Henry Tea Party. There was also a sign with the words "what difference does it make?" which Secretary of State Clinton had said during the hearings regarding the attack on the US Embassy in Benghazi, Libya. Both were reminders that I would soon return to a place I happily escaped from for several weeks. Other messages on road signs, like the one that read "What is your fair share of what someone else worked for?" caught my attention and reminded me that rural and urban America see the world very differently.

I had made it to Bumpass, Virginia, the scene of the extraordinary moment during the TABR 2016 when Steffen Streich awoke at 3:00 a.m., leading Lael Wilcox by 110 miles, and started riding the wrong way. Their dots collided, at which point Streich realized his error, turned around, and continued pedaling to Yorktown. Reportedly, they rode together for a while before Wilcox pulled ahead, beating Steich by two hours to become the first woman to win the TABR.

When I first read about the thrilling outcome of June 22, 2016, my desire to enter the race went through the roof. The story of Wilcox winning in such an unbelievable way was one of the defining moments leading to my decision to enter the race. Seeing Bumpass on this quiet and sunny July 9 afternoon was not the image I'd had of Wilcox and Steich's improbable meeting, riding past the clear blue water of Lake Anna on my way to Ashland.

Prince Purple, a prolific dot watcher from Ashland (population 7,225), had been a frequent supplier of daily updates and made a point to meet racers on the road as they pedaled through his hometown in Virginia. He greeted cyclists and made cameos on North Centre Street, near the site of Randolph Macon University. An Amtrak train shook the ground, barreling through Ashland at 7:05 p.m. The town went silent again. Then, as I rode over Interstate 95, it hit me that I had missed Prince Purple and was getting close to Yorktown. Seeing vehicles traveling at high speed and then remembering a similar image from weeks before, traveling in a bus on Highway 101 to Astoria, acted as bookends to an unforgettable journey with countless memories in between.

I reached Mechanicsville (population 36,348) at 8:30 p.m. I didn't know which way to go when I stopped at a confluence of roads near Interstate 295, surrounded by a large construction area and a newly opened road system. I looked at the Adventure Cycling Map, then at my surroundings, and then at my GPS. My GPS directed me to go in a direction that was no longer possible. The digital files had not been updated to reflect the new roads. I asked a woman walking her dog if she knew the most direct route to the Holiday Inn. She hesitated in her response, not sure where to direct me. After a few minutes, I took a chance and rode on one of the newly constructed roads in the direction I assumed would lead to the Holiday Inn. As dusk set in, I reached the on-ramp for Interstate 295, heading north. I wanted to go east. At the Bell Creek Road exit, I peeled off and followed the road for a couple of miles, winding through side roads until I made it to the Holiday Inn Express parking lot at 9:00 p.m.

I felt a sense of relief. *One more night!* I thought, as I waited for the sliding glass door to open and walked inside a motel for the very last time on this journey. The front desk attendants were expecting me. I looked every bit tired, hungry, and in need of a shave. My haggard appearance didn't faze the two women, Liz and DJ, working at the front desk—I'm sure it was business as usual for this motel that was frequented by cyclists riding through Mechanicsville. I purchased food from the lobby store and walked Tank to my first-floor room. I followed my routine one more time—one *last* time, I reminded myself. I would unpack, shower, prepare for the next day's ride, eat, post a summary of my day on the saddle, and sleep.

Lying on the bed, I examined details of the map that would direct me to Yorktown the next day. The room phone rang at 10:00 p.m. "Hello?" I answered, with a tinge of interest as to why someone was calling me so late at night.

One of the front desk attendants responded, "Prince Purple is in the lobby and delivered food for you." Prince Purple had tracked my location to the Holiday Inn. Since we missed seeing each other in Ashland, he wanted to track me down. When my satellite dot didn't move from this location for 30 minutes, he drove here to greet me. I appreciated Prince Purple making the effort, but I also had mentally settled in for the night.

"I will be down to pick up the food, but it won't be for a little while," I replied, adding, "Please say thank you for me."

When reflecting on and writing about my time in Mechanicsville, I realized I should have greeted Prince Purple and thanked him in person. Later that night, I retrieved the food and then posted a thank-you note to Prince Purple on social media. He replied, "Mystery man, you are the only racer I ever missed riding through Ashland." A dog lover and rescuer, he goes by his dog's name, Prince Purple.

OK. I tried Larry Walsh. I really did try. Before we went out for the evening, your Dot had been in Mineral VA for over three hours, so I figured you were done. But noooooooo! After dinner I suddenly noticed you were cycling again, and you were somehow already past Ashland. Bravo!!! Rushed home, loaded up and headed out to meet you. But it didn't make sense as your Dot was stuck in Atlee Station almost an hour. But I was happy you were NOT in the middle of the road as your Dot showed!! Being a Jersey boy, I figured I'd find you in Dunkin Donuts! Nope! But after going to ALL the food joints in Atlee Station, I knew you had already left. I headed up the road and suddenly your Dot popped up in Mechanicsville. Now I know it's starting to sound a little (or A LOT!!!) creepy, but I tracked you to the Holiday Inn Express. Great choice!!! Right next to the IHOP!! Liz and DJ were very kind and accepted the food I had for you and even posed for a picture... photographic proof that PP was there. Sweet dreams dude!!—Prince Purple, July 9

Earlier in the day, Rolf finished the race. I had closed the gap to 100 miles, but that was as close as I got to catching him. I wondered if Rolf would meet me at the monument the next day when I finished. Forty-four racers had finished. Twenty-four had scratched. Thomas, the 78-year-old Lanterne Rouge, had 2,700 miles to go. Adam had 300 miles, and I had 82 miles to the end.

Two thoughts entered my mind when I placed my head on the pillow: *finish* and *family*.

82 Miles to the Monument
Mechanicsville, Virginia
July 10, 2019

Chapter 41
MECHANICSVILLE–YORKTOWN, VIRGINIA (82 MILES)

July 10, 2019

I f every day could be like the ride to Yorktown, I just might do it again. What a day it was! Warm temperature and cloudy skies, to start. At 9:35 a.m., I stopped at the Malvern Hill Battlefield Historical Marker on SR 156. However, I knew if I read one historical marker, I would want to read them all on the last leg to Yorktown. *I can always return another time*, I told myself. I rode on John Tyler Memorial Highway (Capital Trail) and passed through Charles City to Williamsburg. Just west of the Sherwood Forest Plantation, a cyclist riding away from Yorktown slowed down when he saw me approaching from a distance. "They're waiting for you at the monument!" he said, knowing full well who I was. He'd met Rolf at the monument in Yorktown before starting his own journey to Florida. I now had my answer. Rolf was waiting to meet me at the finish. I was ecstatic when I looked ahead and saw a body of water and a bridge. "I made it!" I said out loud, unaware I had over 20 miles to go when I rode over the James River at Chickahominy Riverfront Park.

At 12:36 p.m., I reached Williamsburg and the Colonial Parkway, connecting Jamestown, Williamsburg, and Yorktown. I reflected on the journey about to end—riding through areas famous for settling the west, where our forefathers freed us from Britain's control. The gold rush, Indian Wars—elements of the history that makes up the TransAmerica Bike Trail. My lesson on the saddle came full circle as I closed in on Williamsburg. I navigated the historic downtown and weaved through the College of William & Mary campus, the second-oldest college in the United States, after Harvard University.

John and Jean, the last two trail angels I would meet on this incredible journey, greeted me at the entrance to the scenic Colonial Parkway and rode with me the last 13 miles. Jean asked what memories stood out. "It's hard to pinpoint one thing… The overall experience was fantastic." To keep our conversation alive, I shared several stories during our hours-long ride together. I couldn't wait to relax and process the journey I was about to finish. For I knew seeing the United States on the saddle of a bike is nothing short of incredible.

John described the final two-mile path to the monument, and then he and Jean slowed down while I continued my pace. John told me, "This is your finish. You should be alone when you reach the monument."

I took a right onto Comte De Grasse Street and began pedaling up a short, steep hill—the *last* hill. When I turned left onto Main Street, the towering Yorktown Victory Monument came alive. So many times, I thought how I couldn't wait to experience the incredible rush I had imagined as I gazed up at the enormous monument.

I scanned the area, looking for Kelley. Then, out of the corner of my eye, I saw her (carrying our dog, Bradley) and running toward me from a distant parking lot. My son, Brian, and my niece Erin reached me at the moment Kelley doused me with champagne. We all hugged.

"What do you think about Dad racing across the country?" I asked Brian, watching him stare at my unshaven face.

"Pretty cool," he responded.

I heard a voice through all the commotion saying, "Ride to the monument to finish!"

I turned and saw a man filming my arrival. I hopped on Tank and rode the last 50 feet on a path leading to the monument's base, the official end to the Trans Am Bike Race.

I saw Rolf standing along the path. He looked the same, minus a few pounds, as I remembered when we first met in Astoria 39 days before. I took a victory lap, riding full circle around the base. When I reached the front, I stopped, hopped off Tank for the very last time, and slapped the concrete exclamation point! At 3:10 p.m., my race was finished.

My right hand stung for a second from the slap to the concrete. I was caught in the surreal sense that the past few weeks hadn't happened. A few people stood around the grass area, circling the bottom of the monument. I set Tank down on the ground. I looked back to the path I had ridden to reach the monument, scanning the handful of people who joined in on the celebration. Kelley, Brian, Erin, Rolf, John, Jean, and a photographer all beamed, congratulating me for a job well done. *Mission accomplished*, I thought. The sun was beating down pleasantly, and I was surrounded by smiling faces.

I reached out to embrace Rolf, thanking him for greeting my arrival. He told me he remembered meeting me in Astoria.

"I tried to catch you the past two weeks," I shared, with a beaming smile.

He added, "You motivated me to keep going. I thought you might catch me."

"You pulled me along!" I said, wanting to get the last word in.

He finally fulfilled the dream he had set out to achieve the year before, when he was derailed due to developing pneumonia halfway to Yorktown. *Determination. Perseverance.*

For a minute, I had forgotten about my wife, son, and niece, who had been standing, chatting, and taking videos. I turned and pointed to each, introducing them one by one. Then I directed my comments to the small gathering. "Thanks for being here everyone!" No music. No bells. No whistles. And yet, it was absolutely perfect. I turned, faced the monument, lifted Tank above my head, and let the moment sink in.

Kelley, Erin, Brian, and I walked away from the monument to the parking lot, where Kelley had parked our QX60 Infiniti. I opened the rear hatch and put all the equipment I carried on Tank inside the SUV. I attached my Yakima bike rack to the rear hitch and secured Tank to it, ready to drive home to New Jersey. I looked up at the white monument one last time. I called my daughters, Tara and Jaclyn, my parents, and my four brothers. I could hear in Mom's voice that she was relieved her son was finally finished, safe and sound. I stared out the passenger window, thinking about all the well-wishes and words of encouragement I had received the past 38 days, 7 hours, and 10 minutes. Every shout-out transmitted a boost of energy though my mind and body—a lifeline to Yorktown.

Two 57-year young riders completed their TABR journeys. Rolf arrived at The Monument Wednesday afternoon (37:07:42). He had ridden the TA as a cycling tourist in 2012 and completed it in 82 days. He more than halved his time this time around! Like a good wine, Rolf just gets better with age!! Awesome ride!
Congrats!

And Larry Walsh finished his TABR experience almost exactly a day later yesterday afternoon (38:07:10). Issues with LW's tracker, at least in VA, made it a challenge to find him, but his family located him at The Monument to congratulate him on a ride well done! Congratulations LW! Chapeau!

And then there were two...
*Adam overnighted in Daleville, VA... ***
*And Thomas spent the night in Jeffrey City, WY... ****
The Trackleaders map is starting to look pretty lonely
now...—dot watcher, July 11

* Time to Finish – 41 days, 11 hours, 40 minutes
**Time to Finish – 99 days, 11 hours, 44 minutes"

Yorktown Victory Monument
July 10, 2019

Tank at the Finish!

EPILOGUE

Why did I enter the TABR? It seemed like a good idea—another chance to test my mind and body. I finished; therefore, I won.

My mind often returned to the days of Lewis and Clark. Riding along the places where gunslingers lived, Native Americans roamed, cattle ranchers settled, wagon trains rolled through, and significant historical figures shaped our history, I brought home a more profound understanding of the past—and how the legacies of the past impact the present. "History matters. It is not just 'useful', it is essential."[100]

Of the 299 towns I rode through, 75 percent had a population of fewer than 1,000 souls, each with its own unique culture—American flags waving in the wind and a blue-collar work ethic displayed with every handshake. Rarely did I hear someone shout, "Get off the road." The weather was not as dreadful as it could have been. I rode through snow one time and hail twice. I pedaled in torrential rain and in darkness three nights. Riding through 38 mph sustained winds coming into Pueblo

---

[100] "History connects the past with the present," Why History Matters, Churchill Archive for Schools, Bloomsbury, accessed July 14, 2022, https://www.churchillarchiveforschools.com/why-history-matters/history-connects-the-past-with-the-present

was tough. I felt like a zombie on Kansas Highway 96. And 300 miles in Missouri was not fun.

That big, blue Montana sky is impossible to forget. Cresting Hoosier Pass was demanding but didn't compare to the brutal climb up Mount Vesuvius. I could taste the finish line then, but oddly, I didn't care. The night in Jeffrey City, I wondered if it was my last. Less than a mile in the following morning, I knew I could deal with it and power through to the end. My fingers were continuously numb, and my feet hurt more times than I can remember.

With less than 1,000 miles to go, I didn't understand why I had no emotion.

Completing a single cross-country bike trip was a worthy goal. But two… Cycling 7,300 miles across 18 states and through 528 towns in 10 months was a unique experience worth sharing. For that reason and others, I wanted to write about it. Reading about Lael Wilcox winning the 2016 TABR sparked an urge that set me on the road to Astoria. Newton Bike Shop owner James Barringer's plea to bring cycling and small-town America closer drew me in.

The cycling community had come together to rejuvenate run-down neighborhoods. That was and is a worthy goal. Kindhearted Kentucky adults and kids sparked a state-wide trend: "Just Be Kind" and "Be Kind," which should resonate with everyone. Surrounding oneself with warm, friendly, and caring people makes the day much more enjoyable.

One week into the race, something clicked. Flabbergasted, I realized I had averaged 99.4 miles per day. It got better from there. Not a single flat tire, for the second cross-country ride. That's pretty remarkable. Most gratifying of all, I can once again say I rode every frickin' inch of the 4,192-mile journey!

AFTERWORD

*Photo taken on June 16, 2019—Wind River Indian
Reservation Fort Washakie, Wyoming*

Photo: Courtesy of Eastern Shoshone Cultural Center (Chief Washakie)

C hief Washakie was the last great chief of the Eastern Shoshones. Born around the turn of the 18th century, he was able to foresee the changes coming to his land with the coming of the white man. He was a fierce warrior, feared by his enemies, but also a peacemaker, and a true visionary. Always considering the welfare of his tribe, he was able to secure the "warm valley", the Wind River Country, as their permanent home. Due to his foresight, the Eastern Shoshone Tribe is able to enjoy the bountiful resources of this beautiful region. His vision for the education of the children still holds strong today. Washakie had many dealings with white men, first by encountering fur trappers such as Jim Bridger who later became his son-in-law, and then coming in contact with emigrants along the Oregon Trail, which cut directly through Shoshone country. He soon realized that fighting the white man was futile—the people that made the guns and poured through the land by the thousands. Peace treaties were made that reimbursed his tribe for lost game along the trail and he always upheld his side of the bargain, allowing passage and helping the emigrants when possible. He found the US troops to be his allies when fighting enemy tribes. His outstanding character came into play when he was allowed to choose the area for his tribe's assigned reservation land. He always stayed true to his word, even when the whites forgot their promises.—**Robyn Rofkar,** *Eastern Shoshone Cultural Center, Fort Washakie, Wyoming*

*Photo taken on June 16, 2019—Wind River Indian
Reservation, Fort Washakie, Wyoming*

Sacajawea is one of the best-known Native Americans, having accompanied Meriwether Lewis and William Clark on their 1804-1806 Corps of Discovery to find a passage to the Pacific Northwest and open trade relations with native tribes along the way. After being kidnapped as a young girl from her Lemhi Shoshone people by Hidatsa or Minnetaree warriors, she was married at age 14 to Toussaint Charbonneau. During Lewis and Clark's winter stay near the Mandan village (North Dakota), they hired Charbonneau as an interpreter. Sacajawea was to go along, as well, to interpret with the Shoshones. The Corps leaders heard that they would need Shoshone horses to cross the mountain passes on their way to the Pacific Ocean. She gave birth less than 2 months before they departed, and her baby son accompanied them on the journey. She proved to be a valuable member of the Corps by finding roots, berries, and nuts that provided food and medicine. She also proved her worthiness by keeping her head when the boat she was on almost capsized and rescued valuable items, while her husband panicked. When the Corps reached the Shoshones, she was brought into council to interpret with the Shoshone Chief Cameahwait and she was overwhelmed to discover that he was her older brother. With the Shoshone horses, Lewis and Clark were able to cross the mountain passes, eventually reaching the Pacific. Sacajawea was so well respected that she was given a vote as to where to build their winter fort (Near Astoria, Oregon). She was also able to request that she be allowed to accompany a group to see the ocean and a whale that had washed up on the beach. Cpt. Clark realized that her presence in the expedition showed all the Native Tribes that they met on their journey that they were not a war party, preventing altercations along the way. He later credited the success of the Corps of Discovery to Sacajawea.—**Robyn Rofkar, *Eastern Shoshone Cultural Center, Fort Washakie, Wyoming***

ACKNOWLEDGEMENTS

"If you dig it, do it. If you dig it a lot, do it twice."—Jim Croce

To the many readers of *Suit to Saddle*: the warm appreciation I received for sharing my story, and your encouraging words were fuel for my soul.

To the cycling clubs, book clubs, libraries, VFWs, senior centers, and business partners: thank you for welcoming me into your organizations. I hope someone was inspired to tackle that sought-after long-distance bike ride or hunkered down to begin writing that book they've pondered for years.

To the Bublish Team: I'm grateful to you for once again ushering me through the publishing process with patience, professionalism, and honesty. And to the incredible editors who encouraged, guided, and coached me to remain disciplined to achieve the book's intent and steer it to the finish line.

To Juliette Fredericks, who brought *Forty to Finish* to life: thank you for sharing your exceptional artistic talent in creating an attention-grabbing cover design, a masterful repeat of the highly acclaimed illustration on the cover of *Suit to Saddle*.

To mom and dad, the world's best parents, and consummate *Suit to Saddle* advocate! Their many friends always received a parting message, "Our son wrote a book!"

And to the four best brothers, Tim, Dan, Dennis, and Kevin, who are still processing, "their brother wrote a book!" With the Walsh brothers, there's always time for a good laugh.

To my loving children, Tara, Jaclyn, and Brian: I love you all dearly.

Finally, to Kelley, wife, best friend, and confidant: you are an incredible spouse, fantastic mother, and a legend among the many people I presented my story to who reminded me, "Your wife is a saint," for supporting my bike rides across America.

APPENDIX: BY THE NUMBERS

- Total distance—4,192 miles
- Total climb—181,052 feet
- Maximum speed—45.33 mph
- Average distance per day—109 miles
- Maximum day distance—148 miles
- Maximum day climb—9,039 feet
- Days away from home—40
- Towns ridden through—299
- Number of towns with populations less than 1,000—224
- Nights camping under the stars—9
- Hottest temperature—85
- Coldest temperature—32
- States—10
- Flat tires—0
- Time to finish—38 days, 7 hours, 10 minutes
- Memories to last a lifetime—too many to count

Made in the USA
Middletown, DE
19 May 2023